ADDICTED TO LOVE
KATE
MOSS
FRED VERMOREL

OMNIBUS PRESS

LONDON / NEW YORK / PARIS / SYDNEY / COPENHAGEN / BERLIN / MADRID / TOKYO

Cover designed by Fresh Lemon

ISBN13: 978.1.84609.755.3
Order No: OP51733

Exclusive Distributors
Music Sales Limited,
14/15 Berners Street,
London, W1T 3LJ, UK

Music Sales Corporation,
257 Park Avenue South,
New York, NY 10010, USA.

Macmillan Distribution Services,
53 Park West Drive,
Derrimut, Vic 3030,
Australia.

Every effort has been made to trace the copyright holders of the photographs in this book but one or two were unreachable. We would be grateful if the photographers concerned would contact us.

Sex And Drugs And Rock And Roll. Words & Music by Ian Dury & Chas Jankel © Copyright 1977 Blackhill Music Limited. All Rights Reserved. International Copyright Secured.

Typeset by Phoenix Photosetting, Chatham, Kent
Printed by Gutenberg Press Ltd, Malta

A catalogue record for this book is available from the British Library.

Visit Omnibus Press on the web at www.omnibuspress.com

D1197864

... a deeply disturbing story of some of the worst excesses in the fashion world ...
- *reFRESH magazine*

It's hard to believe but supermodel Kate Moss once considered having a boob job and was cripplingly shy about her body ...
- *Cosmo*

... revelations and underwear examinations ...
- *This is London*

Vermorel follows his subject from indolence in suburban south London to decadence in the international jetset ... The supermodel was infatuated with the culture of pop debauchery long before she met Doherty ...
- *The Observer*

... remarkable ... a page turner ...
- *This Morning, ITV*

Her life, especially in recent years, seems dizzyingly turbulent ... [An] interesting picture of her upbringing: out drinking and jointing at 14, with a somewhat laissez-faire mother ... really overly intimate, even for the genre ... Vermorel [quotes] extensively from Kate herself ...
- *The Evening Standard*

For Tolsty

Contents

In the realm of fashion, where breathless enthusiasm sings harmony with toxic ennui.
– Jay Mcinerney, *Model Behaviour*, 2000

Thus every Part was full of Vice,
Yet the whole Mass a Paradice …
– Bernard Mandeville, *The Grumbling Hive: or, Knaves Turn'd Honest*, 1705

She used to have one pair of shoes with spikes at the back that she called her sex boots
– because she said she wore them when she had sex.
– *Vanity Fair*, quoting a journalist who interviewed Kate Moss, December 2005

Prequel

Welcome to The Circus.

The Circus is a barn attached to Kate Moss' country house. The place is cavernous, with high ceilings and wooden rafters daubed with black paint. The ancient brickwork is scarred and pitted,

The Circus is lavishly decorated with red, white and black drapes: huge rolls of fabric looping from rafters and festooning the walls, suggesting some kind of occult fête, and giving the sense of an ominous chapel.

This feeling of worship is enhanced by the numinous half light streaming through narrow slits cut high up on the walls and through cracks in the old barn doors. Light also filters through the incongruous crescent – or "lunette," windows, whose panes resemble the rays of a rising – or maybe setting, sun. Again, a feature you might find in a chapel.

Adding to this effect is an enormous and striking portrait of His Satanic Majesty, Keith Richards.

The doyen of sex and drugs and rock and roll here shows a wizened and frazzled profile, pouting a cigarette. The pose is nonchalantly decadent, eyes narrowed and heavy lidded, hair fluffed up, collar turned up, a flare of light accidentally strobing the image and enhancing its insolence: the mood defiant cool.

This image dominates the room, lending the Richards aura to all proceedings. Its position beneath the chapel-like window adds to its icon-like implication: opposite the stage, inciting devilry and sanctioning debauchery – the Edge.

And high above is a large mirrored ball hung from the rafters: hundreds of tiny mirrors that reflect and seem to soak up the spectral light - and which has witnessed some rum goings on, especially on the evening of 16th January, 2004, when Kate Moss and Pete Doherty fell in love ...

ACT ONE:

From Obscurity to Obsession

Beauty is potent, but money is omnipotent.
– English proverb

Forget Croydon. That is a fantasy she likes to spread as much as the media does. A supermodel from Croydon: beauty flowering out of the concrete towered, motorway infested, chav ridden wastelands. Someone on an American web site helpfully explains that Croydon equates to Newark.

But if you know your way around, and leave the everlasting Brighton Road with its boarded up properties and dingy corner shops, and head into some of those side roads towards Shirley … Selsdon … Forestdale … you get a very different picture.

Because it all gets leafier and leafier, until you are near arcadia, or its suburban equivalent, a place – as the prophet of suburbia, CG Masterman announced, fit for suburbans, whom he defined as a happier race than city dwellers: superior in manners and sportsmanship, better fed and educated and even better looking (the prettiness gap is as marked between UK city centres and suburbs as when you go to from London to Paris), a "homogonous civilisation", "detached, self centred and unostentatious", "a state of semi-detachment" … and eventually you get to the leafiest bit of all, you get to Sanderstead … which is where Kate Moss really comes from – spiritually as well as spatially.

"Croydon" may be the general area, and convenient shorthand, but Sanderstead – suburbia, is what's inside her. It accounts both for her timidity and nihilism and for her "state of semi-detachment" - the restlessness that makes her ideal for fashion and search for dream-men to endorse her ethereal fashion self.

Otherwise, her merry-go-round of lovers and "partying" is to pass the time of day - time hurts because it perplexes – which is why we so often find her killing time, and especially on beaches – and most often in Ibiza, that cod-exotic suburban get-away-from-it-all fantasy of her E generation.

Q: What does your mother do?
Kate Moss: Nothing, really, at the moment.
- Exchange in *Vanity Fair*, 1994

★ ★ ★

But the story doesn't quite start in Sanderstead.

Her mother, Linda Rosina Moss was born on the 8th September 1947. Linda was a local girl; her parents lived in Anthony Road, Woodside, about a mile from central Croydon, just three streets from where she would marry and then have Kate.

Linda's mother's maiden name was Emily Louisa Cresswell. Her father, George Frederick Shepherd, was a retail greengrocer. Unlike that other greengrocer's daughter, Margaret Thatcher, Linda failed to rise to the challenge of humble origins. As a child and teenager, and then a wife and mother she lacked ambition. Her greatest achievement was to run a boutique when she was 23. Later in life, in her surprise role as a supermodel's mum, she was prickly about her status as a casual shop worker and bar attendant. (When asked what her mother did for a living Kate would be evasive or giggle: "She'll kill me for telling you!") When Linda married Peter Moss she was selling hair accessories for Carmen.

Peter Edward Moss was born on the 31st August, 1944. The war was still raging in Europe and the Far East, the liberation of Paris had taken place six days before and Peter's father, Herbert Edward Moss, a former post office engineer, was serving as a sergeant in the Royal Signals Corp. His mother's maiden name, Queenie Louisa Stanbridge spoke of British stock. Peter's parents lived just beyond Croydon, though still in its orbit, in London Road, North Cheam. When they married, Herbert was stationed at Buckford camp and Queenie travelled to the military base for their wedding.

Dipping into Moss genealogy we can see the Moss men pursued a variety of trades. They were also partial to the name, Herbert. Peter's father, Herbert Edward, born in 1905, was the son of Herbert Thomas Moss who was a coal merchant's clerk and the son of Herbert, a travelling salesman for publishing houses. But that's where the Herberts end. Kate's great great great great great grandfather, born in Birmingham in 1824, was called John. John Moss was a commercial traveller before working in the newspaper industry, and ending up as what the 1881 census intriguingly calls a "dressmaker".

Tracing back the Stanbridge line from Kate's paternal grandmother, Queenie, we find that her great grandfather, George Henry Stanbridge, was successively a railway guard, ticket collector and porter. He was also a naughty boy. The 1901 census shows him living as a lodger at the home of a plumber's labourer, Louis Parsons. Also in the house were Louis' wife and son, and two daughters, and … you guessed it – George ran off with Georgina, one of the daughters. From the records, it's likely they eloped. Firstly, because they married many miles from Georgina's childhood home, and no relatives witnessed the marriage certificate – unusual for those days. Secondly, Georgina lied to the registrar about her age, adding enough years to avoid the need for parental consent.

The majority of Kate's more recent ancestors from the male and female lines had found their way to South London by the mid 19th century, and there they stayed for over a century.

* * *

Her father, Peter Moss, eventually became a ticket clerk with Pan Am. A diligent and ambitious worker, he was soon on his way up in the company. He met Linda at a mutual friend's 21st and they wed on the 17th April 1971 in the 14th century parish church of St Mary Beddington. Linda cut a modish note in a neat dress suit rather than a conventional wedding dress, which in those days could still raise eyebrows – people muttered, did she think she was in show business?

The Mosses first lived in Pagehurst Road, Addiscombe, in a semi which is a five minute stroll from the house Linda had been born in.

This motif of not straying very far recurs. Which is odd, given that Peter has always been in the international travel business, and that Kate has been on the move internationally since the age of 14. But the area seems magnetic. Even Kate left reluctantly and kept going back, until she realised she was no longer welcome. Equally, tracking her former schoolmates through Friends Reunited with a UK Info Disk was spooky: so many of them in the same area, the same streets, even the same houses as a decade or two ago.

* * *

Pagehurst Road is terraced houses, today remarkable only for identical front porch extensions – the kind of place where a travelling salesman like one of

Kate's ancestral Herberts might discover an anonymous b&b and commit suicide one morning in the carpeted bathroom as the smell of a "full English breakfast" wafts up the stairs. This is where Kate was brought home after being born on 16th January 1974, at St Mary's Maternity Hospital, Croydon. She weighed in at 7lb 1oz – no hint yet of a superwaif destiny.

Recalled Linda,"I thought she was a lovely baby, but she had a mop of bright red hair. I said, Oh God, I've got a redhead. But she quickly turned fair."

The Moss's then moved to Church Way in nearby Sanderstead. This area is only about two miles from Addiscombe, but a social world away.

Property prices alone are deceptive. Today, the average price for houses in Pagehurst Road is £206,000 – as opposed to £296,000 in Church Way. But Pagehurst Road is drab suburbia in the sense lamented by George Orwell, while Church Way is the suburbia celebrated by ex poet laureate, John Betjeman.

Sanderstead village has an entry in the Domesday Book as "Sanderstede." Its 800 year old parish church, All Saints, stands 596ft feet (the website says) above sea level, and from many streets around are spectacular views and sunsets: a big sky of cumuli and jet tracers. Even today, 50% of Sanderstead is unbuilt; the impression is green closes and sleepy streets, gardens lush with wisteria and laburnum and oversize plumes of pampas grass, ornate crazy paving and meticulously shaven hedges. All around is parkland and woodland and rolling golf courses. A local boasts that, "people in Sanderstead live longer than anyone else in Croydon."[1]

The street developed piecemeal as people bought plots and designed their own dwellings. Today, it's a striking and eclectic jumble of dream homes, several with bizarre designs – the reverse of ribbon development. This situation attracted "quite a few doctors and schoolmistresses."

The house the Mosses moved to was detached and built in the fifties. It stands imposingly above a steeply terraced front garden. The dwelling boasts two double bedrooms and one single. Kate had one of the bigger bedrooms, her younger brother Nick the small room. The family cat slept downstairs.

The Mosses had the local paper, *The Post*, delivered. But otherwise took little part in local events, didn't attend church, and Peter wasn't even a

---

[1] This conservation was largely due to an energetic campaign from the 1930s by Malcolm Sharpe. Sharpe ranted on conservation issues in *The Times* from his home in Church Way. No doubt posting his letters in the same red post box that Kate passed every day to and from primary school. His imposing title was Honorary Secretary and Treasurer of the Croydon and District Commons and Footpaths Preservation Society.

member of the golf club. They kept to themselves, taking the children out in the car at weekends, or they enjoyed their back garden.

This, like the front, was sharply terraced, sloping up until it merged with extensive ancient woodland called Sanderstead Plantation. A lush spot, the plantation still resembles what Maurice Sharpe described 80 years ago as "a particularly enchanting spot [with] abounding wild life [that] includes the badger and the brown squirrel and – less welcome, the weasel and the stoat ..."

Today, the house is owned by a Chinese couple whose teenage children, aware of the Moss mystique, allowed me to sample the back garden – hardly changed from Moss days: a compact idyll of levels, steps and grottos, rockeries and nooks, with a pretty pond, all sheltered by numerous mature trees decorated with bird houses.

This was Peter and Linda's house on a hill, where I suppose they thought they would all be happy, and for a time they were. But it was also where the Moss family played out its disintegration

* * *

How fancy romped and played here,
Building this house of moss!
A faery house, the shade here
And sunlight gleams across;
And how it danced and swayed here,
A child with locks atoss!
– Madisun Julius Cawein, "The House of Moss," 1913

Kate's playschool was a community hall in nearby Selsdon. It was well run and stocked with toys and kiddie apparatus like a slide, a Wendy house and bikes to ride round in circles. Kate, who in those days only answered to the name of "Katy," is remembered as bright and pretty: "A sparkling child." "She just fitted in, she wasn't naughty."

She seems to have relished playschool and "used to like painting an awful lot. But she could get into a horrible mess with it!" Starting at 9am there was free playing – "painting, sticking and gluing, things like that" – until milk time at 10.30, followed by "structured activities" like story telling or "musical games." And, occasionally, visits from officialdom when a fireman or policeman would warn about fire hazards or road safety.

* * *

Primary school was Ridgeway, housed in low brick buildings, and less than ten minutes walk from home. This was a sought-after school with an excellent reputation. Kate wore a uniform of grey skirt, white shirt, and grey and yellow tie. In summer she sported a yellow gingham dress.

Her first headmaster, Mr Kershaw, left not long after Kate's arrival. When asked, his successor, William Harris, looks blank and then recalls Kate as "pleasant but not particularly noteworthy."

At primary school Kate was in the "cool" group of kids, hanging out with equally cool kids like Sarah and Naomi, and mindful of her two male admirers, Ian Hawke and Nial Simonds, both apparently "after her". Nial made his move when Kate was nine.

One teacher, Mr Robertson, allowed the children to play records in lunch-breaks and Nial, who'd been eying Kate up for days: "eventually plucked up courage to ask her to dance when a smoochy track was played. It was one of those silly little boyfriend-girlfriend things you get at that age. They'd have slow dances together to the music and have the odd kiss. It was very sweet."

At primary school too, Kate first experimented with style and tried to pierce her ears: "She and another girl hid in the adventure playground and tried to pierce each others ears with a sewing needle borrowed from the needlework room. It was incredibly painful and in the end Kate couldn't face sticking the needle right through, so they had to give up."

There was another, more radical, style experiment. Deciding she was bored with the waist-long hair she wore in a plait, Kate and a friend pro-cured a pair of scissors and locked themselves in the girl's toilet during a morning break.

"When she came out, her hair was several inches shorter and cut in a zig zag across the bottom. It looked very funny – it really was all up and down. Kate was fairly proud of her efforts, but her mum was furious."

Meanwhile, she did the things little suburban girls do, joined the 7th Sanderstead Brownies, and took piano lessons as well as tap and modern dance – but with no great success.

An inconspicuous child.

Though what people did notice was unusual poise and serenity. Also her prettiness.

Friends recall dressing up with her in their mother's clothes, and pre-tending they were models tottering on high heels while smeared with their mothers' make up and lipstick and drenched in perfume.

Some people thought she might have a talent for acting. Peter's boss thought so. "He met her when she was five and immediately said she was going to be an actress or something similar."

Linda confirms, "I'm sure she dreamed of being an actress. She was always putting on little plays and performances with her chums."

She also acted in primary school plays and was often given the main part. Even so, she was shy in front of an audience, especially giving ballet performances, a shyness that has always stayed with her.

In the final year of Ridgeway she went on a school trip to Northern France. Some of the girls were homesick but Kate was no stranger to travel. Her father's job gave him access to cheap flights and the Moss family regularly holidayed in exotic places like Florida or the Caribbean.

* * *

Peter Moss was a notably light sleeper. "An insomniac," specifies a neighbour. A trait put to good use when Peter noticed two burglars prowling in the street and then watched as they broke into the family Passat. "It was the early hours of the morning, and he was watching them. They came over to his car, and broke into it. He phoned the police. But by the time they got there, these geezers had got the radio out of his car ... And up the road was a van, which was their 'hoppo.'"

On another occasion, the insomniac saw "three black men" trying to enter a house in this very white street and raised the alarm.

Otherwise, the neighbourhood was exceptionally safe, "a very friendly road, on the whole," and Kate's routine humdrum. As a pre-teen Kate appeared well balanced and confident. Her father likes to stress the normality of her childhood: quite evenings playing with friends, shopping forays to Croydon ...

* * *

Another element of security was that for a time Kate's uncle Alan, from Peter's side, lived next door, with his wife, Kay, and their son and daughter. This Moss clan formed a club, only admitting selected friends and neighbours.

Recalls one neighbor, "Alan and Kay used to have Christmas parties and both Peter and Linda used to come to them." Jollities included the conga: "I remember once we were weaving in and out of the all the houses and the gardens and I was holding on to Linda and she said 'don't grip me so tightly' and I shouted, 'you're going too fast!'"

* * *

Her mother claims "the only setback that Kate has ever had in life" was her parents' divorce" – when Kate was 13. Linda adds, "And she came through it well."

Others however, tell a different story of a Kate unhappy about the marital tensions preceding the eventual break-up, and who began doing classic "seeking attention" things like playing up and rebelling – testing her family's unusually elastic boundaries.

Kate: "Literally, my parents let us do what we wanted. I was smoking when I was thirteen in front of my parents, and drinking. I'd have parties where I'd come in at three o'clock in the morning because someone chucked me out then."

Adding: "It's actually worked to my benefit, because you end up thinking for yourself because you know you're not rebelling against anything."

It seems some tensions too, arose between the two Moss households due to their differing outlooks. Peter and Linda's laissez faire attitude, as well as Linda's relaxed lifestyle, may have created dissension. Neighbours still recall that Linda seemed to have lots of free time.

Peter, less so. "He was gone all day, and he never used to get home until late, about 7 in the evening."

Eventually, Alan moved his family away to another house nearby, where they still live. Whatever the reasons, there was a cooling between the families which persists today. Even before any scandal surrounded Kate, Alan's family refused to talk about her or about Peter or Linda. "There has been a sort of barrier between them … [especially] about Katy. So we don't say anything, because I think it would be embarrassing for them and for us. They brush it off politely."

The same source clarified, "I remember someone asking 'do you see Katy at all?' or 'where is Katy?' or something like that … And it was a sort of very off-hand answer, and you gathered from that they didn't really want to talk about it." And once he [Alan] told me, "We're one family and they're another family, and she [Kate] is not the same as us'. And it's true – they aren't the same sort of families at all."

* * *

We might also wonder what was beneath Kate's unusual composure as a child. That was a disposition she inherited from her father, who is the original model for that famously far away, detached – even spaced out, Kate Moss gaze. Many sources attest to her coolness and apparent imperturbability. Some thought it concealed insecurity.

But that placidity was not extended to her brother, Nick. Nick was a flash point – and maybe still is. The screaming little bundle Linda brought home in November 1976 turned into a sibling she resented with unusual passion.

Not that Nick was in any case easy to live with. His mother recalls him a difficult and demanding child, unlike Kate. A neighbour confirms, "He used to squeal like a girl. He was a noisy little so-and-so – always screaming his head off." Into his early teens he is remembered by an ex school friend as "quite a naughty boy … yeah, he reckoned himself a bit …"

Battles between Nick and Kate could get scary. Kate would tease Nick and he would tear down the posters in her bedroom or destroy her cassettes by pulling the tape out. On one occasion, Kate was obliged to lock herself in the bathroom while Nick threatened her from outside. The bathroom was also where, exasperated with her little brother, Kate would sometimes lock him inside after having first tied him up with the help of obliging girl-friends. Kate has also reported, "I used to pin him down and spit in his face."

While the animosity eventually subsided, it's interesting that after their parent's divorce the two opted to live apart – Kate with Linda, Nick with Peter.

Moreover, there are indications the friction lasted into adulthood. Spending Christmas, 2003, with her family in a rented cottage in Falmouth, Kate was so high handed and contemptuous of lil' brother, at one point order-ing him to fetch her a drink as she watched telly, that he exploded, telling her he wasn't one of her gofers and to get off her arse and get her own drink.

Nick for his part, was not a neutral observer of his sister's downfall in autumn of 2005. There was a distinct element of "told you so" in his com-ments. And even some remarks which upped the ante.

One cause of this rancour may have been jealousy. Kate wanted, has always wanted, Linda's attention.

* * *

Kate's former primary school teachers as well as neighbours thought Peter was a doting father. They noticed it was mostly Peter who would take Kate to the playgroup and attend her school events.

"Yes, this was the funny thing … he made a point of always being there for her. Even when it came to concerts I remember him coming."

Years later, when she moved in with her boyfriend Mario Sorrenti's fam-ily, Kate marvelled that Mario's mother, Francesca Sorrenti, "is a real mother, I mean, she cooks dinner and everything." Different to Linda Moss. A family friend remarked pointedly that Linda was "hardly an earth mother." For example, rather than cook she would "order stuff in" from caterers for parties and family gatherings.

A woman preoccupied by projecting a sense of her own glamour, Linda was recognised for attention to dress and her modish accessories. One source recalls she styled herself on the svelte and sleek look of Audrey Hepburn, adding cattily, "only she didn't have the figure."

Linda it seems, was also forever mislaying her house keys. This became a running joke. Neighbours would break in for her. Or Kate sent up a ladder to squeeze through an upstairs window and then run downstairs to open up the house. Linda would be suitably flustered. A psychoanalyst might be intrigued.

Sorrenti's mother was not the only surrogate mother espoused by Kate. All her life she has looked for mothers. She turned her agent, Sarah Doukas, into a second mother, referring to her as such. Doukas returns the compliment, "I think my three girls would say Kate's like my fourth daughter." And then there is her unusually intense (and complex) relationship with what you might call her "cultural mother," Marianne Faithful – of which more later.

Certainly, Kate has always striven to appeal to Linda. When she began earning big money as a model, she several times declared the best thing about it was being able to send cheques to her mother. Was there an element of pleading in this generosity, or even control?

Note that no mention was made of cheques being sent to the father. And yet, Peter Moss has been from the start a managing director of the various companies that have managed Kate's finances. This, while continuing his work as a travel agent and managing his own company, The Visit USA Association (UK) Ltd. And, as well as cheques in the post, Linda also gets exotic holidays gratis and shopping jaunts in London and abroad.

Peter and his new wife, Inger, today live in a modest home in Haywards Heath, on a street where the average house price is less than £200,000. Linda meanwhile, lives in a plush Georgian villa on an exclusive private estate in countryside outside Croydon. The dream home of a Croydon homebody, it is more secluded than Kate's own country home near Lechlade. Linda's home is also surrounded by extensive sports and leisure facilities, including a private tennis court. All paid for by her daughter.

Kate is keen to spoil Linda. Late in 2005, after rehab and all that, Kate bought her mother a £50,000 Porsche. No ordinary Porsche, this was "a blue 911 Targa – the sports car her mum had always dreamed of owning." The gift was apparently to thank Linda for visiting her in rehab. A PR source disclosed, "When Kate asked her to go out to Arizona, Linda didn't hesitate – she booked a flight straight away." Unexceptional you might think in the circumstances. After all, it's her only daughter and the girl was in deep shit.

Linda has lived off her daughter's earnings for many years now. She's also lived vicariously off her daughter's fame, relishing the celebs she can rub

ADDICTED TO LOVE

KATE MOSS

FRED VERMOREL

shoulders with, like her "fave rockers", post punk/art rock band The Kaiser Chiefs – blushing to their boyish singer, Ricky Wilson, that she is "his biggest fan".

Some commentators have pointed out that Linda is more like Kate's sister than her mother. That may have posed a problem. Every child needs a mentor. But Linda seems to have resisted that role. Nor is collusion always required from a parent. Linda hardly seems shy of joining in Kate's partying ways. She was for example, present at Kate's 30th and 31st birthday parties, both of which turned into a night-long pageants of outrageous revelry and strange dancing.

The only time Linda openly demurred over Kate's behaviour was over Doherty. But then, Linda, like everyone else, knew the guy might be disaster, that the power of Kate's attraction to him might bring the glittering facade crashing down on all of them.

* * *

Linda has asserted that Kate "had a very stable upbringing with liberal parents and I think that it has made her a sensible girl."

Aside from the glib assumption that "liberal" equates to stability, in retrospect, that seems an unfortunate boast. Sensible is something Kate Moss certainly is not. She has never had to be, or cared to be. She has lived in a bubble since the age of 14. And Linda inhabited that bubble too – until it almost burst.

* * *

Kate's rebelliousness began soon after she went to her comprehensive school, Riddlesdown High. By this time she was known to school fellows as "Katie Mosschops", or simply, "Mosschops".

Like, Ridgeway, Riddlesdown was the posh choice, a school with mostly middle class pupils. A contemporary recalls: "Without wanting to sound snobbish, Riddlesdown was maybe a little bit better than some of the other schools around. The catchment area was Purley, Sanderstead, and Selsdon. And the general class of people that went to the school were pretty reasonable people. You didn't get sort-of council types. I know it sounds so shallow to say that, but you didn't really get that kind of character at the school. And if you did, they stood out a mile ... they came with a reputation – expelled from other schools."

The school buildings were a sixties build, trimly designed and well kept. The location was particularly pleasant. "The school runs along the sides of fields and Downs. And there was this path that went all the way down to the bottom of Mitchley Avenue, called the white path. Which is a very legendary pathway by the school. And if you lived anywhere near Sanderstead or Selsdon, everyone went down the White Path. And if you lived in Purley you went across the Downs."

The head teacher when Kate first joined "was notorious for snooping around the school, and catching any kid that came round the corner to go and pick up five pieces of litter. People used to say 'don't go round the corner, [the Head] is there!' He would end up standing at a really busy point between lessons and not a single person coming round, and wondering why."

"He really hated scruffiness. I remember him saying in assembly: 'The day I turn up scruffy, is the day that you can turn up scruffy.' Because he used to wear corduroy, checked suits, and things like that."

After two years, he retired and was replaced by the current Head Master, who "had a lisp and he came from Selhurst Boys. And I can remember him coming into assembly, with the cape and flat cap. Everyone just pissed themselves, we'd never seen anything like it!"

Another contemporary recalls that "he had a very funny way of speaking – he couldn't say pupils, he'd say 'pooples,' I also remember when we all got dragged into assembly one morning and [he] made this fantastic speech because a first year had been picked on and had his rugby shirt stolen. And in front of 700 kids, he stood up there with his cape having a pop at: 'these people, they took him into the toilet and flushed his head in the toilet and took his rugby shirt and placed it across the toilet – and then decided to shit upon it" [spoken in a mock posh voice].

"And you can imagine – you don't expect that, any sort of language like that – and the whole assembly just cracked up."

Like all schools, Riddlesdown had its share of eccentric teachers.

"There was a Maths teacher who had the biggest, brightest red nose you've ever seen. A really aggressive, scary type character.

"And [another teacher] had a hearing aid, and people used to whistle or do a low-pitched hmmmmmmm like that, so he couldn't hear us. And he used to walk up and down the class, like a colonel in the army, and spin round and walk back down. Then there was a husband and wife. She taught French and was absolutely feared by everybody. And he taught art. They were a really strange combination."

★ ★ ★

But Kate didn't respond very well to any teaching. In fact, she was a dunce. At Riddlesdowne, out of eight GCSEs she scraped through with one C (in Science) and all the rest were Ds, Es and Fs.

Nor did her personality impress. One former teacher sniffs she was not, "a child you would have turned your head to look at." A contemporary confirms, "For me, she was very ordinary, she didn't stand out."

For her part, Kate has boasted, "I went to school to socialize. I never did my homework. I liked English and drama because you never had to work." She puts a glamorous shine on this adding, "I was a rebel who only thought of the next day at school. I didn't think ahead, except in terms of the next day's provocation."

It was an approach that would eventually lose her the one man in her life she truly loved, Johnny Depp.

But one thing she excelled at was sport. At Ridgway she'd shone at trampolining and sprinting. At Riddlesdown she played goal attack for the school netball team and was a star in athletics, especially sprinting, becoming captain of the athletics team.

This contradicts the myth she's since created, claiming that in order to avoid sport she "had a period every week."

She was however, already smoking heavily. Kate was one of a group who would puff surreptitiously behind the school gym. Sometimes the teachers would mount raids on this enclave. Once, Kate was caught when a male teacher sneaked up on her. The punishment was to "spend her lunch hour polishing the brass handles on the doors in the school foyer."

It didn't work. She later graduated to an 80-a-day habit.

★   ★   ★

While Kate (and her mother) have always claimed she was naturally skinny, school friends recall she was careful about her diet as a teenager. She certainly attracted attention "because she was so slim".

Kate herself recalls, "They used to call me 'Stick' and take the piss." But her thinness led to envy from other girls. As did her sense of style. Like the way she wore cheap jeans: "She just had a way of making them look good."

Out of school and released from uniform Kate and her girlfriends would take their pocket money to Croydon and buy clothes from the market, mixing and matching current styles.

★   ★   ★

Sanderstead youth club was one early hangout. This was beside the church and happened every Wednesday from 7-10.30. But there was no pub in Sanderstead. It seems that because the land was formerly church owned there's a prohibition on opening one. So the Sanderstead teenscene had to travel for liquor.

A contemporary: "In the late eighties Croydon was a very different place in terms of nightlife. We call Croydon now, Costa del Croydon, because on a Friday or Saturday night it's like being in somewhere like the Costa del Sol, full of young people, trying to look as good as they can, going to non-stop nightclubs and bars. Croydon now, is unrecognizable to what it was sixteen years ago.

"But there were only a couple of places to go in 1989-91 if you were cool. Bruce Saint George, for example, which is no longer there. It was an underground, cellar bar place that was immensely popular. It was really pokey, with little arches, a little bar in the corner, and it probably fitted no more than 200 people in it. Everybody who was everybody went there. Every week you went there."

"And then there was the Blue Anchor Pub. The place to go in South Croydon. With a tiny, overcrowded nightclub upstairs."

* * *

Kate finessed her rebellion. A contemporary recalls, "I remember Kate Moss as being one of the streetwise types, smoking and drinking from a young age and I seem to remember her always being in a group, bit of a leader."

"She was a 'Purley Dosser', one of the cool types that were out on a Friday night and Saturday night hanging around the phone boxes and the cinema that's now gone in Purley town centre."

Adding, "On a handbag raising tip: I do remember that I thought she was very bandy and that I thought she was a bit of a hard chavvy type (although obviously we must have had a different word for it then)."

The park was another venue for pleasure. Kate has recalled: "Everyone used to go down to this park in Purley, and just drink cider and get off with each other behind the bushes."

Another source adds: "Um ... she ... got on very well with the naughty boys, which were, I suppose, the hard kids of the time."

Her brother Nick has confirmed, "She was a real tearaway, always bunking off school. She used to hang out with a load of older kids and go to pubs when she was only 14."

* * *

Purley, about two miles from Sanderstead, was the hip place. "I remember for a period, for Kate's year there was a real big hangout in Purley. Anyone who considered themselves cool and hip would hang out in Purley. I can remember going to Purley and seeing everyone hanging out there on a Saturday. All dressed as best as they could, loafing around."

"The place to go", confides a ex friend, "if you could into it, was 'Cinderella Rockafellas' in Purley and everybody used to call it 'Spinderellas'. It was an awful glitzy, crappy club but if you could convince the bouncers that you were over eighteen … A lot of people from Riddlesdown went there. Quite a long way out, but it was really the only nightclub.

Otherwise Kate and crew would party at one another's homes. "We'd dance, smoke and lark around." They would also drink heavily. A school friend: "I remember getting rat arsed at a party of [Kate's] drinking thunderbirds."

The drinking wasn't only for after school. Kate has recounted how even at the age of 12: "We'd go to people's houses and steal their mum's liquor on the way to school. Some bloke would have brought a bag in from his Dad's stash – we'd smoke and drink Super Tennents. I was smoking pot then, too. It's South London, innit?"

A boy in the year below Kate alleged, "She was the first person ever to offer me a controlled drug on the top deck of a bus."

* * *

This was the post punk generation, or generation X or Y depending on who you read, or the rave generation or the E generation, or the Acid House or Hip Hop or grunge generation …

But whatever you call it, the prevailing ethos was disenchantment: so many dead ends all reached all at once: utopia mired in an oil crisis, the jobs drying up, the welfare running out, systems running down. Meanwhile the IRA got on with their project of demolishing "economic targets" and dismembering passers-by.

These babies of the baby boomers were also Thatcher's children – Kate Moss was five when the Iron Lady entered Downing Street, she began her teens in the heyday of "Loadsamoney" and Wall Street chic and chicanery, and made it as the face of Calvin Klein in the year Margaret tearfully left Downing Street.

Meanwhile, the chimera of a communist alternative was spectacularly "liquidated" through TV images of uproar in far away places that nevertheless looked familiar. If the defining TV moment of Peter and Linda Moss's generation was the moon landing in 69 – when nothing seemed impossible, that of their daughter's was the moment in 89 when the CP rentacrowd started booing the Romanian tyrant Ceausescu live on TV, and the President For Life had to run for his life – and nothing seemed predictable or certain any more.

A period too, when notions of social cohesion, social justice, and even "society," might safely be deemed quaint. As for education for its own sake: since making money had become the only reasonable project in life, education was simply a means to that end, and schools and universities were themselves turned into businesses. No surprise then, that Kate's teachers at Riddlesdown encouraged her to dump school early.

"My teachers were really supportive. They told me if you can make money now, then don't go to college."

* * *

But Reagen-Thatcher rhetoric was white noise on the Sanderstead teenscene. Here, free market values translated as an unprecedented drugs boom. The mid to late eighties gave British youth culture a drugs bonanza. The stuff had never been so various, so unexceptional, or so cheap.

* * *

Sex and drugs and rock 'n' roll
Is all my brain and body need
Sex and drugs and rock 'n' roll
Is very good indeed

Dury's anthem was a biting celebration of an ethos that spread from the lucky dip bowls on coffee tables in Beatles' sessions in Abbey Road, and trickled down from the anorexic allure of Ziggy Stardust, to settle in the high streets, youth clubs and bedrooms of Sanderstead and everywhere else like it.

The same pattern was seen in the USA. Stephen Fried's Thing of Beauty, the biography of the drug addled supermodel Gia, describes the eighties rise of "what was coming to be seen as the new 'mass hip,' a kind of universal exclusivity where everyone felt they were in on the ground floor. 'It was like what John Lennon was doing in 1965 was working its way down to JC Penney.'"

The advent of rave also spread new thrills like MDMA, and made music and dancing (hence fashion) increasingly drug-fixated. Drugs became an essential rather than a contingent part of a night out – or in – and cocktails and admixtures were increasingly played with. Everything from Ecstasy popped in clubs to mushrooms gathered in the woods to LSD copped on the school bus – with marihuana as innocuous backdrop, "It's not really a drug, is it?" as Kate Moss declared, and heroin – later crack too, as enticingly risqué extras.

Record poppy crops allied with political instability in Afghanistan and Iran meant the opium trade too, exploded from the early eighties. Heroin addiction mutated from the genteel quirk espoused in Alex Trocchi's 1961, *Cain's Book*, to the culture feted in the 1996 movie, *Trainspotters* – from the Parisian left bank to Edinburgh sink estates and the Purley Odeon in a generation.

And with all that came what is often referred to as the "cocaine epidemic" from the eighties when Sigmund Freud's powder of choice became a recreation for millions of Americans and Europeans. (This thanks in part to CIA backed trafficking meant to fund right wing insurgencies in Latin America.)

Remark too, that it was the suburbs that gobbled up most of the hard stuff. They had the cash and the enquiring minds. Weaned on *Sergeant Pepper* and Lou Reed they borrowed Aldous Huxley's Gates of Perception from the local library, and might discuss Jack Kerouac in an English lesson. You could find quality Class A products more easily in Purley than Brixton. As easily as you could shop for nirvana in any Shire or Welsh market town – the provinces also, were bored shitless and looking for chemical ways out.

All that and loadsa sex too. Increasingly, sixties free-love rhetoric was enacted – the children practicing what the parents preached. And it was soon far wickeder to mock single parent families than start one, as eccentric not to "experiment" with sex as with substances.

The result was a generation for which drugs and casual sex was both unremarkable and essential, and oddly equivalent or interchangeable. A generation who, as India Knight (specifically referring to women and Kate Moss) remarked in *The Times*, hitting: "… their late 20s or early 30s [relied] entirely on drink and pharmaceuticals for fun, who put themselves about more than may be wise, who've had group sex more often than they care to remember. ('After a while the difference between a model and a whore becomes tenuous,' says one party lover.)"

Knight continued: "At some imperceptible point these girls go from seeming fun and cool to becoming pitiful. It is appropriate that [Kate] Moss should have become a mascot for an entire generation because she is very generation-specific in terms of her story. That generation – once known as generation X and now in its early 30s – is uniquely acquainted with no-strings hedonism. It also has an absolutely extraordinary sense of entitlement. None of them do much but they want everything: money, fame, happiness, time, travel, technology, life on their own terms, lived exactly as they want it.

"It is a generation that has never been deprived or wanted for anything, that has never known sacrifice of any kind, that stopped valuing hard work when it realised – via recession, housing crashes, Lloyd's losses – that there was no such thing as a job for life, so why bother working at all? Why not drift about being creative and experiencing things? Especially given they were the first young people to reap the benefits of the explosion in cheap travel. And in cheap drugs."

* * *

Oh, that a witch had willed it
That these child dreams come true!
With which the child-heart filled it
While 'neath glad hands it grew,
And, dim, amort, it builded
Far better than it knew.
- Madisun Julius Cawein, "The House of Moss," 1913

As everyone knows, Kate Moss was "discovered" at 14 in an airport. A fairy tale for our times that conflates a lottery win and hair's breath odds – what if? – with Sliding Doors coincidences: fate transforming the unknown into the known, the spectator into the spectacle, nonentity into celebrity.

Almost too good to be true and all the more mythical because that's how it was. Why, it could be you next! Hope burns in the population. And part of her appeal (as she well knows and well plays) is just that: the kid plucked from nowhere, an ugly duckling resurrected, the princess recognized and respected: the fantasy of frustrated schoolgirls all over the planet who didn't ask to be born and chafe at housework and homework.

* * *

It was because of the family crisis over his failing marriage that Peter took the kids on a "bonding" holiday in 1988 to the Bahamas. Kate takes up the story:

"I was on a holiday with my dad and my brother. We'd been in the Bahamas for two weeks and on the way back had been stranded at Kennedy airport for a night. My dad's mother was getting married in England the next day, and he told the airline. They said there was one last flight with three seats left. I was praying, "Please let us get on that plane." We did. There was one seat in economy, one in business, and one in first class. I was in economy, my brother was in business, and my dad was in first class.

"Halfway through the flight – the meal had come and I was listening to my Walkman – a man came over to where I was sitting and said, "Excuse me." I was like, "What? What do you want?" He said, "My sister owns a modeling agency and she'd like to speak to you." We ended up having this chat. To this day she's still my agent – Sarah Doukas."

★ ★ ★

Sarah Doukas, nee Sarah Noelle Chambers, was born in Malta on 21st December 1952. Her father was a naval lieutenant surgeon and she describes her mother as "very eccentric, she was a pharmacist and the model doctor's wife. At 65 she became a pig farmer."

Doukas inherited her mother's rebelliousness, she always looked for work that "left me to my own devices, I never really answered to anyone, and that's the way I liked it. I knew I could never be an employee – it just wouldn't have been me."

She also recalls, "I was put under a lot of pressure from my parents to be academic. As far as my father was concerned, unless you followed medicine or law or a conservative profession, you weren't going to have a reasonable life. But I thought, to hell with it, I'll do whatever I want. I completed one A-level and walked out of the rest. My father was furious. He didn't speak to me for two years."

A pretty, petite blonde, she became a model just after leaving school. She then ran an antiques business based in Antiquarius on the King's Road, and also in Paris where she lived for two years. She then helped manage a punk band, The Criminals. "A friend in Paris wanted to sign the band to his record company and had nobody to look after them in Britain so I started managing them. I did everything from driving the van to loading the equipment to setting up their gigs. I didn't get any sleep but it was a lot of fun."

Married at 24 to a music entrepreneur, it was after she had her first daughter, Noelle, that she thought she ought to get a proper job. She went back into modelling – on the agency side, for Laraine Ashton, founder of IMG Models. In six years she went from a junior assistant to generally managing the place. However, she found the work sometimes mundane and chafed at collecting the boss's dry cleaning and being a gofer. "I was going nowhere, had a boss and was collecting a wage packet – all the things I said I'd never do."

Meanwhile, she was thinking she could play this model agency game better on her own. She had seen a niche: imperfection and character were more intriguing than the air brushed perfection rampant at the time. Plus, she thought agencies might take a more proactive approach to finding new faces.

"Wherever I was going, I was looking. I found a great girl outside a garage in Battersby, in her school uniform."

The classic route would have been to plot a new agency while with IMG and then leave with the contacts book and as many models as possible. But Doukas just left.

"It was a mad thing to do, but I couldn't go to sleep at night or look at somebody at work and think I was organising something behind their back."

So she found herself stranded in the monetarist eighties with no money. "My husband was furious that I was going to leave my job because I was being paid very well."

Luckily for her, she came from posh stock. Following his dreams for an academic daughter, her father had sent her to a very expensive boarding school to do A-level retakes. While there, she shared a dormitory and became chums with Lindy Branson, the sister of the bearded millionaire and serial entrepreneur, Richard.

At that point Branson was flushed with success. In five years Virgin had gone from releasing Tubular Bells and double album epics written by pale hippies in sheepskin coats, to signing the Sex Pistols. That coup gave him the kudos to sign Boy George and then the clout to sign Phil Collins and then the cash to set up Virgin Atlantic … Ten years on, the rest was legend. What next?

While she was painstakingly negotiating a business plan for her agency with the help of U2's financial advisor, Ossie Kilkenny, Doukas got an unexpected call from the great man. Branson declared he'd heard of her plans and might be interested in backing them. After some amicable negotiations the result was a £250,000 interest-free loan for three years.

As she quips, "It is all about who you know in this life."

Belying the story that Storm started out in the apocryphal "bedroom" of rags to riches legends, Doukas admits that Branson also "lent me a gorgeous building he was selling to set up in." In fact, he bought a house in Kensington for Doukas to use as offices.

"I got the company off the ground with just me, an ex-model from IMG who became my booker, a friend of mine's nanny and another friend who was married to a producer. That was my crew, and from that I built Storm."

She chose the name "Storm" because 'I was looking in *Roget's Thesaurus* at the word tempest. I saw "storm", lived with it for a month and liked it.'

Doukas had an extensive network of music biz contacts, including Miles Copeland, manager of the Police. She was also well connected to mainstream showbiz through her sister, Emma Chambers. (Emma was a TV actress who played Alice Tinker in the BBC TV series *The Vicar of Dibley*, and made Hollywood as Honey in *Notting Hill*.)

More crucially, Doukas recruited her brother, Simon Chambers, who left a lucrative banking post to run Storm with her.

* * *

In fact, it was Simon who approached Kate Moss on that plane.

The pair had been scouting for girls in New York but found no one to excite them. They were returning disconsolately to London when Doukas spotted the 14 year old Kate in the airport melee.

Doukas takes up the story: "I still remember it as if was yesterday. I was in such a bad mood because I'd been in America far too long. I was with my brother Simon and my six-year-old daughter. I was razzled and desperate to get home and the last thing I said to my brother before I went to sort out a cab to pick us up from the airport was 'I never want to see another model again.'

"It was then, while I was on the phone, that I saw this wonderful face in a sea of other faces. I saw those wonderful cheekbones. Then she disappeared. I knew she had to be on our flight because she was at the same check-in desk and, as I was in the departure lounge, I was searching for her. We got on the plane and the engines revved up and I thought I'd lost her. Then I saw her getting on with her father. They were the very last two people on the plane. I couldn't move because I was jammed at the end of the row of seats, but as soon as the seat-belt signs clicked off, I sent Simon to give her my card."

Doukas also recalled: "She had a kind of ethereal look about her, a translucency, and such phenomenal bone structure. She was young and absolutely beautiful.

"I saw her and knew instantly I'd struck gold. This 14-year-old girl with amazing bone structure was a vision. Yes, she was smaller than any model on an agency's books, especially in the era of the supermodel, but I knew she had something.

"She was the last person to check in on the flight back to London. But it was a flight that changed both our lives."

Since then, Kate Moss has been Storm's calling card, the foundation of an agency that by 1992 was turning over £2million with profits at "a good six figures," and booking 130 girls and 90 men. By 1997, the turnover was £6.6m and the agency was representing Elle MacPherson, Rachel Hunter, Marie Helvin, Carla Bruni, Eva Herzigova, Sophie Dahl and Iris Palmer. By 2004 Storm employed 29 people and had a turnover of £8m.

Kate Moss has always stayed loyal to Storm, though she is represented abroad by other companies. It is a personal as much as a business attachment. "Sarah's really my second mother. If there's ever a problem or a drama I ring Sarah and she's amazing. She has great strength; she's incredibly resourceful under pressure. She just kicks in, she makes a plan, she stands by you and takes care of you."

* * *

To begin with, the Moss parents were incredulous. Kate has recalled, When we got off the plane I told my dad about it, and he laughed. Then after we got home I told my mum and a few days later we were sitting around the kitchen table, and one of us said, "Should we give her a call?"

We phoned her up and made an appointment and went on the train up to London to see her. She signed me up. They took some Polaroids, put them in a book, and immediately sent me off on castings.

"At the end of that first day my mum said, "If you want to do this, you're on your own because I'm not traipsing around London ever again like that. It's a nightmare.""

So Kate found herself at the age of 14 in the care of an industry hardly known for its gentility. What's more, Storm themselves could be somewhat careless. There was little supervision and arrangements were sometimes chaotic.

Kate has related how: "I went to this guy's house in North London and he was in his bedroom. He told me to come through and there were all these rolls of film on the bedside table. He asked me to take my top off. I took my jumper off. He asked me to take my bra off but I wouldn't. There were other girls who had taken theirs off and were just lying there on the bed. It was really scary. We took him to court and he got done. He wasn't a photographer – he had just phoned the agency and they didn't check him out."

Nowadays, Doukas admits that she would never work with anyone still at school. She has also appeared in a TV documentary advising model wannabes to finish their studies first.

* * *

Of course, back then, Kate thought she was anything but a child. The Sanderstead suburbanite and pupil at the genteel Riddlesdown High, thought herself pretty streetwise.

One day she appeared unannounced at the home studio of photographer, David Ross.

"This kid rang my doorbell. She was quite small and my first thought was she was a child looking for her mum in one of the flats. She said, 'Hi, are you David Ross?' I didn't remember there being any arrangement to photograph her. I was thinking, she's so young, why is she here? She told me Sarah had sent her to do some pictures. I thought someone was going to come up after her, but she was on her own. She was so young and so determined.

"I said, 'I don't mean to be rude, but I'm not allowed to photograph you by yourself.' She looked at me as if to say 'don't be so ridiculous, I'm not a kid", then went off in a huff. But the next day she was back with a friend."

He continues: "Kate clearly didn't realise what she was getting into, she was so young. At the time, beauty photographers used girls aged between 12 and 15 to do make-up shoots because their skin was faultless and re-touching was so expensive then."

Ross adds: "Kate was shy in front of the camera, as if she wasn't sure of herself, in the way of most teenagers. She didn't express the kind of confidence she expresses now, although it might well have been in her. She may have been a wild kid at home, but she wasn't with me. She was nervous, shy and probably thought it was all a bit silly.

"She just didn't know what to do, so I offered her as much direction and encouragement as I could. I showed her how to give me expressions. She was a clueless child, a bit of a blank canvas."

Kate would however, sometimes take her school friends along on casting rounds. "She just never made a big deal of it," recalls one. "We'd even go to the castings with her. She was always conscious of this little bead of sweat which would appear on her lip. She'd whisper, 'do I need a tissue!'"

★   ★   ★

Meanwhile, back in Sanderstead, things had fallen apart. Peter and Linda Moss decided to go their separate ways. Professionals were called in: things had to be done properly.

Kate has related how: "A man came round and asked us which of them I wanted to live with. I said me mum and my brother said me dad."

A flat statement for so much pain.

So Peter found a house in Purley. And Linda got herself a maisonette on a smart estate in Forestdale. And Nick went to stay with Peter and Kate moved in with Linda. And not long after that, Linda's lover, Geoffrey R

Collman, moved in too. (Though the arrangement was more fluid than that and Kate quite often stayed at Peter's house).[1]

*   *   *

Meanwhile, Kate had begun to get more interested in boys. Even though, to start with they were not that interested in her. "She wasn't that amazing," reminisces one. Another chips in: "She was no more pretty than a couple of other girls in her class."

Her father admits she went through "an ugly duckling stage at 13 or so." Linda suggests however, this phase was short lived. "Kate's just lucky. When she was 14 she began to look much the same as she does now." Though she adds, "Still, no one ever thought of her as a model."

At 14, Kate developed an interest in a fellow Riddlesdown pupil, Scott Wilson. She sent him a message on lined school exercise paper, "I really do like you – please meet me at the youth club." Scott ignored this heartfelt plea.

Later he recalled that she just "didn't look sexy in her school uniform – grey skirt, green jumper and white shirt with a green, black and white striped tie."

Even so, he admits, "I'd given her the eye."

But Scott was not a confident lad. "I never thought she would be interested in me. I always thought I'd be too short." He wondered whether the note was a wind up from his mates. But then she "bumped into" him a few days later during a lunchtime break. They chatted and soon after became an item.

However, Scott was perfidious. "I blew it by getting caught snogging her best friend at a party. I'd had a few beers and there was a bit of trouble at the party with a few lads. It was her friend's party and when her dad switched on the lights to throw us all out there I was in a clincher with her pal. It was the abrupt end to our relationship. I wouldn't mind but Kate was a fantastic kisser and her friend wasn't anywhere near as good."

*   *   *

It was also when she was 14, that Kate, as she has famously claimed, lost her virginity: "Well it was just something to lose." She has also been quoted

---

[1] These homes were both two miles equidistant from Church Way – Peter went West, Linda East.

many times:"I didn't want to lose it to some nasty bloke from Croydon, did I?"

The story goes – her story goes – that she waited for a more romantic opportunity which finally came on that fateful holiday with her dad and brother in the Bahamas. And was thereupon deflowered by a handsome young American whom she never saw again.

The story continues that it may even have been the "glow" from that encounter that so entranced Sarah Doukas at the airport.

A nice story, but not necessarily so. For one thing, it seems rosy and pat and like a Duran Duran video. And convenient: that vanishing lover who has never reappeared to claim his prize of publicity …

Other sources claim she had already given herself to more than one "nasty bloke" from Croydon before that holiday.

She has said:"I was the girl that all the boys used to be friends with, not the girl that the boys fancied. I didn't really have a boyfriend – I was just one of the lads that hung out."

Insecure about her looks – "At school I was nothing special, I was never five foot ten and stunning" – she hung around with boys almost as one of the lads; casual sex may have been part of the laddishness.

And another source has called the legend of her defloration in the sun, "absolute rubbish. She lost her virginity to someone she barely knew in a garage in Croydon."

* * *

Whatever the truth of all that, it's certain that her first serious boyfriend was the Croydon born and bred Clark Gregory, three years older than Kate. Far from being "nasty," Clark was well groomed, handsome and debonair.

The affair began when she was 15 and lasted 18 months. They met in November 1989 at the Rue St George, a trendy Croydon night spot. Kate was wearing jeans, T-shirt and black leather jacket.

"I just started talking to her, and we went on to a party and got on really well. We exchanged phone numbers but neither of us called. Then two weeks later I saw her again and asked her to come to a boat party on the Thames. We saw each other regularly from then on.

For a Croydon schoolgirl, Clark was a catch. Apart from his looks he owned a car (a Suzuki GX) and his job as a counter assistant at Next netted him what for those days was the tidy weekly sum of £140.

Clark had enjoyed his share of local talent. But Kate seemed a more serious proposition.

That Christmas he took her to his family home, a posh semi with pink carpets, and introduced Kate to his dad, Peter, an executive in a publishing company, his mother, Maxine, and three brothers.

"They hit it off straight away. My parents were really fond of Kate. She was very mature for her age and always in the kitchen chatting with mum."

For Kate's 16th birthday in 1990 Clark splashed out on a pair of earrings and a bottle of peach schnapps – her favourite tipple at the time.

"We hadn't yet said we were in love, but she knew my family, I knew hers and we really liked one another."

There was nearly a tragedy however. Speeding in Selsdon High Street, Clark's Suzuki smashed into a parked car. The passenger side occupied by Kate took the main impact. The car was a write-off, but Kate escaped with bruises – Clark with a ticking off from his mum.

The lovers would spend evenings in trendy Croydon pubs or the local Chinese restaurant, or cosy times in front of the telly watching Neighbours and so on. But nearly every day Kate would travel to London on modelling assignments that grew more lucrative, and more involved. And she was becoming engrossed in a culture unknown and even alien to Clark.

"She'd show me her latest photographs and told me what she'd done, but she really didn't discuss it that much."

In spring 1990 they spoiled themselves with a holiday in New York, courtesy of cheap air tickets supplied by Kate's dad. Then, that summer they went on a camping holiday in Bournemouth.

"Neither of us was really romantic in the sense of staring into each others eyes across candlelit tables, but we were in love."

Even so, "There was certainly no talk of marriage, though Kate always loved kids and said she wanted them one day, but she wasn't interested in getting married."

In fact, her thoughts were very far from marriage.

* * *

Kate's modelling career began as a bumpy ride.

Storm had made her first booking for Mizz magazine in 1988, when she was still 14. Kate recalls, "My parents were astonished when I started making money. I got £150 for my first job for Mizz magazine. It was like, wow!

However, "I wasn't booked again, but not because I was late. I think it was because I wasn't pretty enough."

She had to suffer numerous rejections and humiliations. She was told she was too short, too girlish, too contrived, too gawky, not beautiful. And that she had bandy legs, a gap in her front teeth and a lazy eye. Nor was she considered enough of a looker for catalogue work.

* * *

Despite being the "wrong" height however, she did get a catwalk gig in Paris when she was 15. This was for John Galliano, who cast her as "Lolita".

Galliano was then panicking. He was four years out of his legendary St Martins graduation show, looking like a one hit wonder sans backer. This was his first Paris show and he needed all the sensation he could muster. The decidedly boyish Moss as Lolita – Parisian gamin fused with spring chicken – spelled controversy.

So Kate bunked off school and flew to Paris, staying with one of Galliano's seamstresses. The evening before the show she was so scared she couldn't eat. She recalled, "I had to come down the catwalk by myself. It looked huge, like an airport runway – I was so nervous."

She also described watching the video of the show later that evening: "Someone had run off with the champagne, so me and this other person drank a bottle of Scotch between us. I passed out at the table and went missing for two days. I was supposed to be back at school but no one knew where I was. I was supposed to be back at school on Monday morning and I was still in Paris on Wednesday!"

(Fashion light years later, in 2005, when Kate was presented by David Bowie with a special award for Style at the Council of Fashion Designers of America, Galliano was unable to attend on account of a "shower accident." But he sent Kate a Humbert Humbert note, "You will always be my Lolita.")

* * *

Sarah Doukas had big ideas for her protégé. She steered Kate away from catalogue and advertising work, even though that was lucrative. Instead, she was angling for Kate's face to show in the editorial pages of street savvy publications like *The Face* and *i-D*. While they paid peanuts, these were the magazines that were scoured by photographers, designers and fashion editors on the lookout for new talent and trends.

Despite the slow start, Storm stuck with Kate. Doukas thought people were tiring of the sleek perfection of reigning supermodels. Fashion professionals were also getting pissed off by supermodel fees and tantrums. Kate came at a bargain rate. And she had a naturally sweet disposition – a major asset, as she cannily realised, in her search for accommodating photographers. She also had that *je ne sais quoi*: street.

* * *

Street was the triumph of a "trickle up" effect of fashion – confounding the former "trickle down", whereby style emanated from couturiers, got paraded on catwalks and then copied in the street. (I recall my mother in the fifties, each season scanning *Elle* for the latest Paris intelligence on hem lengths, then spending all night altering skirts on her Singer to be the first a la mode in Ruislip Manor High Street.)

Street first started to make business sense – and alarm the Paris fashion establishment, in the sixties. Its most totemic artefact was the mini skirt designed by Mary Quant – but only, as she admitted, after it was spontaneously created by London teenagers trimming existing garments. (Quant is cross with the couturier Courrèges, who claimed he created the mini on his catwalk in 1964.) The mini was modernism in motion, summoning the Mod ethos and the clipped, clean, technological pretensions of the sixties. It displayed arse to the older generation and long legs to punters: ready-to-wear revolution.

The other totem, of course, was the model, Twiggy, often seen as Kate Moss's "anorexic" precursor. Twiggy was styled from the Neasden born Leslie Hornby by her boyfriend Justin de Villeneuve (aka Nigel Davies). Just like Kate Moss, Twiggy had all the wrong looks for modelling: too short at 5 foot six, too skinny at 91 pounds, and too flat chested at 31-22-32. But it was precisely all that which made Twiggy street: a bit "wrong" or "odd" looking, a bit human, a flawed gem, not as impossibly beautiful as Jean Shrimpton or Patti Boyd, and not posh at all.

And more successful than any of them. Michael Gross: "Twiggy's appeal was as enormous as it was initially inexplicable. 'Within a year she was on her way … She started being a phenomenon.' She wasn't a model like any model before her; she was a marketing miracle, the first of a new breed. Flying by the seat of his pants de Villeneuve had created a monster. She was the first model to achieve genuine international celebrity." [1]

Twiggy was only the most successful encapsulation of a principle Quant had grasped and put into operation for her first press show. Shrewdly, Quant used photographic rather than catwalk models to show her clothes through a calculated mayhem: "I wanted to show the clothes moving, not parading, and these [photographic model] girls move beautifully and naturally … [Then as the models] danced … literally danced … down the open stairway, a wind machine caught their skirts and blew them this way and that to create an even greater sense of speed and

[1] *Model*, 1995

movement ... We showed forty garments in fourteen minutes and every single minute was packed with incident ... One girl carried an enormous shotgun; another swung a dead pheasant triumphantly round her head. Perhaps too triumphantly because the poor thing, which we had bought from Harrods across the road, thawed out in the heat of the place and blood began spurting out all over the newly painted walls; even over some of the journalists."[1]

From Quant on, London boutiques took it upon themselves to create styles from what they saw around them, a process facilitated by the sartorially audacious British youth cults. A neophilia also catalysed by the Sunday colour supplements, hungry to endorse difference and map what was first called new culture, and then subculture. In those days, Quant just called it, "The Chelsea Look."

This rigmarole was parodied and turned on its head with punk rock, when Westwood and McLaren invented their own youth cult – punk – complete with art school ideology and musical genre – which they dressed up in a kind of war paint that was then tarted up as elegant plumage by Zandra Rhodes and became fashion proper.

Punk also created fanzine frenzy, shaking up magazine publishing. Eclectic new editors and magazine designers fused art and fashion and consumerism into desirable new blends, exposing unsuspected niche markets. In so doing, they created harbingers of alternative style like *Blitz*, *i-D* and *The Face*.

Kate Moss was a model they could recognise and empathise with. She looked like one of their little sisters or the girl you once dated, she hung out in Old Compton Street, hunted style oddities in Pimlico's Cornucopia, she might be in the crowd drinking on the pavement outside the French Pub, or raving in Manchester's Hacienda.

* * *

By the end of the eighties too, music, always the harbinger of youthquakes, had rediscovered gritty realism, jarring rhythms, and tense lyrics. An insurgency was gathering against the big hair and big sounds of eighties studio and stadium monsters like Duran Duran and U2, not to mention New Romantic sweeties like Boy George.

Time for something tougher. Time to get real. Time for creative catastrophes like Madchester and the Happy Mondays, or Seattle and Kurt Cobain's

---

[1] *Quant By Quant*, 1965

end game. Time too, for Ibiza style junkets of E and DJ raving. And time for all those summers of love.

And time for Corinne Day.

* * *

Corrine Day was a suburban school dropout who drifted into a job as an international courier then met a photographer on a plane who said she ought to be model. Braving the incredulity of friends she made a go of it enough to fulfil her dream of globetrotting. When that dried up another boyfriend inspired her to begin taking photos. Eventually, as she recounts:

"I started to take photographs that meant something to me. These photographs had an intimacy and a sadness about them.

"There we were struggling to pay the rent, living in a dump, surrounded by glamorous magazines that were so far away from our own level of living. A photographer friend of mine, Anthony, saw some of these photographs I had taken, and suggested … that I go and see Phil Bicker at *The Face* magazine."

Bicker however, was not impressed with the holiday snaps he was shown of good times in Thailand and Milan. He asked what she thought she could bring to *The Face*. Quick as a flash, Day produced the feminist card:

"I asked if there were any girl photographers working for *The Face*, he said no. I said give me a job, then. I think he thought I was joking, I wasn't."

Day had been away from London for five years and was out of the frame. Who to photograph? What was photogenic? She made the rounds of agencies, scanning their wannabes. One appointment she made was at Storm, which "showed me an out of focus Polaroid of Kate Moss. I said I could not tell if she would be right, and could I meet her."

So she did, and, as she recounts on her website, discovered that "Kate was 15 years old. She was small for a model … same height as me. And there was something familiar about her that made me feel comfortable. That's why I chose to photograph her. The first photographs I took of Kate were in my Nan's front garden. Nan had raised me from the age of five and this was the house I grew up in. Nan made us tea and sandwiches. We went to the park where I had hung out with my brother my whole life. The photographs were snapshots of nothing more than us hanging out in the suburbs where I grew up. The clothes Kate wore were simple, V-neck jumpers, Kickers from the Natural Shoe Store and a bias cut, John Galliano maxi-skirt from Browns.

"I took black and white photographs because I had little experience with colour. I showed six different photographs to Phil, he published one – but not the photograph I liked. I liked the photograph of Kate walking down by the side of the motorway, she was blinking and looked pissed off.

"I suggested to Phil that Kate should be seen in the magazine more, as *The Face* looked like a *Boy's Own* magazine. A couple of months later, he commissioned me to photograph eight pages of fashion. The same week, I was walking down Old Compton Street with a friend of mine – she was telling me of a stylist that she knew called Melanie Ward who like me, collected second hand clothes. That day, we saw her on the same street; we went for a coffee and talked about our common interests in second hand clothes. I asked Melanie if she would like to work with Kate and me for *The Face*."

Soon, Day and Melanie Ward had become close friends. "We went to the markets, Portobello and Camden and others every weekend. We shopped at second hand clothing shops like Glorious Clothing and Cornucopia. We worked very closely together. Both of us being on the dole, we shared the expense of buying clothes. I always bought clothes that I would wear myself.

Day continues: "Music was our inspiration for the "Third Summer of Love" photographs that I took in 1990 for *The Face*. Kate and I liked Nirvana, Stone Roses and Happy Mondays.

"These photographs were about Kate, I wanted to capture her presence, not so much mine. And I liked the way that she was skinny. I was teased at school for being thin and clothes would never fit me when I was a model."

Day dispensed with as much "fashion" artifice as she could. She preferred minimal or no make-up, and sought spontaneous or casual poses.

"I thought fashion photography was about the photographer, instead of the person they photographed. Fashion magazines had been selling sex and glamour for far too long. I wanted to instil some reality into a world of fantasy."

* * *

The results of those strategies were striking. They defined what became a "new wave" of fashion imagery, launching several careers, as well as Kate Moss.

Kate had found the perfect foil, and Corinne Day the perfect muse.

But Day's account above dwells on the fashion and styling aspects of the collaboration. It misses out on a more crucial dimension. Which was that Kate got her kit off.

* * *

From Kate's perspective some of these shoots were problematic. "I was quite shy, believe it or not, then. I was definitely more aware about my body. Didn't want to take my clothes off. When I was fifteen, with Corinne, I cried. I was so self conscious! We used to fight all the time. Those shoots would take weeks and weeks. Nobody was getting paid – it was in my school holidays. (In fact, the most she normally got in those days was between £50-£100.)

But, she continues: "It was a really exciting time. I was working with Corinne. We were really close friends. I ended up living with her for a while and we'd just hang out all the time. And talk about fashion and what we were going to do and draw pictures. She had very strong opinions and very strong ideas about what she wanted to do. We did lots of the images that she wanted to do. And I think she did succeed in changing things a bit.

"… it captured what was going on in England at the time. It wasn't eighties glamour. It was about the street. Everyone was saying, "Let's get off our tits and have a laugh. Be more real and not have to grow up so quickly. And have fun."

And: "I was only fifteen then. It was completely contrived – you know, hunch over, whatever. I didn't want to take my top off, I didn't have tits and stuff. The pictures were about fashion, not documentary."

But those injunctions to flash her parts still rankled years later. "I still love those pictures. They're still some of my favourites even though I look so ugly in some of them. That topless one – I'd left school by then, but my brother really caught it. All of his mates were going, 'I've seen your sister topless!' I can appreciate it now – it was a great picture. But at the time it was like, 'Corinne, how could you give them that picture of me looking so gross with my flat tits!'"

* * *

We all got familiar with those flat tits. And a lot else.

If you google "Kate Moss" in "images" you will see a classic Corinne Day style of image. According to google's ranking system, this is perhaps the most hit upon image of Kate Moss on the planet. The image depicts Kate Moss shivering knock kneed and clutching her crotch against a brick wall with a smidgen of pube peeking out. The picture fills your eyes immediately with her tits squeezed between taut and skeletal arms, forming a triangle with disturbingly protuberant collar bones. We notice that darling mole on her left breast and her nipples erect and darkly ringed – miniature mouthfuls.

A screwy composition topped, or illuminated, by an awkwardly toothy and unconvincing grin that scars her bashfully tilted and withdrawn face.

This display of her nakedness is as enticing and scary as her boniness. It is an exposure in every sense.

The image references firstly a Romantic rock and roll iconography of the pared, almost flayed, self: fashionably excoriated torsos of shamans like Iggy Pop or Ziggy Stardust. "This is me. This is what I do for you."

But in the defensive pose, the brickwork backdrop, the shallow depth of field, the flat grey tonality and obliterated context, and in this model's female gender and adolescence, there is also a furtive distance and calculatedly banal obscenity.

Kate scrunched and starved and skewed like that recalls pictures of starved and naked Jewish women, rounded up by Nazis, clustered by a pit, holding on to whatever dignity they can conceal, at the disposal of the cameraman or the marksman, for we realise they are about to be shot and this picture is a trophy of that moment.

In the same way (albeit on a different scale), this picture by Mario Sorrenti, based on the look created by Corinne Day, is a trophy of Kate's nakedness, of the fact that she was stripped. Which as we shall see, became her entrée into fashion, both here and in America.[5]

*   *   *

Not that *The Face* editorial committee wasted much time on semiology. They gasped at the beauty. And so Kate was adopted as the *Face's* house model, appearing on its cover five times.

*   *   *

Around this time Kate confided to her boyfriend, Clark Gregory, that she was thinking of having a breast enlargement operation.

Modelling had made her insecure about her looks. Especially about those "flat tits" exposed by Corinne Day. She worried that her 33A-23-24 figure was not up to the mark and that she ought to look more "womanly". Ungallantly, Clark did not demure.

"I thought she looked great. But this would make her look even better. She was so serious about having the enlargement done that she had it all priced. She found out it would cost her £2,000 and planned to save it from her modelling fees.

"But she still wasn't working much at the time and the money came through in dribs and drabs, so she never scraped enough together. Then she hit the big time and of course, she couldn't change her image.

*   *   *

[5] While this book was being researched, and up to mid 2006, this image was the most looked at picture of Kate Moss on the Internet. It subsequently disappeared. An account of this censorship is given in Act 5 of this book. The disturbing impact of the image is hard to convey – it has to be seen. Despite this airbrushing of Kate Moss' photographic origins, assiduous googling of "Kate Moss" or "katemoss" can sometimes get results.

While that image was being sorted Kate was still living with her mother in Forestdale. Linda and her new partner, Geoff Collman, a television dealer and repair man – and Barry Gibb lookalike – shared Kate's adventures vicariously, at that stage not taking them very seriously.

Looking back in 1993, Geoff marvelled, 'It's amazing to think that just a few years ago we were arguing with her about not doing the washing-up. I remember when she did one of her first jobs and she was having to learn to rollerskate. We didn't have any carpets down and she was flying around the room. She hurt herself and I thought: 'This is a silly old game, this modelling.''

In those first days too, she supplemented her income with part time work around Croydon. A school friend recalls: "I can remember her working in a clothes shop called Radius in Croydon, North End High Street. I remember going in there and talking to her one day, buying a polo shirt. It was a part-time Saturday sort of job."

However, the same friend also recalls: "I went to a party in Addiscombe and it was about 89/90, because everyone was in the old hooded tops with stars all over them, or Egyptian writing, it was all very 'rave-y'. Coming back, I jumped on a bus at East Croydon train station, and Kate was on the back of the bus. And she had just come back from Austria, modelling, and she earned £2000 from it."

The contradictions in her lifestyle were getting acute.

★ ★ ★

The culture gap was also widening. This especially through Kate's protracted stays with Corinne Day and her crowd.

Nine years older than Kate, Day was worldly-wise, if not dissolute. Her photos mostly starred her junkie friends and specialised in squalor.

Discussing a retrospective of her work in 2000, *Village Voice* commented that while it: "could be dismissed as a British knockoff of Larry Clark and Nan Goldin, with a similar circle of chums at loose ends enjoying dangerous drugs and casual sex … Day's world seems even seedier and her grip on life more fragile."

In *The Times*, Waldemar Januszczak thought that: "The most surprising thing about these photographs – apart from the fact that the people in them are not all in jail – is their lack of depression. They are dark. Scary. Bruised. But they are not depressing. The junkies in them are not depressed. Far from it. They appear to be having a whale of a time with their foaming white noses and their instinctive settee sex. The rooms they inhabit are squalid, the things they do are grim, but not one iota of self-pity communicated itself to me."

This is the higher education Kate had. This was her university. And the context of the images she and Day created.

* * *

Day has been frank, (see for example, *The Corinne Day Diary*, BBC4), about her own longstanding and even heroic appetite for drugs. (Though she's since given them up for health reasons). It is unlikely the presence of adolescent Kate Moss would have inhibited her. Especially since Kate was a dab hand at rolling joints herself, and also handy with a bottle.

(A source who met her in Paris around this time expressed astonishment at the amount of booze this skinny thing could knock back. Indeed, so legendary was teenage Kate's drinking prowess, she was nicknamed by her new fashion friends, "the tank.")

During this formative time for Kate and her image the two friends lived in proximity, going as a duo to the same parties, hangouts and squats. Kate often stayed over at Corrine's apartment and the two became much more than photographer and muse, they became intimate. That proximity: the good times, the dead times, the shared jokes and scandal and music and girlie banter, the shared cigarettes and joints and bottles and friends and beds, all that was bound to make the world of her boyfriend, Clark Gregory, and what he stood for – a shop assistant who still lived with his mum and dad, a little unexciting.

* * *

Clark knew and cared little about the painstaking work of styling and crafting and shooting a look. He'd never tasted the adrenalin surge and orchestrated frenzy of a catwalk show. He had nothing to teach her and they had less and less to talk about.

They started to row.

Not only was Clark miffed that he now saw so little of Kate, he objected to the arty fashion crowd she was mixing with. He thought them pretentious.

Clark was a robust hetero who didn't take to fashionista squeals and bitchy double entendres. He blanched at the continental style double cheek kisses Kate's new friends delighted in. "I found a lot of them quite false. I'm not really one for all this 'darling' stuff. She was going around with stylists and hairdressers and they're not my scene." And while Kate took her boyfriend to the grungy Subterranean club in London, he preferred the local dives.

* * *

Kate also found herself the object of "the old green eye" from other girls who thought she was getting above herself. Talking about his wife, who like him was at school with Kate Moss, one informant said, "The only thing my wife always says is that Kate Moss was completely and utterly up herself. She was in love with herself."

Recalls another school friend: "I think there was a certain amount of jealousy amongst the young ladies, you know … certainly the ones that thought they were better looking or whatever if you know what I mean. Kate's quite unconventional looking. I mean, what I really remember about her is that she was stick thin, no real shape to her, a bit like a 12-year-old boy. So yeah, no doubt there was a bit of jealousy there."

Stick thin or not, the pictures of her topless caused a predictable commotion at Riddlesdown. And yet more jealousy. Who did she think she was? Kate was stung. Clark confirmed that: "The jealousy did become a problem. People wouldn't be speaking to her on the same terms they used to. They would be offish and it did bother her, no matter how much she tried to hide it."

Explaining why they became separated he said, "I think she became lonely and it was then that she really started to make friends in the modelling world and that we started to clash. Also, I wasn't riding high like her. She was the one that they wanted to meet. I was living a normal kind of life."

In May 1991 they tearfully parted. Clark recalls: "It was a Sunday and we hadn't seen one another for a while because she had been jetting off to Tunisia and Spain. We drove to the White Bear pub in Warlingham and decided we were arguing too much to stay together. Afterwards we pulled in at a lay-by and agreed to split. Then I drove her back to pack because she was flying away again."

"It was pretty emotional, when I left her at the station. Kate was crying and I was holding back my tears. We said we'd get back together again, and at the time I think we both hoped it was true.

"But then I found someone else, and so did she, and it just never happened."

But Kate had found someone else even before splitting with Clark.

★ ★ ★

Mario Sorrenti looked remarkably like Clark. But Mario was an ex model turned photographer. He was not only in Kate's trade and of her world, he might also prove useful. As indeed, he did.

Sorrenti was born in Naples in 1971: "Naples is a really cool place to grow up. It was very free, a lot more open than a normal city life. Maybe I got a better education – not in the sense of schooling but in a broader sense – because of that. It was also very family oriented. My family's very close. We're an Italian family. It was all about good vibes, good people, good parties …"

When he was ten his family moved the US. "My parents were splitting up. I was really excited to move away. I'd travelled a lot and been to New York before. When you're young these things are a little bit easier. I had to learn the language, meet new people. It was a completely different culture. In Naples I'd be going to the beach, having lunch with my family. New York was all about break dancing. I was 10 years old and here was this intense city full of people. I got heavily into graffiti and hip-hop culture."

Sorrenti began studying at the School for visual arts in Manhattan. He recalls he took his first picture at the age of 18: "It was a picture of my father and a friend of his. She was a photographer and she took me straight into her darkroom and we processed them straight away. After that, that was all I ever wanted to do."

Then, after eight months of college he dropped out. He'd been noticed by the established fashion photographers, Steve Meisel and Bruce Weber, who began using him as a model. He also modelled for a Levis campaign. But meanwhile, he practiced his craft, cultivating the autobiographical take that is still his trademark. "I kept a photographic diary of my life."

By the age of 19, Sorrenti had moved to London where he continued to record the scene around him. He naturally gravitated towards the work of other young photographers like Corinne Day and Juergen Teller.

For aspiring snappers then – as always, fashion was an important starting point. The new style mags especially, were open to unknown and experimental photographers and fashion could pay the rent. (In the sixties, David Bailey had strayed into fashion photography for the same reasons, and stayed there, almost against his will.)

Like all unknowns, these photographers were crafting a manifesto against the status quo. In this case defining a new "look" against the superstar image makers and their supermodels. They opted for monochrome, minimal props, banal backgrounds, flat lighting, unfussy and unhurried poses, subdued moods – and an ironic cachet of ugliness.

Meanwhile, the ultra handsome Sorrenti continued to model in London.

Kate: "I met Mario Sorrenti. He was modelling at the time. I was kind of seeing a friend of his, and then his friend went away and he kind of pounced on me. Which is a bit naughty [laughs] but I'm glad he did."

Sorrenti used a classic pickup line. He wanted to take pictures of her. Did she want to be a model? Well, she already was, sort of. But he amused her. And she believed in his talent. And soon they were lovers.

Mario: "I was sleeping on different people's couches when Kate and I met and she was in the same position. She was living with her mother in Croydon. We just had this amazing time. You know, we were all very young."

Before long Mario was staying at Kate's mother's place in Croydon. In an interview, Linda confided: "Kate liked him and so did I. So I didn't mind at all when she asked me if he could stay at our house. They lived together and just did their own thing while I did mine."

Kate: "We were together and we would do pictures as well, because he wanted to be a photographer. Then I went to New York with him, and met other photographers."

* * *

New York was crucial. While Kate had been a success in the small – albeit resonant – world of British style mags, Doukas now had her eyes on the USA. The *Face* would never pay the mortgage. She introduced Kate to Paul Rowland, who had recently set up Women Management in a tiny office in New York City.

A muscular figure with an aggressive manner to match, Rowland had been a model himself. He subsequently became a booker for male models. But he wanted in to where the real money was: female modelling. Summarising his pragmatic world-view Rowland explained, "The way my life works is things just come. I can never tell you what tomorrow is. I keep everything moving and fluid. The thing that works for me is, I'm not afraid to attempt it. And I don't care what people have to say."

Thus far however, Women Management was an agency without any models. So Rowland was willing to gamble on inviting an unknown Kate Moss – who looked nothing like any conventional model at the time, to New York.

Sorrenti went with Kate and they moved in with his mother, Francesca, sister Valida and brother Davide. Sorrenti's family was intense, voluble, and very Italian. Quite unlike Kate's. But she was drafted in, becoming especially attached to Sorrenti's mother, and chaperoned by his sister.

Rowland now sent Kate to see the photographer, Steve Meisel. Meisel was struck by how different Kate was from most models in town. He cast her for a Dolce e Gabbana catalogue and a cover for *Italian Glamour*.

Even more fatefully, Kate was introduced to *Bazaar's* model editor, Sara Foley-Anderson.

Foley Anderson claimed later that her staff "fell in love" with Kate. She explained: "We believed that models and fashion needed to be less hard-edged, more pared down and accessible, less complicated and more open and real than they were in the eighties. Kate was the original herald of this movement which at its extreme became waif."

The result was a nine-page spread: "Wild: fashion that breaks the rules."

* * *

That started a panic. In fashion as in rock music, panic is contagious. It spells wealth and beauty and announces the next big thing. And you better move fast because otherwise you're history: if you can see the bandwagon you're not on it.

Michael Gross:" ... by Fall 1992, the waif look had conquered fashion. Corinne Day and Mario Sorrenti ... began snatching up jobs that would once automatically have gone to Demarchelier or Meisel. That season Moss walked the runways in fashion shows for the first time, wearing grunge, gamin and bohemian fashions that seemed inspired by the new wave of models. That December she made her first appearance on the cover of Bazaar. Early the next year she appeared in a campaign shot by Helmut Newton for Yves St Laurent."

Helmut Newton. That really was big time.

But the biggest boost for Kate's career came from the canny designer, Calvin Klein.

* * *

Klein started off designing women's coats in the sixties and then moved into sportswear. He was a designer who understood image and could play the media. Never mind the frock, where's the shock? Or even the schlock.

In the late seventies Klein invented "designer jeans," a new spin on an old story that revitalized, as they say, the market.

Klein equally relished the power of scandal.

For example, he cultivated the use of "underage" models in ads with erotic panache designed to maximise controversy.

The first starred Brooke Shields, who was previously eroticised by Louis Malle in *Pretty Baby*. Shields breathed that "Nothing comes between me and my Calvins."

What, no knickers?

The resulting fuss over nothing burned the company name and logo into American folk memory – and marketing lore. The ad was credited with shifting 200,000 pairs of jeans in the first week alone. Feminists protested: exploitation, paedophilia, male gaze, might as well be rape …

Sales rose.

Outraged graffiti was sprayed over ads.

More sales …

Not that Calvin was against knickers. In fact he created another fortune in 1982 by plastering his logo on the waistbands of boxers and briefs. He also made men's underwear sexy, segueing these previously humdrum garments into the discourse of feminine lingerie, and further twisting the androgyny knife by designing "masculine" underwear for women.

* * *

However, the hyperactive supermodel Janice Dickinson has revealed in her autobiography, *No Lifeguard On Duty*, that Calvin's own underpants were less desirable.

She recalls being propositioned by the great man in the presence of Bowie's wife, the model Iman: "And Calvin makes us drinks and he keeps ogling me and saying, 'You look hot, Janice. No seriously, really hot.'

"And Iman says, 'I think she gets it, Calvin.'

"And Calvin leaves the room and comes back a few moments later, having slipped out of his pants, to get comfortable. So now he's sitting there in a boxy silk shirt and no pants and Fruit-of-the-Loom underwear and fucking knee socks. It was bizarre. Maybe he thought he looked hot. So I told him, 'You look really hot, Calvin. I mean, hot. I love the socks.' But he didn't catch the irony. Then I said, 'Why don't you do a line of underwear? Just put your name on it. I bet it'll sell.' And his eyes lit up. But he didn't say anything. He should have said, 'Janice, you're a genius. I'll cut you in for ten percent.' But he didn't."

* * *

It was called branding.

To the despair of thinking people, from the eighties consumers began wearing, even flaunting, the labels of the very fashion houses that were oppressing them with false needs and fake desires.

Klein was right in there. From his jeans to his boxers to his perfumes, Obsession and Eternity, the CK logo, the Calvin Klein name or aura or whatever, shifted product.

Clever Calvin. The man was a legend. Everyone studied his methods.

However, by the time Kate Moss arrived in New York, the CK logo looked dated. People were beginning to find it tiresome. People were starting to talk. Maybe his day was over. Had CK peaked?

* * *

... the process of daydreaming intervenes between the formulation of a desire and its consummation; hence the desiring and dreaming modes become interfused, with a dream element entering into desire itself ...

Colin Campbell, *The Romantic Ethic And The Spirit Of Modern Consumerism*, 1987

* * *

By the late nineties Klein had started redesigning his products to look mimimalist for added street cred. And naturally, because what you see is what you get, revamped his image. He chose Fabien Baron to organize this. Baron had been art director both for *Italian Vogue* and Warhol's celebrity fixated *Interview*, he knew the games.

Rap seemed the in thing then, the street-cred thing. Baron chose Mark Wahlberg, AKA Marky Mark, to signify it.

Wahlberg and his band, The Funky Bunch, had enjoyed street-cred hits like Wildside and a remake of Good Vibrations. Wahlberg had the added frisson of being a redeemed petty criminal and racist who had spent time in jail for beating up two Vietnamese men after trying to steal their beer.

The rap artist styled his bad reputation into an onstage persona who dropped his pants and ripped off his clothes to reveal the beautifully toned muscles gained working out in prison.

It was his record boss, David Geffen, a close friend of Calvin Klein (Geffen once even bailed the designer out of bankruptcy), who suggested to Klein that Wahlberg might be a suitable new face for CK.

But a female face was also needed.

Kate Moss was an incongruous but effective foil to Wahlberg's muscleman poses and extremely well-filled underpants. She was pictured clinging to – or draped around, him. More to the point, they were both naked from the waist up. Once again, Kate had her tits out. But this time in America.

It seems though, there was little electricity on set.

Wahlberg: "Kate is a very, very nice girl. Umm, there's definitely specifics that catch my eye, but like I said, everyone is different. But ... see, 'cause Kate is very thin ... she's very small. I like a little bit of meat, you know what I'm saying?" Gotcha, Mark.

Kate: "We weren't each other's types. He was this young homeboy, like really young, and he liked girls with big butts and big tits and shit and I don't really fit into that category."

Anyway, it worked. The media howled, the feminists cussed, even the supermodels joined in, since such a rampant display of flesh called the bluff of their own displays. Some of them got so petulant they clucked, like Claudia Schiffer, about "unnecessary" nudity.

Schiffer's rebuke got this back from Kate: "That's how she made her fortune. She's got an amazing body and big tits. She sold her body like I sold mine."

Meanwhile, US TV stations banned Kate's topless images from TV versions for being overly "suggestive".

But who cared? The market was the MTV generation and there it was a hit.

Klein now realised Kate's potential for revitalising his brand. "She has this childlike, womanlike thing that I haven't seen in a long time. It's a new type of beauty. Not the big, sporty, superwoman type, but glamour which is sensitive, more fragile."

Meanwhile, Kate started getting more exposure in high class magazines like *Harpers Bazaar* and *American Vogue*.

The Times journalist Sarah Mower, analysed the fascination: "along comes Kate Moss, with her mousy hair and poor-girl clothes looking so sweetly anti-everything. Bingo! She reminds the baby-boomer generation now the oldies in power of their own youth. Bingo! She's also from England, the birthplace of all authentic youth movements. Hey, they start asking are there any more like you at home?"

"We call it Tramp," Ms Day said. "The Americans call it Grunge, but we've been dressing like this in holey jumpers and second-hand clothes for ages."

* * *

There were several well placed Brits eager to encourage this "new wave."

Liz Tiberis for example – who'd been chosen by Hearst Publications to tart up Harpers. Tiberis was an energetic socializer who liked to scatter titbits from her "close friendships" with Lady Di and Hilary Clinton. She was also a modernizer who transformed *Harpers* with a minimalist look partly borrowed from *i-D* and *The Face*. Tiberis championed experimental photographers like Patrick Demarchelier, David Sims and Peter Lindbergh and further blurred art/fashion lines by working with "difficult" artists like Cindy Sherman.

And she adored Kate Moss: "The second she walked into our office [everyone] knew they were looking at a true beauty – someone whose face and attitude were the personification of our time."

As another plus for Kate, her former Calvin Klein champion, Fabien Baron, had just become *Harpers* new creative director. The result was that Kate became for a while *Harpers* virtual house model, as once she'd been *The Face*'s.

* * *

But just as we marvel at happy coincidences, here is a sharp article in the management trade magazine, *Folio*, teasing out the incestuous pacts and slippery margins between bluff and hype, fantasy and reality that have always prevailed in fashion:

"Once again, the lines between advertising and editorial in a fashion title are blurring. The July *Harpers Bazaar* contains a tangled web of coincidences: Fabien Baron, the magazine's creative director, also designs ads for Calvin Klein. His best-known ad campaign – featuring Marky Mark and top model Kate Moss in nothing but their Calvin Klein underwear – catapulted Moss to the top of the modeling world and made the 'waif look' an industry standard."

"Moss strikes a pose on the cover wearing a linen crewneck sweater from the Calvin Klein Collection. Her shampoo and conditioner? Eternity by Calvin Klein, of course.

"The Baron-Moss-Klein nexus marches on in an article about fashion designers' second-tier clothing lines, which features Klein's CK line. Klein products appear again in illustrations for "Body of Evidence," a self-serving editorial feature rebutting readers' charges that *Bazaar* and other magazines are contributing to eating disorders when they use superslim types like Moss. In one of the illustrations, the seated wonder waif wears a Calvin Klein sweater, and even her fragrance is credited as Calvin Klein's Obsession Body Spray."

The piece concluded: "With all the free publicity, we wonder why the omnipresent designer bothered to purchase five advertising pages for his Escape and Eternity fragrances. Bazaar de-Kleined to comment on the apparent synergy."

* * *

From that point Kate's image was crafted by renowned pros. Contracts for campaigns proliferated: after Dolce and Gabbana came Yves St Laurent and Banana Republic ... She was on the move all the time. It became her "whirlwind phase."

But was she happy?

"Sometimes, I really don't like this job. I mean, do you know how many times I've been on a plane this week? Nine. London to Milan. Milan to Paris. Paris to New York. New York to Paris. Or was it Milan … anyway, it's knackering and it's given me spots."

Later, she recalled of that period: I was on planes all the time. And I didn't see my friends. I cried a lot and was alone a lot. It was quite terrifying, actually."

And: "I started to get really nervous-panic attacks. I couldn't get out of bed. It really didn't hit me at first and then I thought I was really ill and the doctor gave me Valium."

At the same time, she was finding fashion industry people, "terrifyingly tense and calculating". On one occasion she spent a week on an assignment without anyone speaking to her. "Well, they were French and maybe they didn't speak English, but it would have been nice to have the chance to find out."

* * *

After meticulous negotiation, Kate finally secured a deal to become the new "face" of Calvin Klein. Things began to settle down.

For £2 million the contract guaranteed Klein 100 days of Kate's time over the next five years. It also barred her from advertising for other designers. It did however, allow her to do editorial work for magazines as well as runway shows. Now she was in a position to be pickier about what she took on, and maybe relax a little.

* * *

Clinching such a high profile deal was seen as remarkable. After all, Klein could have chosen names like Claudia Schiffer, Christy Turlington or Naomi Campbell. But he had an inkling their day was – if not past, at least passé.

Then again, Kate was on the up in New York – hardly an unknown any more. In the weeks before the contract was signed she was splashed over a four-page spread in *Vanity Fair*, sporting Calvin Klein jeans – and in some images topless.

As Rebecca Tyrell put it: "In all the major fashion centres of the world, from Linda Evangelista's boudoir to Karl Lagerfeld's office on the Rue Cambon, the question on everybody's lips was: 'Where did this girl come from?'"

To make sure we got the point, Tyrell added: "How did a girl like Kate become the new darling of the fashion industry?"

One reason "a girl like Kate" could make it so apparently suddenly and effortlessly had to do with the celebrity culture that had come to saturate the planet.

★　★　★

"Celebrity is the main currency of our economy, the prime value in our news and the main impetus in our charitable works. It is the predominant means of giving and receiving ideas, information and entertainment. Nothing moves in our universe without the imprint of celebrity."
- Ziauddin Sardar, 2001

★　★　★

Kate Moss came from a generation weaned on celebrity, especially through TV and its "personalities". They were glued to soaps like Neighbours that spawned all purpose singing and dancing opinion spouting designer friendly celebs like Kylie Minogue. Celebs that began as fiction and ended as fable. Who were stories wherever they went, whatever they did, whatever they neglected to do. And whoever touched their gold was also transmuted into celebrity.

★　★　★

The decade Kate grew to maturity in saw a massive boost in the power of famous faces. To start with, the eighties are inseparable from the movie star, Ronald Reagan, who from 1981 to 1989 starred in the greatest role on earth: Mr President. Ronnie, dubbed "Celebrity-In-Chief," imported Hollywood into global politics and everything was movies, from 'Star Wars' to the telespectacular collapse of communism.

Lauren Bacall once said of actors and politicians: "We're doing what they can't do – we can sing and dance and act. They're doing what we can't do – they have access to power, real power. I guess we all have fantasies about the other."

Reagan was his own fantasy. And during his reign celebs started to pine for real power in earnest. Right in the middle of the decade came Live Aid, when the celebritariat made a determined bid for global dominance through a variant of what Umberto Eco has called Ur-fascism. Hailing us from the Live Aid stage Madonna asked: "All right, people of the world, are you ready to get into the groove?" And: "People of the world – now I know you're mine."

Madonna's MTV allure meshed with her Malibu marriage to Sean Penn in 1985, attended by 13 helicopters laden with paparazzi. Celebrity-based media mushroomed. *Lifestyles Of The Rich And Famous* debuted in 1983 and became the most syndicated and popular TV "glamour" series in the world, the prototype for *Hello!* And *OK!*

The eighties also saw the ascendance of that uberceleb, Princess Di, whose wedding to Charles in 1981 pulled in around 1,000 million oglers and eavesdroppers. Di's subsequent career broke all records for celebrity obsession and her funeral was a watershed in celebrity led hysteria.

* * *

So Kate and Co were the first real connoisseurs of celebrity: saturated with the stuff from birth, with unlimited access to a media increasingly tied to and indistinguishable from its celebrity remit.

What's more, the only antidote – the pre-celeb culture you may find in say, novels or books in general, was not available to her. We can safely say Kate's trips to Sanderstead Library in Farm Fields were infrequent. And like everyone today who doesn't read, she became a media junkie, unable to imagine, think or emote beyond a celebrity framework.

* * *

Celebrity depends on visuality and visual style; it must be seen to be believed. So the eighties was also a voyeuristic decade.

It saw the beginning of MTV, which welded music to fashion and visual appeal. And spawned bands like the "filmic" Duran Duran, entwined with models in "filmic" locations.

In Sanderstead, as everywhere else, the top cop show was *Miami Vice*: heroes and villains chasing one another in designer gear to rock scores. In 1985, the model Nick Kamen strip-teased down to boxers to wash a pair of 501s to Marvin Gaye's 'I Heard it Through The Grapevine'. By 1986 there'd been an 800% rise in sales; factories were overburdened and Levis were forced to pull the ad. Kamen got his recording contract and a one hit wonder with 'Each Time You Break My Heart'.

Designers arbitrated this visuality. Stylists like Terence Conran were now celebs in their own right. Philippe Starck ascended to celebrity-designer par excellence with a campaign of "Chinese whispers" PR tactics. Peter Saville's minimalist chic was intrinsic to the appeal of bands like New Order. Jean-Paul Goude designed his girlfriend Grace Jones so well her look was better than the music.

In this visual age, good looks were paramount. Hence model mania, hence supermodels.

These women became more celebrated than the couturiers employing them, and more bankable. They launched "signature" accessory lines and migrated to other entertainments. Rachel Ward went from Revlon Scoundrel perfume girl to Hollywood actress. Brooke Shields from *Pretty Baby* to Calvin Klein and omnipresent cover girl.

Seeing this, everyone rushed to become a model. Sports stars like Steffi Graf became branded sex symbols with sponsored "lines" – like Adidas' revealing "Steffi Graf tennis skirt".

By the end of the eighties, supermodels, "remote confections of cultured image and cherished dreams" as Michael Gross puts it, or in *ArtForum*'s lengthier definition, "professional surrogates for the frustrated emulative instinct of the mass pecuniarily deprived," were omnipresent.

And had become tiresome. Especially the so-called "trinity": Christy Turlington, Linda Evangelista and Naomi Campbell. It was Evangelista who uttered the notorious line about not getting out of bed for "less than $10,000 a day".

Which caused even Turlington to have a nightmare: "I was on the Arsenio show, "covering Linda and Naomi's mouths with my hand!"

* * *

Those three achieved ubiquity on the catwalk. They then transferred to imagery. By the time Kate Moss arrived, the catwalk was dispensable. It was media exposure that counted. The Twiggy story all over again. With the difference that while Twiggy was an exception, Kate Moss happened where promo was God, the media King, and designers mere fixers.

What you needed for this kind of celebrity modelling was a "personality". Or at least, you should look like you had a personality. Kate was perfect for that. Her face was a Rorschach puzzle. It signified your heart's desire, reflecting whatever whimsical or indolent thought just crossed your mind. Her features were a jigsaw not quite put together, subtly dissonant, suggesting realignment. A face that looked like it told a story but was really a blank page for you to write your own.

* * *

Talking of celebrity, and how contagious it is, we might spare a section for the singular modelling career of Kate's brother, Nick Moss.

Back in London, while Kate was still working with *The Face*, Mario Sorrenti persuaded Nick, then still at Riddlesdown High, to model solo and also with his sister.

Nick was hardly the part. He lacked Kate's fragility, presence and poise. And he was, well … ugly. Or to quote Louise Atkinson of the *Daily Mail*:

"His sunken hairless chest, unhealthy pallor and narrow hips jar incongru-ously in the world of tall, tanned Adonises."

Another journalist weighed in with: "the face of a jock who spends his evenings at the local pub."

Nick himself had few illusions: "I hate my height, my nose, my chest, my lips … I could keep going for ages. At 5ft 9in, I'm too short to be a model. I should be at least 6ft, but I'm pretty reconciled to the fact that I won't be getting any taller. My nose is a mess. I've broken it playing football at least four times now, so there's a really thick bit at the bridge. When I'm older I might have the bone shaved by a plastic surgeon, but I've got to wait until all the bones stop growing – my mum looked into it for me. My lips are a bit too big – that's the bit of me that looks the most like Kate. I don't con-sider myself attractive: I know I'm not classically good-looking. I never thought I was model material. This whole model thing took me completely by surprise. When I'm on form I think I'm okay and I'm quite good at a bit of small talk, but in the mornings I'm pretty horrendous. When I see all those topless pictures of me I do wonder why they want my shirt off. I wouldn't mind a more muscly body, but it's such hard work."

Nor was Nick's image enhanced by a pony tail secured with an elastic band.

In a move that recalls the wonderful moment when Warners signed Johnny Rotten's little brother, Martin Lydon, because they thought some of the Rotton-ness might be hereditary – Storm signed the 16-year-old Nick Moss as a model.

His appearance was glossed by Sarah Doukas: "He's not conventionally handsome, nor is he a hunk, but he has a very 'now' look". Adding hope-fully, "All the international male-model agencies are clamouring to get him on to their books."

Kate was underwhelmed: "I never thought he'd be a model." Then, loyally volunteering, "But I always thought Mario would be a top photo-grapher."

Nick's father too, was doubtful. He regretted that Nick had the ability to become a professional footballer but lacked the "dedication and commit-ment". He added, "He doesn't like me to push him too hard. But I mean a career in male modelling is not as easy as female modelling is it? He needs something to fall back on."

The Storm headsheet, distributed in New York, Paris, Milan and London, stated their latest discovery had a 34in chest, a 30in waist, a shoe size 8-12, brown hair and brown eyes, and was five foot nine and a half. Nick added, "and I'm still growing."

Kate's brother was duly portrayed by Glen Luchford decked out in a pink fake fur coat for *Interview* magazine. Even Luchford admitted that "Moss's looks are an acquired taste – he is quite odd-looking [but that] is the look of the moment."

For a flash that seemed to be the case. Nick was flown to New York for a Gianni Versace shoot along with his sister and seven other models.

"When I arrived at the New York studio, Kate hadn't turned up yet. I was just with all those girls. I was very nervous. Some of them were really nice. Some were a bit bitchy."

He also appeared in *The Face*, *Vogue Homme*, and *Harpers Bazaar*, did a campaign for Banana Republic, and trod catwalks at the menswear collections in Paris. But he was still the jock who likes a pint: "I went out on the town the first night I was in Paris for the catwalk shows. It wasn't so much a bad evening, it was just stupid to go so crazy when I was working early the next day. I had been flown over to Paris, landed at the airport and discovered no one spoke English. It was terrifying. I found the show, someone handed me four outfits and stood me in line and I just had to stagger out there and face a huge bank of photographers. I had no idea what to do. That night I went out with one of the other models – Rob English – and met up with my sister. But we lost her after a couple of hours. Rob and I carried on partying and got back to the hotel at 8am. I had to be at a job by 10am. I looked and felt awful."

Kate remained unimpressed, remarking, "After his first job he got really big headed. He was going on about Versace this and Naomi that. It was really embarrassing."

For his part, Nick riposted about his sister, "When she's bitchy, she's very bitchy. That's always been in her blood."

Bitchy or not, her doubts were justified. After that initial flurry, Nick faded from the fashion scene. Perhaps he was glad to. At the height of his 15 minutes of fame he confessed in an interview, "I miss Croydon."

Moreover, he was uneasy and resentful about being in big sister's shadow. "I hate talking about her. That's all I ever hear. What I love talking about is football or sex."

And: "I'd never be doing this [modelling] without Kate. I wanted to be a footballer, like most boys. Sometimes it's good and other times it's really annoying. I was walking down Oxford Street and these girls came up to me and said 'you're Kate Moss's brother', and I'm like, 'no, I'm Nick'. I don't see Kate often because she's got so big now. I'm not doing this full time. I'm going to college to do travel and tourism."

In 2002, the *Sunday Mirror* tracked Nick down working at a mobile phone centre.

* * *

It seems that Doukas hadn't quite got the hang of Kate's allure after all. She put her appeal down to being "different". Nick too was "different". So she launched him. Only "difference" wasn't enough. It also took the ambiguity – the slippage that makes us want to dwell on Kate's face – check whether her eyes really are that far apart, whether her mouth is actually skew-whiff, and whether that "pretty vacant" gaze is for real.

And, of course, even more rewarding than the story of her face was the story of her body …

* * *

After the Calvin Klein deal, Kate's catwalk career also took off.

Catwalk was another world. As she admitted, if she'd tried that route into the business she could easily have failed.

"In photographs it doesn't matter, but on the runway I think clothes look better on taller women. It must be a bit weird for them, everyone saying this [the waif] is the new look when they've got the perfect face, the perfect body, the perfect everything, and somebody who's not at all perfect comes along and starts taking all their jobs. It must be really horrible. But I don't think it will ever change that much. They won't ever be out of fashion because they're beautiful, and at the end of the day that's what people want to see – beautiful people wearing beautiful clothes."

But now she had celebrity allure, and that was beautiful enough. For designers, that was the Mona Lisa.

For some of the other models it was poison: "There was a bit of a weird thing going on – some of the girls were getting fucked off."

Even so, she was welcomed into the brat pack of supermodels like Christy Turlington and Naomi Campbell. Christy and Naomi, as she was soon calling them, took the newbie "under their wing" and inducted her to insider techniques and gossip.

"We had so much fun that first season. The Galliano shows! It was amazing, like a high – the adrenalin, and 'You're on, and you're going to be this character,' and you get so into it because of the energy. It was Versace, and the parties; every night there was something you had to go to – and then you had to be up at six – I mean, it was fun!"

Asked if she thought she was beautiful: "I don't feel beautiful at the moment. It depends. Sometimes I feel all right and sometimes I feel, 'O my God.' Depends on who I'm with. If I've been hanging out with Christie and Naomi for a couple of days, I feel like a piece of shit.

"When I started modelling, I didn't really care if I got rejected. But now, because I'm doing so much, I kind of expect to get jobs, and get upset when I don't. Like, I went to Valentino yesterday for the rehearsals and I'd been confirmed for the show, but they hated me – I was just awful. They called me back and I am doing it now, but at first I thought he didn't like me at all. That was the first time I ever felt very rejected and upset. But the more success you have, the more pressure it is, because there's more pressure to stay there. Before, I was just having a laugh; now I'm doing better jobs – I care more. You want to be good at what you do, but if you start wishing you'd got a certain job, you find yourself being jealous. As long as you're aware of it, you can stop it – you don't want to end up bitter and twisted. I mean, we are lucky."

★　★　★

Another reason Kate was a hit in the States was the folk memory of the first British youthquake back in the sixties. That was about music as much as fashion – or about the inextricable fusion of both into cool and style.

The stylist turned designer, Anna Sui, thought that: "Kate's look really reflects what has gone on in the music world and that has influenced fashion. The spirit seems to be less 'look at me, look at me.' The same has happened with clothes and it's now far less 'look how much I've spent.'"

She continued "Kate's look is very subtle – she's not like the exaggerated Amazon types that had dominated; hers is a more delicate, quite look. For me, there's an inner beauty that has come through with the best new clothes. It is not about ostentation."

There was also her laid back manner and flair for stylishly mismatched clothes. A hippie feel that became defined as boho.

Jo Matthews, the bookings editor for *British Vogue*: "There's something quite special about Kate. There's an intelligence there – and not just the shrewdness about money that quite a few of them have. She's actually not very materialistic. I can imagine in the Sixties she would have been hanging around Woodstock sticking flowers in people's hair."

But there was more to it than instinct. Several observers have recorded the detached professionalism with which Kate Moss from early on transformed her gangly awkwardness into gangly and awkward poses. She knew how to act – at least for a photo shoot, and realised that reality is not as photogenic as a masquerade.

While she drew on her body and biography for her image, what you saw was all her projection.

She has many times been quoted – sometimes exasperated, sometimes wondering – or as if stating the obvious, that what we see is not her: the photos are not me. In her eponymous book, *Kate*, she even got philosophical: "the more visible they make me, the more invisible I become."

A gnomic observation that got one theorist, Bela Chatterjee, hot and bothered: "Who is viewed and who is viewing is no longer clear. Visibility and invisibility are seen to exist at the same time, almost sounding like a contradiction in terms. If it isn't Kate Moss, then who or what is it? Kate Moss herself is not being seen, it is her image to which we react. As I see it, her statement echoes the confusion – perhaps conflation at times, if that is possible – between reality and simulacra, and subject and object, that postmodernist theorists have drawn attention to."

But Chaterjee, underestimates the wily and willed aspects of popular culture. Like Roland Barthes, she presumes – or fabricates, a "naïve" object she can then deconstruct through her specialised and ironic viewpoint.

In reality, the designers of the images she ponders – and Kate Moss is one of these – are perfectly well aware of the subterfuges and layers they employ.

And of what they conceal or traduce.

What's more, any trendy young designer today is quite likely to have graduated in a degree that breezed through Freud, Baudrillard and Derrida as much as Walter Gropius, Magritte, and Warhol.

You can't teach these suckers nothing.

But in the end, of course, from Kate's perspective, the images will have their revenge – they evacuate, they exhaust her, and what is left are increasingly improbable protestations.

* * *

As Kate was getting on board the CK wagon, her boyfriend Mario Sorrenti, was still taking photos of his increasingly famous girlfriend. Still dreaming of a career in photography.

Eventually his pictures started to trickle through. Kate's first US magazine cover for *Harpers Bazaar* in December 1992, went with a fashion editorial by Sorrenti featuring Kate with her brother, Nick.

Partly on the basis of that, Sorrenti was considered for the next stage of Calvin Klein's master plan for Kate Moss.

This was to be a campaign for Klein's perfume, Obsession, a scent traditionally, "promoted in print ads showing photos of multiple nude bodies in darkened rooms going at it every which way."

The clincher came when Sorrenti showed Klein his rather "personal" book of writings and erotic photos featuring Kate. Klein declared: "It was perfect for Obsession – his real obsession with her. You can see the love he has for this girl. I said let's give him a camera and let him shoot his feelings for her."

The two lovers were sent to the practically deserted island of Jost Van Dyke, just off St. Thomas, V.I. Here they were instructed to spend their days recording themselves being obsessive about one another, so creating images suited to the perfume.

However, they were not as "alone" as has been claimed – or fondly remembered since by Kate, since they were accompanied by "a crew from Epoch Films."

Sorrenti insisted that Kate should be naked for most of these shoots and that moreover, she should not even wear any makeup.

Kate: "Mario was like, 'You have to be naked, man – it's about purity; you have to be pure. And I'm like, 'What's the difference if I have a pair of knickers on?' But at the end of the day, you know, he had the control."

Not all the control. Neil Kraft, Klein's senior vice president of advertising went to oversee things after six days. "I insisted for the last two days that we have hair and makeup people and a major director," he explained. Adding, "But we didn't need any of it."

Klein was chuffed with the results. He'd correctly banked on exploiting Kate and her lover's genuinely torrid passion: "It's believable. It was the same thing with Marky Mark. I got him because he had a thing for my underwear. It's incredible how Marky associates certain dates and what's sexy with his underwear. It's just like Mario feels about Kate. People want that reality."

Sorrenti also filmed Kate – he'd been given a crash course in using a low-tech Bolex, and that footage was turned into a commercial. It featured a sexy – albeit clothed, Kate Moss gazing rather vacantly into the lens with a breathy voiceover by Sorrenti.

Adweek enthused: "It's not stagey, it's not lit, and Kate's not all madeup and styled. A lot of it is photographed in and under the water, and our waif Kate has turned into a sea urchin, shot lovingly from the bikini top up. In some shots, he closes in on her eye; he also frames and flattens her lips."

It continued: "Some of the more death-like portraits of Kate suggest the photographer Sally Mann, who photographs her children in sexual, ambiguous ways. Other shots (the way Moss' face is framed against a stark white wall, for instance) suggest Richard Avedon, the dean of Obsession ads. He and Doon Arbus wrote and produced the original, now classic, TV spots that included the line "between love and madness lies Obsession" – a line Kate actually delivers again."

"There's a lot of white, blank screen, which is appealing, and a natural soundtrack (waves and heartbeats), which is nice. If there is any problem, it's with their voices: Kate has a reedy little one, and Mario (in the spots for Obsession for men) is allowed too much heavy breathing to say too little ("I love her … I love you Kate … love is a word you can't explain …")."

Kate recalled less tender moments: "We fought the whole time. 'Obsession' is the way to describe our relationship. Calvin was very clever. He saw that. But we did the pictures and that really worked. I remember hearing Mario's voice in the other room going, 'I love you Kate. I love you Kate.' And I was like, 'What is that?! He was like, 'Well it's true man! It's true! And I was like, 'You're mad!'"

She also confessed, "I think it was a bit much actually. I didn't really think about it – yeah, he's doing the pictures, great – then when it came to the commercial, and his voice over – 'I love you' and all that …"

Opined Lynn Tesoro, head of Calvin Klein PR in her PR way: "Maybe this is just cinema verite for the MTV generation. If you know Kate and Mario's history, you'll have a real connection to the story in these ads. What makes these commercials so special is that the message goes beyond fragrance."

Tesoro added, "[Kate Moss] has a real purity to her beauty. Calvin thinks that she represents the new spirit of a nineties woman."

* * *

Just to make sure everyone got that message, the Calvin Klein apparatus went to town on promo. They teamed up with America-on-line and SPINonline to push the product in virtual space, and also went olfactory with scented strips in major publications like the New York Magazine, Vanity Fair, Allure, Vogue and GQ. They also plastered Sorrenti's images of his lover over billboards, TV screens and bus stops.

* * *

Today, looked at as photographs, Sorrenti's pictures of Kate Moss are strikingly derivative of Corinne Day's early pictures. You could say they are a more stylised and accomplished version of an image – a look – that Day had created.

Stylistically they have the same pared down, black and white – or muted

Portrait. At the Burberry Spring Show, September 2004. "I'm drawn to the eyes..."
The supermodel who became a bigger brand than the brands she represented.
(RSR/Rex Features)

Alexander McQueen's holistic Kate Moss at his Spring 2006 show in Paris. As in this bizarre catwalk apparition, the story of Kate Moss haunts as well as taunts the fashion industry. *(Andy Paradise/WireImage)*

The Moss family's detached suburban home in Church Way, Sanderstead. An idyllic house on the hill where the family nevertheless fell apart. *(Vermorel/Dowle)*

Linda Moss (mother): "Kate was always her own person with her own mind. She wasn't one of those children who start crying if you told her off. She was quite defiant." *(TDY/Rex Features)*

"A sparkling child" – but with unnerving self composure. *(TDY/Rex Features)*

Kate's Primary school: the scene of her first radical style experiments where she cut her own hair in the toilet and tried to pierce her ears with a sewing needle. *(Vermorel/Dowle)*

An early instance of Kate Moss "partying". *(Artellus Ltd)*

Peter and Linda Moss in October, 1983. Their relaxed lifestyle and way
of bringing up children sometimes raised eyebrows. *(Artellus Ltd)*

Peter Moss. The life and soul of any party, as at home with real ale as tinnies. A hardworking and shrewd business man, Peter became the mainstay of Kate's £multimillion fortune. *(Artellus Ltd)*

Kate and brother Nick enjoy a temporary truce. Their battles were ferocious. "I used to pin him down and spit in his face." *(Artellus Ltd)*

Riddlesdowne High. The secondary school where "Mosschops" failed to shine academically and was nicknamed "The Stick". A teacher: "She was not a child you would have turned your head to look at." *(Artellus Ltd)*

WOMAN STYLE

have their say about waif who became a star

NATURAL: Kate began modelling at 14   ONE OF THE GANG: Boys at Kate's school remember her as "nothing special"

HOME TRUTH: Childhood friends Oonagh (left) and Lucy (right) still adore Kate   CHIC: As a girl, Kate was a trend setter

SHINING STAR: Kate's looks have earned her a fortune and international fame, but a few of her old friends feel a little for her but resentment

really well for herself — and good luck to her."

There are not many regulars today in the Blue Anchor who would say the same. As they make do with designer jeans, she sports the latest in designer year; they are lucky to earn in a year what she earns in a day.

The ordinary Croydon girl has had to face the bitter fact that she has left them all behind — and that instead of congratulating her on her success, many of those she grew up with resent her for it.

Kate's rise began seven years ago after being spotted at 14 by Sarah Doukas, boss of the London model agency Storm. By then Kate was well on the way to creating the waif look which was to propel her onto a hundred magazine

covers. Kate's friends remember that she suddenly stopping eating in her teenage years.

"When she started losing weight it was very noticeable," says schoolfriend James Wilkinson, now a 19-year-old university student. "I never saw her eat a proper meal.

"She wouldn't touch pudding because she wanted to be slim. By the end of school she stood out from the other girls because she was so slim."

But while Kate's thin looks left the boys cold, it worked wonders among her girlfriends. Long before Kate's waif-like features were copied by teenage wannabes around the world, her childhood girlfriends worshipped her look.

"We idolised her,"

recalls Nicola Howe, who met Kate when she joined the 7th Sanderstead Brownies. "I remember when she got her ears pierced before us and we all wanted ours done."

Grunge

As a 14-year-old at Riddlesdown High, Kate was the youngest of her gang, but her grunge look set the trend. Sniffing a chance to be a supermodel, Kate gave it all she could. She embarked on a nonstop hunt for modelling jobs, attending one casting session after another.

Kate was even prepared for cosmetic surgery. Her first serious boyfriend, Clark Gregory, says that in the beginning Kate was desperate for a bust that would get her noticed.

One day she told him: "I'm going to have silicone implants. She was so serious about having the enlargement that she had worked out what it would all cost," Clark reveals.

"She reckoned she could have the surgery done for about £2,000 and planned to save it from her modelling fees. But she still wasn't working much then and the money came through in dribs and drabs, so she never scraped enough together."

But while some in Croydon have turned their back on her, Kate can still rely on the friendship of two of her childhood girlfriends, Lucy and Oonagh Connor.

As children they used to dress up together, pretending they were models as they smeared on their

mum's old lipstick and eyeshadow, spraying themselves with perfume.

Two Christmases ago, Kate came home and Lucy and Oonagh saw their old dressing-up partner for the first time since she became a star.

"We were really nervous," says Lucy. "We didn't know what to put on.

"When she arrived, she was wearing Manola Blahnik shoes with very high ones with pointed toes and a little black mini dress, a denim jacket

and a leopard-skin handbag." But the highly-paid super-stylish model was still the same goodnatured Kate they remembered.

"She came in and hugged us all and we were all talking at once. She sat there with a box of Quality Street munching away," says Oonagh, quashing any rumours their friend was anorexic.

"Now she's in every magazine you pick up. That's why it was lovely seeing her, she's still the same person, she'd just matured. She is so down to earth, that is the amazing thing. Not many people have done what she's done for Croydon. Terry and June put Purley on the map, Kate Moss did the same for Croydon."

"She was a real tearaway, always bunking off school." Kate: "Everyone used to go down to this park in Purley, and just drink cider and get off with each other behind the bushes."
(Mirrorpix)

Thrown into the fashion maelstrom at the age of 14, her mother declared that if she wanted to carry on she was "on her own". There was at least one unfortunate incident before she reached 16. *(TDY/Rex Features)*

Sarah Doukas. Bankrolled by Richard Branson, she "discovered" Kate Moss in an airport. "It is all about who you know in this life." *(TDY/Rex Features)*

Angelic in one of her first photo shoots after signing to Storm at 14. But this sexually experienced member of the "Purley Dossers" was already an accomplished drinker and smoker and also partial to marihuana. Kate: "Well, it's South London, innit?" *(David Ross/Mirropix)*

An uncertain and fitful start in 1992. Just like her "anorexic" precursor, Twiggy, Kate Moss had all the wrong attributes for a model. She had to suffer numerous rejections and humiliations. She was told she was too short, too girlish, too contrived, too gawky, not beautiful. And that she had bandy legs, a gap in her front teeth and a lazy eye. But also like Twiggy, she eventually outshone all her contemporaries.
(Vic Singh/Rex Features)

grey, tonality, equalising and equating flesh with drab or minimal surroundings.

They are often framed or cropped to make the viewer uncomfortable, the viewpoint ambiguous or voyeuristic: what is concealed is seemingly as arbitrary as what is revealed (glimpsed). We might move a a little this way or that to reveal a little more – and in that way they are meant to frustrate.

They are also self-consciously "dark" – clipped visions of an austere project probing supposedly disconcerting margins. And sometimes mocking and cod apocalyptic – an avant-gardist's revenge on the commercial beast that feeds the artist.

Twenty-three of these images are reproduced in the book, *Kate*, twenty of them in a double page spread. Kate's nudity gleams through the veil of a mosquito net, against a mottled wall or a black sofa, often out of darkness.

The pared down context emphasises that you, the viewer, and she, the beauty, are alone in a room stripped of reference that looks like an underused or abandoned space. Maybe we are in an attic which imprisons this naked woman like the "mad" females of Victorian legend. This suggestion of captivity is enhanced by some of Kate's poses, which evoke the uneasy tedium of confinement.

Kate Moss here is "distressed" – aesthetically as well as physiognomically: abandoned to glamorised and recherché abjectness, her body stylised as a crisis that is impending: maybe a voyeuristic intrusion, or something more threatening. She is posed to seem to display her attractions – eyes – tits – nipples – arse – unawares.

And at the same time she watches us through the lens with studied enigma.

Pictures which celebrate the seduction of an innocent.

Of course, the Riddlesdown raver was not exactly innocent in any sexual sense. But emotionally and professionally she was an ingénue ready for plucking. And plucked she is – of her clothes and residual modesty, of her pretensions, of her beauty.

* * *

This mood was created by Corinne Day. She was the first to strip a protesting, humbled and humiliated Kate as the subject of her portraits.

Kate: "For my first ever modelling job for *The Face*, the photographer [Corinne Day] wanted me to go topless and I was just like dying, and I hated it and she'd go, 'no, no, no' and so then I kinda …"

And: "I don't mind nudity so long as it's an artistic form. My body's still private though it's easier with Mario [Sorrenti] to take my clothes off, but it's just weird because sometimes I want to keep them on ..."

Such were the efforts and strategies, the subterfuges and overriding of protestations that went into the game that became the subject that became Day and Sorrenti's pictures of Kate Moss stripped naked. Stripped, not in spite of her protests but precisely because of them.

* * *

There is another aspect to these images, brought out by Val Williams: "Day has subverted an entrenched notion of women as consenting objects of desire. The complicity between model and photographer is absolute; both are playing a subtle game which centres on the fantasies of childhood, adolescence, day-dreaming and make-believe with which all women are so familiar. Perhaps this is why the critics are so confounded, for these are women's stories, secret and exclusive, enacted outside the arena of the gender battle. Women photographing women in this way make some men anxious; they create bewilderment and unease."

There is truth in that. But in the end, maybe Williams is simplistic. For what are we then to make of Sorrenti's appropriation of that game? Or Calvin Klein's relish?

* * *

If anything, Sorrenti's pictures are less vivid than Day's since they allow themselves the artifices of a college educated eye. In the double page spread reproduced in *Kate*, it's clear that Sorrenti's images hark back to 19th century cheesecake. The person who took them was colluding with the subject in a game, a game of love, but he was also looking at his lover through a syllabus that runs from Fox Talbot to Weejee, to Taschen re-editions of Victorian erotica.

Whereas Day's originating images were monochrome only "because I had little experience with colour, "Sorrenti uses sepia tinting as well as artful blemishing to simulate effects of time and light and chance and to give his images a patina of the antique.

Corinne Day created the look Sorrenti later recapitulated. A look gradually and fitfully created with the help of Kate and the stylist Melanie Ward.

This was one of those fateful encounters – the kind of baffling and absurd chemistry that popular culture revels in and depends on. Twiggy's "Bambi" haircut in Leonard's Hair Salon, John Lydon wandering into the Sex boutique with a subverted Pink Floyd T-shirt ...

Without Day and her milieu and fantasies and drugs, without her desire to witness this 15 year old with no clothes on, to sexualise her, to fix her and have like that in her lens and in her Brewer Street, Soho apartment – what chance for this skinny waif? How many pretty girls are there in the world, and how many pass through model agencies every day?

"I can't think about that, it would drive me crazy," Kate once exclaimed.

* * *

Whatever Kate Moss did next, and she did plenty, she would never wipe out the trace of that brilliant and disturbing "waif" look, that "anorexic" look, which is also, as I suspect Day well knew, the look of gay jailbait.

Or child whores from Acapulco or Havana, blinking scratching stretching, or just wary, in a blanching light, oblivious to the lecherous stares that will follow their images for ever after.

* * *

The point of these images was not nudity or eroticism per se. There was soon a plethora of Kate Moss images posed naked or semi naked with all kinds of intriguing come-ons, erotic dramas and fetish accessorizing. But the punctum in these later images – the detail that leaks affect and that jars or makes us remember them, is that we enjoy and conspire in her nudity at the same time, and for the same reasons, that she reveals it, and also revels in it. It is not tricked out of her. These later pictures are also the shrewd gifts of a knowing woman to hype.

Or just a laugh.

When the 28-year-old Kate Moss reunited with Corinne Day for a video made by Day's partner, the supermodel sprawled disgracefully on a bed, naked except for a fireman's helmet, and with the ever present fag, caressed her nipples with warmth, crooning to camera: "My nipples used to be so little. I used to have really tiny ones. Now they are huge like fighter pilot's thumbs."

When the photographer asks her to stop playing with them, the response is: "No. I like it! Jefferson [Hack, her lover at that time] likes them. All boys like them like this don't they? [pouting into the lens and whispering] Don't You?"

Or think of the 2004 portrait of Kate Moss by Lucien Freud. Pregnant and naked, Kate opens her arms and legs to the viewer, curled before the master's forensic eye, luxuriant and expansive, mistress of her desires, the proprietor of significant investments and a pile in the country, and gazing at us with sardonic ennui … More Lady Hamilton than Liz Siddall.

* * *

The backlash against the Obsession campaign was unusually intense and protracted.

Media Watch, a feminist consumer organisation, fulminated against the images. They were incensed by what they saw as the infantalisation of women. One of them, objecting to Kleins's promo postcards declared that, "The cards feature an image of Moss that looks like she's been busted on the lip, where she has her hand over her mouth and looks hurt. We are particularly opposed to showing images of women who are both nude and look hurt."

A picture of Kate in a white bikini emphasising the space between her thighs also enraged them.

Graffiti, sneering "Anorexia" was sprayed on Kate's stomach on bus shelters across Manhattan, and "feed me" stickers plastered over her mouth. "Give me a cheeseburger" was another slogan. Skulls or skeletons were spray-painted over her figure. The ads were also attacked by Boston-based militants calling themselves Boycott Anorexic Marketing. A spoof ad featuring a picture of Kate, "Feed the Waifs," appeared in *Esquire*: "For just 39 cents a day, less than the cost of a cup of coffee, you can keep this girl and other supermodels just like her, alive." It was reported that over 2,000 people got (or missed?) the joke and called the phone number given to make the pledge.

Even so, that same year, 1993, Kate's face began to dominate American newsstands, gazing soulfully or scornfully or vacantly from the cover of practically every fashion magazine. Even *Cosmopolitan* lent her its prestigious cover that May – though they arranged her clothing to simulate a little extra flesh. The fuss was set to die down. Then Corrine Day reappeared in Kate's career.

* * *

It was Day's images for *British Vogue* in June 1993, a kind of sardonic coda to the Kate Moss she had previously created, that inflamed the outcry caused by the Obsession campaign and upped the ante. It seems that *Vogue* imagined they might be able to do a Sorrenti and neutralise Day's original Kate-Moss-as-erotic-waif look. But maybe Day was either too obdurate or obtuse to take the hint.

It all started innocently, with a phone call from Anna Wintour (dubbed

"Nuclear Winter" by her staff on account of her frequent tantrums). Day, who was on the dole at the time, flew to New York, taking her 77-year-old granny along as a treat – the same granny who'd brought her up as a surrogate mother. Granny insisted on being snapped next to the flash car sent to whisk them to *Vogue* HQ. Later, Day remarked, "The best thing is that my granny finally believes."

But the rest was not so good. Day resented the glitz and the pressure. She bridled at the aura of money which she found creatively suffocating. "I think it's beautiful not to have money. Not having money makes you use your imagination more." And even though her visit coincided with Kate's triumphant appearance in that year's New York fashion shows, she defiantly chose not to attend. "I don't like fashion shows. I'd rather be down town in the second hand shops."

Her attitude translated to the images she took for *British Vogue*. Far from prettifying the waif, her pictures took the piss. They upturned every convention of fashion photography, negating fashion values, and ridiculing the allure and erotic charge of the fashion model and fashion itself.

Framed and lit like family snapshots, here was a gangly Kate with hardly any makeup, her hair hardly combed, looking distraught, and set against minimal props – if they were props at all: a nylon bedspread, a TV remote control … whatever happened to be around – a negative styling that complimented these jaundiced images. And what was Kate wearing apart from a sullen expression?

Day explained, "I bought some underwear from Ann Summers sex shop in Brewer Street which is where I live. I also bought some American tan tights, [and] I got Liza Bruce to copy some T-shirts of mine so there were some designer credits in the magazine."

She then explained, "The photographs looked cheap and tacky – everything that *Vogue* was not supposed to be. Kate had had a fight with her boyfriend that day and was crying so a few of the photographs were naturally sad."

"Cheap" was the motif, indeed. The images played with "cheap" as the obverse of the luxury *Vogue* represented. They rammed the message home through Kate's throwaway poses, pantomimically sexy undies, and a dingy London apartment setting.

They also hinted at another kind of "cheap". These apparently informal snaps harked at the sniggering and bragging genre of Reader's Wives. Only here was a Reader's Daughter.

Whether "Nuclear Winter" was happy when she saw these pictures is not on record. And what the team at *British Vogue* discussed as they spread this "dirty realism" (as the style was later dubbed) over the editorial table, is also a mystery. But they published them.

* * *

That now infamous *Vogue* featured a cover picture of Kate looking perky in Chanel. But Day's pictures inside, spread over eight pages and headed, "Under Exposure," caused consternation. You weren't supposed to see that kind of thing in the bible of fashion.

Marcelle D'Argy Smith, editor of *Cosmopolitan*, complained: "The pictures are hideous and tragic. I believe they can only appeal to the paedophile market. If I had a daughter who looked like that, I would take her to see a doctor." Looking back in 2003 she further lambasted these images of "superwaif Kate Moss wearing scruffy see-through knickers hollow cheeks, blank, staring eyes and bones" adding, "You looked at her the way a doglover looks at a battered, starved, pup at the Battersea Dogs Home. With horror."

The *New York News* thundered that Kate "should be tied down and intravenously fed."

In *the Guardian*, Judy Sadgrove, in an article headed "Are this year's models creating next year's anorexics?" made the alarming claim that "Breasts have now disappeared altogether", tendentiously suggested that "Kate Moss – ironically, the star of a new semi-skimmed milk ad, praising its low-fat quality – has the body of an 11-year-old." Followed up swiftly with yet another rhetorical question: "So will there be another surge in the epidemic of eating disorders afflicting women in the west?"

Marion Hume in *The Independent* lamented that *Vogue*: "has sanctioned images that resonate with the sexualisation of children. That is irresponsible. Sexual abuse of the young is a harrowing truth of our times and *Vogue* is a magazine with influence that extends far beyond its readership. It is the bible of British style. By choosing a photographer, a model, a look, it gives its sanction, an esteemed seal of approval. And *Vogue* makes waves; it is a source book, used by lesser magazines, by advertisers, by television commercial- makers who wish to emulate its opinion on where fashion, not just in clothes but in photography and in faces, stands at any given time. *Vogue* is also a social document that records the changing aspirations of the British."

And with a nimble twist commented that: "It is just as dangerous for a woman to play a child as it is for children, who do not know what they are doing, to play roles too adult for their years."

Jenny Barnett, from *Marie Claire*, meanwhile sniped: "From a fashion point of view, it's neither modern, nor innovative." The editor of *New Woman*, joined in: "*Vogue* is trying to experiment, but it hasn't worked. They're meaningless pictures."

* * *

Vogue drew back, startled by the uproar. Sarah Doukas too, was not amused. Day then suffered the same punishment the ancient Greeks visited on errant philosophers – exile. She didn't work for *Vogue* or photograph Kate for ten years.

But her images had made the controversy simmering over the Obsession campaign boil over. They underscored the rawness of what Sorrenti and Klein had tried to gloss with art and sentimentality.

They also made Kate Moss a household name.

In September, *People* ran an article, "How Thin is too thin?" with a cover shot of a naked Kate with skinny arms crossed over skinny chest, and a red banner: "Skin and Bones."

Seeding the storm it was supposed to be reporting on, the article began "Moss looks as if a strong blast from a blow dryer would waft her away, let alone the winds of discord now whipping around her."

The magazine then wheeled in: "Suzanne Henrick, a registered dietician and counsellor at Wilkins Centre for Eating Disorders in Greenwich: 'I wouldn't say Kate Moss causes anorexia, but I had an anorectic in here just yesterday who said she wanted to look like Kate Moss. A lot of them bring in her picture as an ideal. I haven't seen that with any other particular model before.'"

It also quoted, the feminist Susan Faludi, author of *Backlash: The Undeclared War Against American Women*, that the Kate Moss waif look was: "a man's fantasy of shrinking women down to a manageable size. The look is about being very weak and passive. It is a very Victorian portrait of a woman where you are so weak you can barely get off your chaise longue and on to the retirement home."

It moderated all that however, with Sheyll Garrett, editor of *The Face*, suggesting that: "I don't think you can mistake a 19-year-old girl for a 12-year-old. [Day's photographs of Moss] are not going to make people want to go out and sleep with children. They are just quite real documentary shots of what Kate is like."

* * *

It is hardly surprising these images fostered a moral panic. That was their purpose. And facetious of critics like Robin Muir to affect surprise at the public disquiet these commercially honed and destined images caused: "Accusations against Day ranged from child exploitation to promoting anorexia and, incredibly, condoning under-age sex."

We were no longer on reasoned ground. This was now what Theory merchants call "a media discourse." A shrill but indistinct noise that was about everything and touched everyone. To ignore or dismiss it marked you a barbarian or pervert.

This was a conflation of worries, arguments and fantasies that distilled roughly down to the pleasures and obscenities of ecstasy in our consumerist civilisation. Here was every red herring chasing every explosive suggestion: the buliminia scare, the anorexia panic, fears about media contagion, teenage bodies out of control … plus tall or alarming tales about desire and wickedness, money power fame beauty and destruction – and how one thing led to another … all going round and round until it was one of those "controversies" that won't go away, that will never go away – and has dogged and defined Kate Moss ever since.

* * *

"What do they want me to do, get fat? Oh, fuck off."
– Kate Moss

* * *

Her own reaction has ranged from stunned to hurt to defensive. Of the *Vogue* images, she said: "The styling was slaggy in a way. But I love those pictures … and I looked my age. Lots of women haven't got big tits, but we still wear lingerie …"

Of the controversy in general: "That felt a bit weird. I could have said something about it at the time but that just would have meant entering into their game so I didn't. I knew the pictures weren't intended to be what they said they were, and it was really nothing – they just made a fuss about it. They're going to write things about you that aren't true at all all the time – it just goes over your head at the end of the day. I mean. I was like, 'Oh, my God, that's really horrible saying that.' Paedophile, Ugh. But you can't let it get to you."

In the face of incessant hounding by the media about her "bad" influence, she protested: "Women are always going to worry about what they look like. When it was Cindy [Crawford] who was flavour of the month, everyone wanted to get silicone implants to get big tits. Now they say people are going to be anorexic because models have a thin body type. I don't think women are so stupid that they look at a magazine and say, 'Oh,

God, I've got to be that thin to be fashionable.' As long as they feel good about themselves, they're not going to worry about what's in a fashion magazine. At least, I hope not."

The accusation she was promoting anorexia particularly riled her.

"At the end of the day, they're blaming me for diseases I don't have any control over. I think it's the adults putting the blame on some public figure instead of taking the blame for their child's anorexia themselves. I'm sick of it. I go to restaurants and people come up and say, 'Oh, I'm disappointed you're eating.' I wasn't even the skinniest of the girls. I don't know why they picked me."

Later on, she recalled: "At first I got defensive. I was like, 'What are they talking about? It was upsetting, absolutely. I was a scapegoat. The media had to put responsibility on somebody, and I was chosen. They felt free to say that, because someone is thin, they were anorexic, which is ridiculous. And just because one person brought it up, then everyone was like, 'Oh, She must be anorexic.' And no matter how much I say over and over again that I'm not, they don't want to hear it. They want the opposite to be true. And that's even more upsetting."

* * *

As reported by Kate herself, Sorrenti's sweet nothings whispered on the Obsession ad had alarmed her. Maybe too, although she's never admitted it in so many words, those Obsession pictures of reluctant nakedness had undermined their intimacy.

The pair now had a flat in London to stay whenever they were there. (This was the set of Day's *Vogue* images.) But Kate also had an apartment in the Pigalle district of Paris. This was spacious and smart, with high ceilings and large windows curtained in white, stripped pine floors and modish wrought iron and glass furnishings.

Kate rented this place for tax reasons – at the time, she was officially domiciled in France. Asked about this arrangement she was coy: "I'm not telling you! I can't really, the tax man will be after me. I don't talk about money." She continued, "It's completely insensitive. You get paid ridiculous amounts of money to do ridiculous things, you know, and if you talk about it to normal people, they're just like, 'Fuck, why weren't we born beautiful?'" She clarified, "That's what someone said to me the other day. I mean, I do work hard, but it's a different kind of work. I don't like talking about it though."

So as well as having her own bolthole, Kate was financially independent. All this may have widened the growing gulf between her and Mario. Asked around then about their romance, she was evasive: "Um … well, we're just having a break. He lives in London and I live in Paris." Adding cryptically, "I dunno. You know how it is – relationships."

* * *

Highlighting the problems of working with a lover, Kate commented: "We do our best work together, but it puts such pressure on the relationship that we just, like, argue all the time and it's such a nightmare."

But she also hinted at another, perhaps deeper reason that frightened this 19 year old: "He's a typical Italian: very macho and old-fashioned, a real drama queen. He says, like, 'Kate, have a baby!' I don't wanna have kids because I'm too young. He wants me to have kids because then he thinks I can't run off with his baby, but I wouldn't do it now, especially for a reason like that. He'd like to see me in the kitchen. It does sometimes annoy me. His mother is like my second mother, and she says he's just like his father."

By September 1993, it was a crisis. They'd been obliged to cut short a holiday in Tuscany after rowing furiously over the arrangements – Kate objected to sharing a villa with another couple. When they got back to London Kate decided she should move out of their West London flat. She began looking for an alternative pied a terre, helped by her long term friend, celebrity hairdresser, James Brown.

If anything, the split was a relief. In any case, by January next year, she was back in New York partying with Jenny Shimizu, the "dyke supermodel". Shimuzu was good company for forgetting soured affairs. According to Andrew Morton she had also become Madonna's "doppelganger" in the aftermath of the Material Girl's split with Sean Penn.

* * *

But with all of that jet setting lifestyle, there was still a part of Kate that hankered after Croydon.

That Christmas she went home to her family. She also tried to go home to her former friends. The face of Calvin Klein turned up at one of her former haunts, the Blue Anchor, (nowadays tarted up and renamed The Treehouse).

The place was packed with familiar faces and her former friends, but none of them were impressed or pleased to see the supermodel. They ignored her. Or insulted her. An observer commented, "It was a sad Christmas for her. Everyone slagged her off and shouted comments at her. She rang a lot of friends up to meet her, but we all had other plans."

Even Clark, her former boyfriend, stood her up. He promised to meet her there but failed to show.

Kate ended up sitting alone on a widow ledge by the pool table.

* * *

Obsession's bad press was no hindrance to Klein's fortunes. He was the darling of the fashion industry in 93-94. A love affair maybe helped by his apparent masterminding of a plot against the dictatorship of the super-models – or what was seen as their stranglehold on designers.

The Council of Fashion Designers of America (CFDA) who award the equivalent of the fashion Oscars, also run the New York Fashion shows. In 1993 the CFDA decided to house the normally scattered and anarchic New York season in one venue under two 30-foot-high white tents in Bryant Park. Partly to rationalise the event, partly to rival the similar French shows at the Louvre, and partly, to outfox the supermodels and their agencies.

Women's Wear Daily reported: "A 'top secret' preliminary meeting Wednesday evening at Calvin Klein's offices … was attended by Calvin Klein, Donna Karan, Nicole Miller and CFDA president Stan Herman and executive director Fern Mallis. It also included representatives from Ralph Lauren and seven modelling agencies …"

The ploy was simple: since shows under the tent would be shorter than normal the designers would pay the models less – up to 70% less.

Predictably, the agencies fumed. So did the models. One, who spoke on condition of anonymity, declared: "I was up in arms about it. The ironic thing about it is, models are self-employed, and nobody's telling us about it."

After two days of "heated discussions" in Klein's offices the agencies wouldn't budge. So the designers negotiated individually with models.

They won a partial victory that season. But the power of the supermodels was based in the celebrity culture of the media. That was not negotiable. A Name is a Name. And soon the supermodels were back – with their super-fees.

* * *

Meanwhile, it was announced that Klein had been awarded the prestigious designer of the year award not once, but twice – both for menswear and women's wear. The first time any designer had scooped both. The awards ceremony took place the following year, February 7th 1994 at Lincoln Center's New York State Theatre.

The theme of the gala was, "the bankable power of the industry." Klein's own bankable supermodel, Kate Moss, accompanied her employer. The awards were presented to Calvin by his buddy David Geffen – who once rescued Calvin from financial disaster. It was a fashion story with an uplifting moral and a happy ending. The 500-seat students' balcony exploded with applause.

Afterwards, the Klein party went to celebrate at the trendy Café Tabac. Tabac, founded in 1992 by a former model, Roy Liebenthal, was "the white-hot nexus of East Village grunge and supermodel chic," and patronised by celebs like Bono and Donald Trump. It was where an aspirant Madonna had once served her dues as a waitress. And it was at Tabac that evening, that Kate looked across a crowded room and saw Johnny Depp.

ACT TWO:

From Depp to Devastation

"The most pain I ever suffered was at the dentist." - Kate Moss

Eleven years Kate's senior, Depp had already carved a niche as a Hollywood bad boy. Born on June 9, 1963, in Owensboro, Kentucky – "barbecue capital of the world", Depp's father was a city engineer, his mother, Betty Sue, a waitress.

The family moved to Florida when Depp was seven and travelled rootlessly as Depp's father tried to find work. Depp recalled, "We moved like gypsies. From the time I was five until my teens we lived in 30 or 40 different houses ... But it's how I was raised so I thought there was nothing abnormal about it. Wherever the family is, that's home. We lived in apartments, on a farm, in a motel. Then we rented a house, and one night we moved from there to the house next door. I remember carrying my clothes across the yard and thinking, This is weird, but it's an easy move."

Depp was destabilised by this existence. He rebelled at school, disgracing himself by mooning a teacher. "I wasn't learning. I felt the teachers were there to kill eight hours and get paid."

Like Kate, he experimented with sex early, "I was about 13, playing guitar at a club, and this girl who was older had been hanging around listening to us. She was a virgin, too. That night we just ... partook. It was in the bass player's van, a blue Ford. I knew what to do – I had studied the subject for many years. And I remember us laughing, having a good time together. It's a sweet, sweet memory."

Like Kate too, he was smoking by twelve and drinking soon after. And then came drugs, vandalism and petty crime.

He chose a classic way out: through rock and roll. His mother had given the adolescent Depp a guitar and he taught himself to play. He joined a punk band, Flame, which transformed into The Kids. They played Florida nightclubs, supporting The Ramones, The Pretenders, Talking Heads and even Depp's hero, Iggy Pop.

"[The] night we opened for Iggy. It went great. After the show I was pretty drunk, and in the Iggy tradition I wanted more, so I started screaming at him. Just sophomoric insults: "Iggy Poop! Who the fuck are you? Iggy Slop!" He got in my face and said, "You little turd." And walked away. So of course I was delighted. I looked over at the bass player and said, "Yeah, that was Iggy. He's a god."

In the wake of such glamour the band moved to Los Angeles looking for the big time.

The big time proved elusive and Depp was reduced to selling ballpoint pens over the phone. "The best thing about that job was using the phone – I'd call my family in Florida on the pretext of selling them pens. The boss, the pen boss, would circle the room, but when he went by I'd say, "How many pens would you like, 288?"

By this stage, Depp had married a make-up artist, Lori Anne Allison. She suggested he try his hand at acting. She also introduced Depp to the film-maker Nicholas Cage. Cage's agent then got Depp an audition with Wes Craven. Craven, known for his slasher and gore style in *The Hills Have Eyes*, cast Depp in *A Nightmare On Elm Street*.

Depp then took classes at an LA drama school, The Loft. He was next cast as Private Lerner in Oliver Stone's Vietnam war drama, *Platoon*. This Oscar winning movie however, only led to small-time TV work.

Then he was cast in a new cop series, *21, Jump Street* as officer Tom Hanson. This smash hit turned Depp into a TV heart throb with an appropriate bag of fan mail. "Nude pictures in the mail, yes. Tons of them. Some are beautiful -nicely lit, black-and-white, mysterious. Some are out-and-out primitive. Then there are the pubes. I've gotten a lot of pubic hairs in the mail. I don't save them. I guess you could get ritualistic about it, burn the pubes in a fire, but I'm not sure I want to touch them so I throw them away."

Depp chafed at his cute stardom. He hated the studio machine and felt trapped. He had higher aspirations; he wanted to make art. He grabbed a way out by collaborating with the scandalous filmmaker, John Waters, credited with "dragging bad taste into the mainstream". (A teenage fan once wrote to Waters, "I'm 15. I make movies like yours. Why do you get sent to Europe and I get sent to the school psychiatrist?" Waters riposted: "I used to get sent to the school psychiatrist. Keep doing it until you get to Europe. It's just a matter of lasting.") So Depp starred in Water's perverse and anarchic, *Cry-Baby*, playing alongside his hero, Iggy Pop.

Depps's next part made him. Tim Burton's low budget and bizarre horror masterpiece, *Edward Scissorhands*, featured a convincing performance by Depp as the disfigured lover cursed with steel blades for fingers.

By now, Depp was notching up gossip column inches. Particularly for his complicated love life and serial engagements to the celluloid beauties, Sherilyn (*Twin Peaks*) Fenn, Jennifer (*Dirty Dancing*) Grey, and his *Scissorhands* co-star, Winona Ryder. This last pledge resulted in a tattoo (one of many): "Winona Forever. It was altered after they split to, "Wino Forever."

The tag was appropriate. Depp had become notorious for brawling, drinking and drug taking: "Pretty much anything I could ingest. And I was soused, drinking heavily, really doing myself in. When it gets constant, when you're going to sleep drunk, waking up and starting to drink again, that stuff will try to kill you."

Perhaps to facilitate his lifestyle he co-started a club called Viper Room: "After a group of musicians in the Thirties who called themselves Vipers. They were reefer heads and they helped start modern music."

"It became a scene instantly when we opened it. I never had any idea it was going to do that. I really thought it was just gonna be this cool little underground place. You can't even see the place. There's no sign on Sunset [Boulevard]. It's just a black building and the only sign is on Larabee, a tiny little sign, real subtle."

Viper Rooom held about 200 people. Its dance floor was small, and there was a corner stage where Depp and friends might jam. The interior was done up art-deco speakeasy style, with cigarette girls who prowled the venue to enhance the period feel.

Naturally, the place was dark: black walls, black upholstered booths, mirrors: "I'm fascinated by the dark and the absurd. I'm drawn to what's behind that. And don't we all have a bit of the ambulance chaser in us?"

★   ★   ★

One lesser known feature of the club was Depp's upstairs private office, sometimes known as the "secret room". The office wall was glass. But this was one way glass – the people in the club below were unaware they were being watched. It's rumoured that select members of the club sometimes had sex, pressed against that wall.

"My idea," Depp mused, "was to play Louis Jordan and to segue to the Velvet Underground."

The place quickly turned into a scene for celeb "partying". It was dubbed "the gold standard of cool, and the place to behave badly".

* * *

However, the "ambulance chasing" got a little too real when the Viper habitué, River Phoenix, died on the sidewalk just outside the club. The fanatically Vegan movie star had overdosed on a heroin-cocaine "speedball".

Depp was defensive, even shrill: "When River passed away, it happened to be at my club. Now that's very tragic, very sad, but they made it a fiasco of lies to sell fucking magazines. They said he was doing drugs in my club, that I allow people to do drugs in my club. What a ridiculous fucking thought!"

"Hey, I'm going to spend a lot of money on this nightclub so everyone can come here and do drugs. I think that's a good idea, don't you? We'll never get found out. It's not like this place is high profile or anything, right? That lie was ridiculous and disrespectful to River. But aside from River, and his family trying to deal with their loss, what about people who work in the club? They have rooms and dads in, like, Oklahoma, reading about the place where their daughter tends bar and thinking, Jesus, she's out in Hollywood swimming around with these awful creatures!"

He went on, "It was awful for my nieces and nephews to read that stuff, to have every two-bit pseudo-journalist speculating viciously … viciously. And it hurt."

"[So] I closed the club for a few nights. To get out of the way so River's fans could bring messages, bring flowers. And I got angry. I made a statement to the press: "Fuck you. I will not be disrespectful to River's memory. I will not participate in your fucking circus."

Depp's own circus continued. The club blossomed in the wake of this ghoulish incident and for years after tourists would pose for pictures on the very spot where River vomited to death.

* * *

It was four months after that incident that Depp found himself sitting at a table with friends in Café Tabac. He noticed Kate sitting with the Calvin Klein crew.

"It wasn't all that romantic" he recalled. "She was sitting at a table with some friends and I knew one of them." Depp invited them both over.

For Kate it was more auspicious. "I knew from the first moment that we talked that we were going to be together. I've never had that before. He's sweet."

* * *

Kate had fancied Depp before they even met. He was her pin up.

Kate: "I was doing pictures for Calvin Klein and the photographer had stacks of pictures of Johnny. He wanted the style of the advertising to be like the pictures of Johnny. There was Johnny everywhere. And this photographer was like all the time: 'Find me a girl, find me a girl.' And I said, 'Introduce me to Johnny and I'll find you a girlfriend.'

"So I had these pictures in the house months before we ever met. And when we meet it was fate. I was reading this book on the plane, *Celestine Prophecy*, and it said there are always signs and divine intervention. You see the sign and you can take it on. The book says that you must be aware of coincidences in your life because they're not coincidences. For instance, compare the way you got into your career and into your relationship. Well this was weird because they were both the same. My career started because I got stuck in JFK and then approached by the agency. When I met my boyfriend I was stuck in a hotel room. Good or bad, things are meant to be."

She continued the story: "I'd gone out with him the night before in high heels and this tiny skirt. I went back to the hotel and we got snowed in. By six in the morning there was a snowstorm up to my knee so I couldn't move. My friend had to send my clothes by courier from uptown to midtown and it took seven hours for the clothes to arrive, so I was stuck with him [Johnny]. If that hadn't happened I don't know, we may never have phoned each other."

* * *

Two weeks later the pair ended the inevitable speculation by appearing as an item at the mid February premiere of a short made by Depp, called *Banter*.

This was during one of those worthy events when the fashion industry likes to display its heart of gold. In this case at $100 a ticket. The *LA Times* reported on the gala's dress code, nodding at: "*Vogue* Editor Anna Wintour's leather mini with silver buckles [and] Cher's skintight leather pants. Both ladies were surrounded by circles of adoring men."

Women's Wear Daily gushed that: "Some of Hollywood's trendiest names packed Smash-box, a Culver City photo-studio-turned-party-house, to welcome the designer Tuesday night at a Neiman Marcus party to benefit DARE (Drug Abuse Resistance Education) ...

"Depp and Kate Moss, his new amour, were there, but so was Depp's recent ex – model Tatjana Patitz – who didn't give him the time of day."

* * *

Depp's film was also worthy. A grainy and gritty plea for the kids to stay away from substances. *Esquire* commented it was "a gruesome but provocative excursion into the world of hard drugs."

But according to the *LA Times*, "the crowd ... wasn't terribly attentive". The paper speculated, "Perhaps they were distracted by the likes of Heather Locklear, Linda Evangelista, Tatiana Patitz and Jeanne Tripplehorn." It also commented, "And we're not sure what exactly distracted Depp and sweetheart Kate Moss. They stayed out of sight most of the night."

After the party a select group retired to Viper Room.

* * *

As a couple, Kate Moss and Johnny Depp were tabloid manna, and packs of paparazzi chased them everywhere. In the first blush of love, the pair obliged with photogenic displays of necking and nuzzling.

Particularly on beaches.

That March, vacationing in the West Indies on a luxury yacht they were spotted snogging on the island of St Barts. Then, in April, they were pictured "nuzzling" on the island of St Barthelemy. *The News Of The World* quoted an excited "holidaymaker": "They couldn't keep their hands off each other and were getting quite raunchy. Every time we looked at them they were kissing and canoodling, totally oblivious to anyone else on the beach."

A friend of Depp's reported, "Johnny is always falling in love. But he's absolutely besotted by Kate." Kate was equally entranced, "I can't believe it. It's like nothing that has ever happened to me before. I knew this was it."

In early April, the tanned "couple-of-the-moment" appeared at the New York premiere of John Water's black comedy, *Serial Mom*. It was a fashion event. Rubbing shoulders with Kate and Johnny were Thierry Mugler, Linda Evangelista and Naomi Campbell. Not to mention the intriguing combination of Quentin Crisp and Patty Hearst.

Maybe it was this happy atmosphere that inspired Kate later that month to anticipate marriage. When a fan asked for her autograph at yet another premiere she signed "Kate Moss Depp". Johnny was annoyed and was said to have "scolded" her.

* * *

A few months into the relationship, Kate introduced Johnny to her mother.

Linda: "Kate rang and asked if I'd like to come on holiday to Necker Island in the Caribbean with her and Johnny. He was renting the whole island for privacy. She only gave me a week's notice, which is usual for her, but as I only do a little part-time work I was able to go.

"I was pretty excited about staying on a private island and I wasn't nervous at all about meeting Johnny, although I wanted him to like me. I flew out to somewhere or other, then on to Necker by helicopter. Johnny and Kate ran across to meet me, then took me to this lovely villa with a cook, a maid and everything was taken care of.

"I'd read some of this bad stuff about Johnny but I never judge people till I meet them. And when I met Johnny, I liked him a lot. I found him quiet, shy, well … nice. He was probably more nervous than I was. Of course, it doesn't really matter what I think; I've never interfered with Kate's choice of boyfriends and I'm not going to start now.

"We spent a lot of time together lazing around sunbathing and talking over dinner at night. Even though was very luxurious and we went out on a yacht and all that, it was very relaxed and not at all nerve-wracking.

"The villa was so large, we were able to have our own privacy. Johnny was very sweet, very attentive to Kate and I could see he cared about her. I think this bad boy image is all hype. And seeing them together, I feel they are equally crazy about each other."

* * *

Back in London, Peter Moss also approved in his clipped accent: "She said he's quite a nice chap. She seemed to be quite keen on him. Kate's not a silly person. She knows what she likes. And he apparently has been quite nice to her." Volunteering, "Johnny Depp is not dissimilar to Mario."

* * *

Kate also introduced Johnny to Croydon. They visited Surrey Market and bought sausages, then on to Linda's.

Linda: "Kate called me called to say she'd be round in half an hour. I was lying on the sofa recovering from a minor Operation, so I couldn't even tidy the house or cook dinner. She and Johnny turned up in this huge limo. Kate said she'd been showing Johnny all her local haunts.

"They cooked sausages and mash for us all and Johnny told me he really enjoyed it all. Johnny [had] shaved his beard off and I told him he looked much better – and so young. He's so shy that he was really embarrassed."

* * *

But Johnny was not always so sweet. A bouncer at Viper Room reported, "I've heard people describe Johnny as shy and well mannered. He is when he's sober. When he drinks he gets a bad, bad temper." It was reported that on more than one occasion he objected and could become moody or belligerent when other men seemed overly interested in Kate.

On Geraldo, an American syndicated talk show, the host related how, "Johnny's just as jealous as Brad Pitt. The second most gorgeous guy in Hollywood, another one totally possessive. He worries about Kate Moss all the time. Remember, she did a campaign for Calvin Klein with a really gorgeous model named Michael Bergen. And I guess they did some ads together and they really clicked. They're just about nude. In fact, these pictures are so hot, a lot of magazines turned them down [and] someone brought in an issue with one of the pictures into the Viper Room and Johnny flipped out, ripped it to shreds and said he never wants to see Michael Bergen again."

* * *

Another display of temper occurred in the $1,200-a-night presidential suite of the Mark Hotel in New York. This was on September 13th of their first year together.

Depp was firstly annoyed he couldn't find a room at his preferred hotel, The Carlyle. Then he took exception to the attitude of the night security guard, Jim Keegan. "The guy was a little froggy and he decided he was going to 'get in the famous guy's face'. I don't really take too well to that."

In the suite next to the Moss Depps was Roger Daltrey of The Who. Daltrey was ill and became annoyed at what he called "crashing" throughout the night – but oddly, no arguments or shouting. It seemed some destruction was going on.

Daltrey, of course, was a member of a band that became rich and famous for wild antics, and whose drummer Keith Moon turned trashing hotel rooms into a fine art. But that was long ago. Daltrey called the front desk to complain.

The security guard, Keegan, went to investigate. An altercation then began between Depp and Keegan. In Depp's account, "The guy probably had too many cups of coffee that night. He was particularly feisty and he decided to call the shots in a way that I didn't think was particularly necessary."

Keegan assessed the damage to the hotel suite. According to a news report the damage amounted to "two [broken] 17th-century frames and paintings, a china lamp stand, a Chinese pot, a glass table top, the legs of a coffee table, a vase and some shelves. Depp also left cigarette burn marks on the carpet and a red desk chair."

Not so wicked. As Daltrey later wryly commented, The Who would have done a better job in a fraction of the time.

Depp offered to pay. But Keegan was having none of it. He demanded Depp immediately check out. Depp didn't see it that way so Keegan threatened to call the cops. Depp still refused to leave and 30 minutes later three officers from the 19th precinct turned up. They arrested the movie star and, to the joy of paparazzi, led him out of the hotel in handcuffs. Kate then left the suite and stayed the night at Naomi Campbell's apartment.

For the following 48 hours, Depp was detained at Precinct House in Central Booking, and in the "tombs" behind the police HQ. He was then obliged to pay what his lawyers considered a preposterous amount.

The incident did him no harm. John Walters commented laconically that, "The hotel thing didn't hurt his career. He looked good under arrest. I loved the handcuffs – they always work. Criminal movie star is a really good look for Johnny."

* * *

Depp himself, later made light of the incident. He denied it had been any sort of set-to between him and Kate. "It had absolutely nothing to do with Kate. You want to hear the honest truth about what happened in that hotel? There was a cockroach in that room the size of a baseball, and I was chasing it, and I missed." And: "This thing had tried to attack me and tried to suck my blood – a big cockroach. And I tried to get it, I tried to whack it. I'd miss and I'd smash a lamp."

The incident had another surreal coda. On recovering his belongings from the hotel Depp discovered that while he'd been under arrest someone had annotated an autobiography of Marlon Brando he'd been reading. Its pages were scrawled with remarks like: "Fuck you, Johnny Depp", "You're an asshole", and "I hate you". No one claimed that Kate was the culprit, so it may have been the hotel staff.

* * *

The Kate and Johnny saga continued. They were made for news values. And apparently, for each other. *Playboy* pronounced that Depp "and his latest love, ubermodel Kate Moss, are the prom king and queen of young Hollywood – beautiful, thin chainsmokers with an air of sex and tragedy."

The association certainly put Kate in the limelight. Just at that point, people were tiring of waifs and stick-like mannequins. Her career may have faltered in the fickle ambience of fashion; she might have retired to the UK with just her scrap book for consolation. Several models who enjoyed a brief success in that waif boom were eclipsed as trends changed.

★ ★ ★

"Yeah, my life hangs from these cheekbones."
- Kate Moss

★ ★ ★

There's more to modelling than being a pretty face. In some ways it's one of the most fraught and exacting occupations in the fashion industry. You are the toy of multiple and shameless egos – from designers to photographers to agents to editors. The physical toll – especially in the travelling involved, can be devastating. Michael Gross' book, *Model*, documents the surprising number of ex-models that end up broke, doped, suicided or otherwise destroyed. "This is a world in which ... Loyalty is nonexistent. Betrayal is everywhere. But what else", he continues, "do you expect from a world that caters to envy and lust?"

As a model you are also uneasily aware, and frequently reminded by others, of the ambivalence the term "model" attracts. It may stand alternatively for airhead and floozy, muse and mistress, pinup and whore. But whatever terms you can use to describe a model's talent, substance or longevity do not leap to mind. After a certain point it's necessary to move on. But to what?

If your fame is sufficiently established, if papers can shift copies by inserting your name into headlines, if merchandisers can create successful products with your "signature", then you might consider a career move to other areas of showbiz.

But all such crossovers emerge from a critical mass of celebrity. After a certain point, a "Name" becomes a magnet, attracting attention and accumulating value as a value in itself, whatever the occasion or issue.

★ ★ ★

There are parallels in how celebrity works and how money works. Both celebrity and money are formless and yet endlessly mutable: phantas-magoric substances that create worlds of "spectral objectivity". They both originate in magical belief, and their extraordinary power to reproduce and migrate across culture comes from their "super-objective" quality: they are beyond everything yet inside everything.

The stock exchange and hit parade both float on fetishes of reputation – and of number. As the sociologist Simon Smelt put it: "number is money's personality". In the same way, the essence of any celebrity is not anything intrinsic to the person who bears the Name – the magic is in the numbers – of hits, of clicks, of number ones and top tens, the millions of fans or $s or £s that accrue to that "personality".

To get where she eventually got to in the reputation and number stakes, Kate Moss needed that extra and timely boost – the borrowed charisma of Depp's reputation.

* * *

At first she didn't realise how potent this Hollywood magic was. "The first time I went to Johnny's house in L.A. is when I suddenly realized what I was getting myself into. I didn't realize it when we were in New York. I knew he was famous, but I didn't really know what that entailed."

That was the kernel that created the spectral "super-objectivity" of Kate Moss today, and enabled the Moss industry to carry on beyond any model's normal sell-by date. And without any crossover whatsoever – not even a perfume, not even a line in tights.

Note too, that in guest appearances in pop videos and movie bit parts she acts herself – that is the only talent and value she has. But it is a consider-able value and partly accrues from another talent, which is picking useful lovers.

* * *

January 16, 1995 was Kate's 21st.

Kate: "Johnny said, 'We're just going out to dinner.' He's like, 'Put a dress on.' So I had this satin dress, down to the floor, and he got the scissors, and he's like, cutting it up to the knee, literally, while we're walking out the door. I'm wearing, like, red satin up to the knee, all jagged."

But they didn't go to dinner.

Linda Moss takes up the story: "Johnny's secretary, Jess, rang me to say he'd get me a ticket to fly over and to ask if there were any other special friends he could fly over for her, too. I did think of some old school friends but none of them could go because of work, babies or other commitments. Even Kate's brother Nick couldn't make it in the end because he had a model booking."

"[Then] The night I was leaving for Los Angeles, Kate rang me and said that nothing much seemed to be happening on her birthday. When I told her I had posted her birthday card and only hoped it got there on time, she sounded really disappointed that it might not. Then I left to catch the plane."

"Johnny booked me into an out-of-the-way hotel in Los Angeles and told Kate he was taking her to a lovely restaurant for her birthday."

"He said he just had to pop into his club on business, but when Kate walked in with him all her model friends – like Naomi Campbell, Helena Christensen and Elle McPherson were there. One of her friends [the hair-dresser James Brown] popped out of a huge paper cake and we all sang Happy Birthday. Aretha Franklin, Thelma Houston and other artists entertained us all evening.

"It was a great night, laughing and dancing, and talking to everyone. [But] I do wish Kate hadn't told everyone Johnny hid the diamond necklace he gave her in his underpants. I was so embarrassed – but it was true!"

Kate herself recalled: "They opened the curtains, and there was my mum, my dad, everyone had flown from London and New York and John [Galliano] had come from Paris – It was amazing, I was like, shaking – you know, when you start to dance and your legs don't work? I had to go into the office for ten minutes till I'd calmed down."

During that evening and into early morning, several major artists performed. Gloria Gaynor sang 'I Will Survive', an Elvis lookalike sang along with Thelma Houston, and Johnny strummed on stage with the INXS singer, Mike Hutchence.

* * *

These celebrations were almost upstaged when one of the guests, ex *Neighbours* soap star and pop idol Jason Donovan, collapsed in the early hours. A guest reported: "One moment he was the life and soul of the party, the next he was slumped on the floor, completely out of it."

Kate, Johnny and the other guests looked on as Jason, clearly in difficulties, was stretchered out of the club by a medical team. The star had a coat thrown over his face to prevent him being identified. He was nevertheless recognised through his "scruffy jumper and pink jeans".

Donovan was taken to the Cedar's Sinai Medical Centre – where two years earlier River Phoenix had been pronounced DOA. Doctors diagnosed "a seizure" but no other details were forthcoming. Donovan claimed it was all down to "asthma." But, as reported in *The Observer*, when he collapsed, Donovan had been "snorting cocaine". A report in *The Sun* went further: "the Australian heart-throb admitted he had taken 'two lines' of cocaine."

* * *

Kate tried to impress on Johnny just what she did for a living. "I said to him, 'Have you ever been to a fashion show?' I told him about John Galliano, because he's such a good friend of mine and he's so genius. 'You should come,' I told him. I wouldn't ask him to go to any other show. The other boyfriends go. Naomi's. And Linda's. And Christy's. And Helena's ..."

Eventually, Johnny got the point. "When I did the Isaac Mizrahi show in L.A., Johnny was there and it was the first time he'd ever seen a show. I was like, 'Pleeeease, don't come.' The show itself was the most fantastic I've ever done because it was this fan-tastic, fabulous, dadadaaaa ... It was fun, but it was just knowing he was there, and I cared what he thought about my job."

As a reward she gave him a ring-shaped rattle made of platinum and filled with black pearls. In return, he gave her a string of diamonds.

* * *

Whatever Johnny thought about Kate's job, he also thought she should improve her mind. He introduced her to Iggy Pop and the maverick writer, Hunter Thompson. Asked what she was reading by a reporter she confided, "Jack Kerry ... Jack Karri ... er, you know." "Jack Kerouac?" she was prompted. "Yeah, that's it. Johnny recommended it. I love to settle down on planes with my book."

A friend remarked, "Kate says she always feels she's learning something with Johnny." Impulsively, he might insist they fly a 1,000 miles to hear a band. Or they would spend an evening drinking and talking poetry.

They also went in for less intellectual pursuits. Like trampolining. Or riding the magic rollercoasters at California's Magic Mountain. Johnny: "I love going there with Kate. We go on all the fastest rides. It's great. We both scream our heads off."

Meanwhile, she put on weight. Being happy seemed to make her hungry. By June 1994 the papers were reporting she'd hit nine stone. Stories circulated of her pigging on Big Macs, chips and chocolate milk shakes.

At the end of the foreword to her eponymous book *Kate*, which she put out the next year, she wrote, "PS. I am just on my way out to dinner, to eat a massive steak and loads of very fattening potatoes, with loads of butter."

★ ★ ★

Kate's book was put out reluctantly. She wondered what a 20 year old was doing publishing a retrospective of her work. But then again, why not? She and Johnny had supported Naomi Campbell's novel, *Swan* by appearing at the launch party at the London Tramp club. Books were OK. Johnny read lots of them.

The *Observer* review of Campbell's book, mentioned that while, "A turkey is large and can't fly … [*Swan* was] more of a goose failing to lay a golden egg." In *The Sunday Times*, Gilbert Adair pondered that Campbell's "airport novel" had taken Barthes' prediction of the death of the author to a new level, since as everyone knew, it "had been written by her 'editor', Caroline Upcher." "In short," Adair continued, "Campbell modelled Upcher's text, she wore it as she might have worn some flimsy see-through confection by Vivienne Westwood. To employ a metaphor that she herself ought to be capable of understanding, she was merely the peg on which it was hung. What we are talking about, in other words, is fiction as a fashion accessory."

Swan eventually sank. Though not quite. In 2005, a New York fringe theatre group created a hit by reading aloud from the worst books ever. *Swan* featured in these "Lit Lite" events. Explained one of the organisers, "To pick something that's bad enough to be entertaining is really a lot of work."

★ ★ ★

The foreword to *Kate: The Kate Moss Book* (Universe Publishing, 1995), announced her authentic voice in courier "typewriter" face, ranged right. Otherwise, it was free of bullshit: a nicely produced coffee table book full of classy pictures of a good looking woman.

Sorrenti's Obsession pictures appeared under the heading, "For Love, Not Money." There was even a picture by Corinne Day from the *Vogue* shoot. The fashion images were supplemented by family and childhood snaps, news cuttings and magazine covers.

The promo mostly depended on Kate giving interviews, doing book signings – and being unusually accessible. At one signing a man asked her to sign a proffered buttock cheek. He was hustled away. A tabloid arranged for Kate to be ambushed at another by two old school friends and reported delighted squeals.

80

The *Guardian* interview, by Jan Moir, described Kate, "wearing under-stated, grown-up clothes; a black Prada sleeveless dress because, 'I just liked their new collection.' Her shapely little leggies are thrust into pastel sling-backs which clipper-clopper over the marble floor,"

Moir continued: "In her room, she orders a bacon sandwich, pours two sachets of sugar into her coffee, kicks off her shoes, rings her mum and puffs on a Marlboro Light. What a day! So far she has been on the *Big Breakfast*, been interviewed on a double-decker bus for a new kids' pro-gramme called Delicious! and will shortly record an insert for Richard and Judy.

As the interview begins, Kate: "... pads over to the sofa in her bare feet, her pal sits on the floor nearby, her agent takes up sentinel position on the armchair and everyone has their own role to play. The agent is there to laugh at Kate's jokes and the pal acts as a giggly foil for any awkward ques-tions. Every now and again, the two girls pop their eyes and titter at each other, in the manner of seven-year-olds who have just been asked if they have a boyfriend."

* * *

In New York, the book launch at James Danziger Gallery in SoHo was more stylish. Kate and Johnny arrived a fashionable two hours late, Kate in "a secondhand black gown and delicate high-heel sandals that showed off her very grown-up red toenails [as she] moved from one room to the next with guests trailing her so closely that they seemed to be a part of her outfit."

Depp, "with biker sunglasses wrapped around his neck," avoided the fash-ionaisti and conspired with Iggy Pop. Eventually, he went into a back office and emerged brandishing a poster that Pop had drawn, opposing the current bout of French nuclear testing. Kate applauded and shouted, "Don't buy French! Don't buy French!" Then, realising she was holding a glass of cham-pagne, caught herself: "Oh dear, I'm drinking Champagne, and all Champagne is French, isn't it?"

Then: "Well, it's only a gallery opening, so maybe it isn't."

* * *

Depp's occasional flamboyance and mood swings could upset his lover. His volatility was also sometimes self-destructive. From childhood he'd engaged in dares and madcap sensation seeking. Once, he'd blown a mouthful of gasoline onto a fire. His face exploded in flames and only the intervention of a friend saved him from serious burns. And his arms are multi-scarred with self-inflicted knife wounds which, he says, commemorate important events in his life.

"I have a funny relationship with my body … it sounds so stupid, but for me there shouldn't be any halfway."

* * *

As far as possible, Kate and Johnny tried to keep their love affair private. They rarely discussed their relationship, and when they did, were vague or blandly effusive.

Asked about early rumours of an impending marriage, Depp replied: "Kate as a wife? I would not be against that, but it's something that needs to be discussed in private."

Quizzed by another reporter, Depp responded: "My relationship with my girl isn't something I'm going too discuss with anybody, especially a guy with a tape recorder. Whether Kate and me are together or not is not going to save anybody's life. It's nobody's business but mine or hers. I'd rather come out in the press and say I'm screwing dogs, or goats, or rats than [rely on the press] to write anything real about my relationship."

Kate marvelled, "He's really wild, but wild in a nice way. I don't want to tame him." "He's complicated, but I like that. There has to be some mystery." "He's always surprising me. Johnny's a complete and utter romantic."

The actress Faye Dunaway concurred, "He is incorruptible. He always believes in this pure way about love. He's got those kinds of values and it's instinctive with him. This isn't something he's worked out in his head. I love that he believes in love."

Getting philosophical on the topic, Johnny mused, "I think the beauty and poetry you should get in a relationship between a man and a woman has been missing for a long time. We lost a lot of the romanticism that was there in the Thirties and Forties."

Like the surrealist, Andre Breton, he compared his woman to the city of Paris, "I'm fascinated by the city. Every time I finish a movie I escape there. There's something in the air that's magical, an appreciation for art and artists … And I also have the same affinity for Kate."

He affectionately described Kate as "The closest thing a human being can get to a cat. She likes Abba and Big Macs and she can make me laugh like no one else can and when she walks in a room I see her face and she's like my angel. She's so beautiful it amazes me." He also admired her "high water booty [high tilted behind]".

Putting aside his jealousy, he accepted she might be admired by other men – albeit at a distance: "If you can offer someone a little escape by simply looking at your picture, it would be silly to object."

* * *

However, an attentive media began to see cracks. Especially in the time the couple increasingly spent apart. Always, the excuse was work – schedules and conflicting international commitments. And these excuses were invariably Depp's. Kate complained about his absences, with her stuck in LA or New York, when life got "so boooooring – and Johnny [just] says, 'Well, go shopping then.'"

* * *

But maybe Depp too, was getting bored. Depp, after all, is a self made intellectual. Curious and adventurous, he is a man who devours books, a devotee of the arts and patron of artists like the gritty hyper realist, Robert Guinan.

Fanatical about his acting ("the only actor who ever asked director Hallstrom how to say, 'I have a rat down my throat' in Swedish") he prepares for parts with diligence and relish. Preparing to play the part of the drug addicted reporter in Hunter Thompson's *Fear And Loathing In Las Vegas*, Depp, ever the method actor, insisted on living for four months with the author – a highly-strung practitioner of drugs, guns and high explosives. Depp later recalled, "It was fine until I discovered a keg of gunpowder and decided to stop smoking." (Depp once brought Kate's mother to Thompson's compound-like estate. "She just thought Hunter was a madman and horribly dangerous, and we should escape as soon as possible.")

* * *

Depp came from a culturally complex background. He was part Cherokee, but the uncle that nurtured his musical talent was a fundamentalist Christian preacher. Though he rebelled at school, Depp was inquisitive as a child. At eight he was a fan of the daredevil stuntman, Evel Knievel, and reading up on the history of World War II. Depp was also a skilled and sophisticated musician who could hold his own with the best.

Kate's own background was hardly exotic: British suburbia spiced with naughtiness. And her love affair with the local yobbery blew the cultural capital of her middle classness. Nor was her family home electric with cultural contradictions or stuffed with books. Her brother Nick confessed: "I don't read books, my bedroom is full of magazines – *The Face, Vogue* – I'm obsessed with them. I think I've only ever read two books in my life: *Steaming In*, written by a football hooligan, and *Of Mice And Men* in an English lesson."

Kate generally resists ideas, unless absorbed in a Pygmalion role, when they have a secondary purpose. Deprived of her adolescence, in many respects she's clung to the endearingly daft chatterbox persona she had as a teenager. In many ways, she never grew up – she never had to. While her own mother, Linda, is equally a Peter Pan, Kate also had the security of that other, more practical mother, Sarah Doukas, to take care of business. There was also Peter Moss, her stalwart father, to keep an eye on finances. And unlike Depp, Kate never had any real reverses in her career. Apart from the uncertain start, everything from Corinne Day on flowed and clicked like it was meant to be. Nor did she ever really test herself. Though she aspired to singing and acting, she never went much further than dreams.

* * *

Johnny worried about Kate's "immaturity". He called her both his "addiction" and his "little girl".

Of course, as the French saying has it: people have the vices of their virtues. And it was partly that uninformed and spontaneous naivety in Kate that attracted the more jaded Depp. A friend commented: "Kate still seems to look at everything with fresh eyes. She's always enthusiastic and gets excited very easily about the simplest things like going out for ice-creams, or going shopping at the drugstore with Depp. She treats everything as an adventure with Johnny, and he loves that. He says she has a truly unspoilt and original spirit. She has this childlike thing about her, this British charm that he falls for every time."

But another friend added, "I've seen Kate in tears over Johnny and Kate on cloud nine constantly mooning over some photograph of them together. They never do anything normal. They spend weeks moving from one hotel to another, going to clubs and parties at night and sleeping all day."

And: "Whenever they split, it's because she says she can't put up with his weirdness any more, but that's what attracts her in the first place. She's basically quite normal, but she loves people who are weird. She goes for so long and then she just has to see him again. It's the same with him."

In other words, their relationship was as unreal as her life and his life and their life together. How could it be otherwise? Some time later, looking back, Kate recalled, "I was in love with him and I haven't been in love with anyone since. It was an intense relationship for four years and for a while there it seemed as if it wasn't real. But it was."

Only, it wasn't.

*   *   *

Throughout 1996 the love started to cool. Depp had once said of romantic attachments, "If you're in a room you can explore that place completely. You feel the texture of the walls, and you can smell the room without smelling it, and you learn everything about it. Then there comes a time when you say, "All right, I've learnt it, so I have to go somewhere else. Somehow."

Tally Chanel, a former girlfriend warned: "The truth about Johnny is that he asks almost every woman he goes out with to marry him. He's been engaged five times. He craves security, but he won't get it from Kate." Chanel added cattily, "She's too young and she's too thin to have a child. Her hips couldn't take it."

She also added that Kate was not the influence Johnny needed in his life. "Johnny needs an accomplice to end up in trouble, and it's obvious Kate has a lot to do with his recent behaviour."

Here she put her finger on something that troubled some observers later on, through Kate's Pete Doherty phase – was Kate really being led along by a wild man, or was she pretty wild herself?

*   *   *

Meanwhile, Depp had other things on his mind. Like work. He was frenetically busy during this period. In an interview he wondered whether he'd been using his work as a kind of sedative: "I was working constantly, or I was getting fucked up. Trying to hide from whatever feelings or weirdness might have been inside me. I was trying to numb it by getting loaded or whatever. I was postponing the inevitable – that I would have to wake up and stare at the guy in the fucking mirror."

To her dismay, Kate found herself increasingly at a loose end, taking second place to Depp's demons and projects. Her own schedule of modelling also separated them. But unlike Depp's, her work was not a mission. Asked why she continued to appear in runway shows, she responded, "The money. And it is fun when you have all these models staying in the same hotel." Adding, "It's just that that the constant working and partying and travelling can catch up with you."

In June '96 Kate and Johnny holidayed in Mustique with the Oasis guitarist and songwriter, Noel Gallagher, and his wife Meg Matthews. But as the others frolicked on the beach, Johnny kept working. He was putting the finishing touches to a script for *The Brave*, a feature-length movie based on the novel by Gregory McDonald, which he would soon star in and direct.

* * *

The story of *The Brave* was a long way from the celebrity lifestyle the famous four were enjoying in Mustique. In Depp's words: "It's about a guy and his wife and their kids. They live at a really intense level of poverty, out in the middle of nowhere. And the guy is given a choice to make a lot of money, or what seems to him a lot of money, that could bring his family out of this soup bowl. He's given the choice of doing a snuff film in which he would be tortured and killed."

The theme had resonance for Depp. It referenced his part-Cherokee origins and made a socially committed statement about the plight of modern day Indians. It also echoed his feeling that America had become a rapacious and irresponsible society, focused on winning at all costs. The movie accused the former president Andrew Jackson, whose face appeared on $20 bills, of genocide – millions of American Indians had died through his influence.

Then the quartet flew back to London together for the Sex Pistols '96 reunion concert at Finsbury Park stadium.

John Lydon, AKA Johnny Rotten, sneered from the stage: "We're fat, forty and back."

* * *

In December 96, it was reported that Depp had moved into Moss' West Village apartment in New York. Was this make or break time? The media speculated about an engagement – maybe marriage?

Women Management issued a tantalising statement, "The couple decided to get an apartment together in New York as a trial situation before they made it official." Made what official? A spokeswoman for Depp stated, "They are not engaged yet. He is still keeping his L.A. residence."

"Not engaged yet." Meanwhile, the *Sunday Mirror* told its readers Kate had insisted on separate fridges, disapproving of Johnny's eating habits.

* * *

In February 1997, Depp confessed to *Vanity Fair*: "I am amazed. I am doubly amazed at how great it still is. It's still fun. It's still very naïve – even though we have all the history together now and this luggage. But it's still a good time. She makes me laugh. And, man, you can't beat that South London accent."

86

In May, Depp flew to Cannes for the premiere of *The Brave*. He'd played in the movie alongside his long time hero and mentor, Marlon Brando.

"Marlon, God bless him, didn't make a dime. He did it for nothing. He's the pivotal role, he plays the man who I make a deal with ... He's the devil in a way."

Kate also went to Cannes. It was noticed however, that they rented separate villas. And never visited one another.

★   ★   ★

The movie was well received at first screening. However, as Depp related: "One of the producers premiered it at Cannes, and it was placed in the competition category. I don't like the idea of competition, so I was frightened, because all eyes were on me and I felt like a schmuck. I was surrounded by a bunch of people in that world I didn't wanna be around. But the audience stood up for the film. The next morning, all the trades cut the movie to shreds. I was in misery. It was bizarre, because the reviews were the exact opposite of the screening."

The disappointment threw him. And making it had drained him: "It was the most difficult thing I've ever done and I was an idiot to attempt it. It's way too much work for one person. You get up before anybody, you go to bed later than everybody and then when you're asleep you're dreaming it."

★   ★   ★

The Brave also took a fatal toll on his relationship with Kate. She felt squeezed out. Depp was as obsessive as Sorrenti had once been. But not about her.

★   ★   ★

Almost immediately, Depp plunged into making *Fear And Loathing In Las Vegas*. Within a month the press was reporting the couple had broken up. *The Sun* commented that Depp's previous move into Kate's apartment was supposed to cement the relationship. But instead, "the couple found they got on each other's nerves." The break-up was cordial. Kate would continue to attend Johnny's premieres. They would still see one another.

★   ★   ★

By early July Kate had been linked with a certain, Tarka Cordell. Cordell was the son of sixties record producer, Denny Cordell, and according to his friends, a "consummate womaniser". He was also an occasional musician who owned a "celebrated" record collection and "a beat-up, but state of the art, pale blue Capri". *The Times* reported, "He's tall, handsome, rich and named after an otter." Confided Gawaine Rainey, a friend of Cordel's:

"His pursuit of Kate has been a long one and she is really big on him, too. He met her in America a couple of years ago and there's no doubt they really do gel. Tarka has had a lot of beautiful girls in the past, one relationship continued for four years, but I've never seen him carry on like this. Maybe it's love."

* * *

Looking back, Depp blamed himself.

"I have never got that emotional over a woman before. I have been so stupid because we had much going for our relationship. I'm the one who has to take responsibility for what happened – I was difficult get on with, I let my work get in the way and I didn't give her the attention I should have done.

"The whole thing was crazy because I should never have got so worked up over what people had to say about my work. Sure I should care about my movies, but when I get home I should try to leave that stuff behind. I couldn't do that and I was horrific to live with. Trust me, I'm a total moron at times."

All very gallant, but we can wonder. Maybe they were not in the end so much incompatible as unequal. She unequal to him.

He, principally through his work, was developing and changing. Kate's work on the other hand was static. For a model, this year's catwalks are much the same as last year's. The poses and grimaces and flurries are transposable. The club class cabins look the same. The champagne tastes the same. Only the clothes change. Kate seemed – still seems, satisfied with that. Depp wanted much more.

He also hinted at another reason. He was tired of "partying" and all that went with it. In fact he really wanted to be a parent. He was broody. "Why shouldn't a guy get broody? Some people imagine that because of the movies I make or just the way they perceive me to be, that I wouldn't make a great father. They don't know me at all."

Maybe in the end Kate didn't know him that well either.

* * *

It was while filming in Paris for Roman Polanski's, *The Ninth Gate* that Depp met Vanessa Paradis. Paradis, two years older than Kate, had by that time already fulfilled most of Kate's dreams. At the age of 14, her first single 'Joe Le Taxi' had conquered the international charts. Paradis subsequently worked with svelte and sinister Serge Gainsbourg. When she met Depp she was already an accomplished and acclaimed actress – and about to earn the Caesar award (the French equivalent of an Oscar) for her acting in the cult movie, *Noces Blanche*. She was also a model: the face of Chanel, and muse of fashion photographers like Jean Paul Goude and Jean-Baptiste Mondino. What's more, a coup de grace: Paradis, who many say resembles Kate uncannily, had turned down Calvin Klein's offer to front the same Obsession campaign that launched Kate Moss. Even on that score, Kate was second best.

A few months after they shared their first drink in the bar of the Hotel Costes, Johnny and Vanessa were sharing a £700 a week apartment in Monmartre. A few months after that, Vanessa was pregnant with Johnny's child.

The news devastated Kate.

ACT THREE:

Country Matters

The fields from Islington to Marybone,
To Primrose Hill and Saint John's Wood,
Were builded over with pillars of gold;
And there Jerusalem's pillars stood.
- William Blake, c1820

I can't believe I was in bed with Kate Moss last night.
- Anon, attributed to a female Hollywood star after a night on Primrose Hill

HAMLET: Lady, shall I lie in your lap?
  [Lying down at OPHELIA's feet]
OPHELIA: No, my lord.
HAMLET: I mean, my head upon your lap?
OPHELIA: Ay, my lord.
HAMLET: Do you think I meant country matters?
OPHELIA: I think nothing, my lord.
HAMLET: That's a fair thought to lie between maids' legs.
OPHELIA: What is, my lord?
HAMLET: Nothing.
– William Shakespeare, *Hamlet*, c1600

Kate's search for a London base after she left Sorrenti took some time. It was not until two years later, in March 1995, that she finally bought a three-bedroom apartment, in the top two stories of a Victorian house in London's Shepherd's Bush. The price was £320,000. Linda was aghast: "God, you could get a place on the Webb Estate [a garden village in the Croydon suburbs] for less than half that."

It was a shrewd investment; the area was adjacent to trendy Notting Hill Gate, but more affordable. And the price reflected the fact that the place needed doing up.

The doing up took some time. Kate was abroad so often she could only occupy herself with the property intermittently. She meanwhile mostly stayed in swanky hotels like the Halcyon at 81 Holland Park – "Frequented by local residents and media-shy celebrities."

Her lack of attention meant that wires were crossed, things went wrong, tempers got lost, and money got owed.

Initially she'd planned on £100,000 worth of conversion work. This included a steel staircase with sandstone treads. The street was closed to allow a crane to lift the staircase through a window. And then Kate decided she hadn't asked for the staircase. Or maybe it was the wrong staircase. It seems that she blamed the architects and parted company with them. She also dismissed the builder, Frank Neale, who claimed he was owed £23,000. Through her solicitors, Kate refused to pay the builder, citing a contractual breach. Neale, fearing bankruptcy, threatened to sue. He commented, "It's a bit like a flea taking on an elephant." Eventually it was sorted to everyone's apparent satisfaction.

But in any case, Kate never actually lived there. She sold the place in 1999 for £400,000. By that time she reportedly also owned a four bedroom flat near Hampstead Heath and a two-bedroom flat in Notting Hill Gate. She'd also developed a taste for property development.

In early 1999 she bought a run down eight bedroom 150-year-old mansion near Marlow, Bucks, for £1 million. This came with five acres of lawns and woodland, an octagonal swimming pool, a poolhouse and barbecue area. She had it extensively refurbished and added a conservatory at a cost of £25,000. Again, she never moved in, selling it six months later for £1.7 million – a £600,000 profit.

While all that was profitable, it also underlined her rootlessness. At the age of 25, already a millionaire, she still didn't have a home to call her own.

* * *

Kate's career continued apace. In 1996, Calvin Klein renewed her contract as he'd done every year since 1993. Richard Avedon did a shoot for Versace with Kate in frizzy brown curls, frozen in motion. She was on more covers than ever. Meanwhile, she got a taste of styling on a shoot by Glen Luchford for *Mirabella Magazine*.

"I had a really good time doing it. It was nice. I said, 'I wanna see it full length, and I wanna see it like this, and I wanna see it like that' and Glen listened. As a model you don't really have a voice.

The role reversal was temporary: "Two weeks after, I did a shoot with him as a model again. At one point I said, 'Glen, can't we do it like this?' and he was like, 'Shut up.' So it just went straight back to normal."

* * *

At the same time, she was developing her own style off the catwalk. Fashion editors and gossip columnists were paying attention to what she chose to wear on her own account. This was an eclectic mix of second-hand and readymade with casual, almost irreverent, dashes of couture. It became defined as "boho".

So she was becoming a "style icon." As well as a feminist icon. Or any kind of icon. A peg for journalists and others to hang agendas on.

In 1999, Julie Burchill, simpered in the *Mail On Sunday*: "Kate Moss has grown up in public into one of the most singular and shimmering icons this damp little island has ever produced."

Burchill warned anyone who might demur, "Like Marilyn before her, Kate's sweetness has always brought out the beast and the bully in certain people."

To underline the supermodel's iconic standing, Burchill recalled that Kate and Naomi Campbell had once met Fidel Castro.

* * *

The two models had gone to Cuba on a shoot for *Harper's Bazaar* early in 1998. Intrigued by the style conscious dictator – with his bushy beard, guerrilla fatigues and combat boots, they requested a meeting. As credentials, they reported they'd recently met with Nelson Mandela whilst in South Africa raising funds for a children's charity.

Kate recalled how, "Two days later, this guy came to meet us for lunch. He was very official looking. He had hooded eyes, sunken cheeks, he was drinking Cuban coffee and smoking cigarettes, he said, "What kind of modelling do you do?" and things like that and eventually he said. 'Mr. Castro is a very busy man, but I will see what I can do.'"

Meanwhile, unbeknownst to the supermodels, Mr Castro was eavesdropping on them.

Like most tyrants, Castro was prone to paranoia. But then, he'd survived dozens of assassination attempts, from bombs and poison to exploding cigars, plus a special shoe polish developed by the CIA and "intended to make [his] beard fall out, so that he would lose his 'charisma.'" He boasted, "If surviving assassination were an Olympic attempt, I would win the gold medal." So Fidel kept tabs on anything that stirred on his territory. He also kept fat files on foreign celebrities – in case they might prove helpful.

Explained an ex Cuban secret policeman: "… famous Americans are the priority objectives of Castro's intelligence. When word came down that models Naomi Campbell and Kate Moss were coming to Cuba the order was a routine one: 24-hour-a-day vigilance. Then we got a PRIORITY alert, because there was a rumor [unfounded] that they would be sharing a room with Leonardo DiCaprio. The rumor set off a flurry of activity and we set up the most sophisticated devices we had."

Fidel must have liked what he heard because not only did he agree to meet them, he gave him 90 minutes – 30 more than he'd given the Pope. He also said how "very spiritual" it was to meet them in person and signed a book for Kate.

Then, as Kate recalled, "He walked us to the elevator, and as the elevator doors closed – he's in his army greens – he saluted us. That and the thrill of meeting him made me feel as if I was on a roller coaster. I was screaming all the way down the elevator, all the way to the car, and all the way back to the hotel where we had to do a press conference which we were late for."

* * *

Another kind of screaming came from the thousands of political prisoners banged up on the island for everything from bad mouthing el presidento to trying a runner.

Screams reported by Juan Carlos Gonzalez Leyva – the blind lawyer and president of the Human Rights Foundation in Cuba – who described in a letter to his wife how Cuban prison camps are "catacombs where people scream, but the sound is drowned out by a hermetically sealed door".

Some of the screamers might have been Versace, or Galliano, or McQueen. For Castro had dubbed homosexuality a "bourgeois perversion" and imprisoned hundreds of these undesirables, including many artists and academics. In the same spirit, his response to the AIDS crisis was forcible testing and incarceration of anyone found HIV positive.

Cuba, the sunshine police state, with its tourist apartheid and open trade in child prostitution, where a pair of Levis might be exchanged for a night with a ten-year-old …

* * *

Many others, older and wiser than the two excitable South Londoners, had overlooked the nature of the regime behind the man behind the cigar. Jean Paul Sartre sparkled: "Castro is at the same time the island, the men, the cattle and the earth. He is the whole island." Steven Spielberg enthused, "The best seven hours I ever spent was actually with Fidel Castro." The CBS anchorman, Dan Rather, dubbed him, "Cuba's own Elvis."

AA Newsfeed reported Naomi Campbell's reaction to the meeting: "[It] was a dream come true. I'm so nervous and flustered because I can't believe that I met him." Praising Castro as "very, very intelligent", Campbell compared him to Mandela: "These are two men in the world that I think are an inspiration to everyone, they have fought with integrity to stick to their beliefs." When asked whether she and Kate had felt "seduced" by Castro, she retorted: "No man has ever seduced me and I wanted to meet him, so, no."

Later, Campbell expanded: "He knew that I was the first black woman to appear on the cover of *Vogue* and Kate started the revolution of the little models. So I suppose we were both revolutionaries in his eyes."

The two then made a contribution to the Young Pioneers' Union. Asked whether this was wise in view of US sanctions policy, Campbell riposted: "We're not politicians. We have the freedom to help any charity in the world to do with children. If we choose to help a charity in Cuba, that's what we choose."

The Americans disagreed. In May 1999 it was reported that: "The U.S. government has fined *Harper's Bazaar* $31,000 for sending Naomi Campbell and Kate Moss to Cuba for a photo shoot last year. The fines were for violating the U.S. embargo by "trading with the enemy", paying airfares and hotel and meal expenses. The government was said by the British newspaper the *Observer* to have been particularly annoyed about the supermodels' having tea with Fidel Castro."

* * *

In the aftermath of their break-up, and before the announcement of Vanessa Paradis' pregnancy, Kate and Johnny Depp remained friends.

Depp had stated they both knew "there's no going back. But every witnessed encounter ignited rumours of a reconciliation. The tabloids wouldn't let such a good thing go.

When they went together to the 1988 Rolling Stones Madison Square gig, the *New York Daily News* headlined, "Johnny Depp and Kate Moss appear to be back together again." When Kate travelled to Cannes with

Claudia Schiffer as a guest of L'Oreal, and went to the screening of *Fear and Loathing in Las Vegas*, speculations again flew. At the Las Vegas premiere it was noticed Johnny was wearing the very same large silver skull ring Kate had once given him. What could that mean?

Wearily, Depp insisted, "She was in town and she was going to be seeing the movie anyway. Everyone's thinking, 'Oh my God, they're back together.' But we're not."

Then, when Depp visited London, Dominic Mohan of *The Sun* tattled, "They spent an intimate evening together at a private party in Notting Hill, West London, where my sources tell me they were nattering for hours." Continuing this innuendo, Mohan then gasped: "And although they left separately, Johnny's car and driver were spotted minutes later outside Kate's nearby home …" "Spotted" is a nice touch.

* * *

The clearest sign it was all over however, was in Kate's increasingly desperate, even manic, "partying". She seemed to be looking for the oblivion of excess: chemical, alcoholic and sexual.

Perhaps the first indication of this was back at Cannes in 1998, when even reconciliation rumours were eclipsed by the carry on at the Hotel du Cap in Antibes. It was a foretaste of post-Depp hellraising that became a pattern.

Such was the noise from Kate's £1,000+ a night room, that there were numerous complaints from other guests. Asked to quieten down by the concierge, Kate apparently refused. The concierge then summoned the manager. He told Kate to pack her bags. Then she was escorted from the hotel at five in the morning and driven to the less exacting Majestic Hotel in Cannes.

A hotel manageress explained that Kate and her party (which did not include Depp): "were drinking and partying and making a lot of noise." She continued, "During the film festival there are many parties and situations where people meet and have fun and enjoy the atmosphere. This we do not mind when people behave in a civilised manner. But the behaviour of Kate Moss was undesirable. Other guests were very upset with the noise at five in the morning. The behaviour was unacceptable for any establishment, not just for a hotel with the reputation of the Hotel du Cap."

She concluded, "We don't want her any more. She will not ever be welcomed here. Not this year or next year or ever again."

Kate's version was different. "My room was next to the bar and their music was blaring, so I thought they wouldn't notice mine, but they just got cross, and they asked me not to wear a bikini around the hotel and it was like, excusez moi!"

★ ★ ★

Whatever the truth of all that, it is certain that from this period, with Depp out of the frame, Kate Moss went into freefall. The press gleefully lapped up stories of incessant "partying" – their coy euphemism for sex and drugs and rock and roll – and also enumerated the bewildering number of men Kate began dating. It was as if she was trying to reassure herself that she really was attractive and desirable.

★ ★ ★

In October 1997 Kate had bought a town house in the classy St John's Wood area of North West London. This was in a secluded cul de sac where prices today start at around £600,000. It was a fashsionista's home in a fashionable area.[1]

Already by 1901 Kate's street had an arty character. The census of that year lists for example, an artist/sculptor and an 18-year-old actress, Maud Clark. By the 1930s, it could boast as residents the flamboyant conductor, Sir Thomas Beecham and the prolific metahistorian, Arnold Joseph Toynbee, who gloomily prophesied the disintegration of Western civilisation. By the swinging sixties, the film director Val Guest had moved in and shortly after hastened the anticipated disintegration with his soft porn comedy, Confessions of a Window Cleaner – inaugurating the infamous "Confessions of …" series. Meanwhile, adjoining Kate's house was the home of the legendary art connoisseur and dealer, Edward Speelman – it is still occupied by his descendents.[2]

As for Kate's house itself, at the turn of the last century it was the home of a barrister Charles Morris. A Commander of the Royal Victorian Order,

---

[1] Even this home was not it seems exclusively Kate's domain, for also officially resident was the retired couple George and Shirley Hart, previously connected to the exclusive West End boutique, Shirley Leonard – Conduit and South Audley Streets. They lived at the house until 2001, when they moved to a nearby house.

[2] Speelman served as an intelligence officer in WW2 and eventually had the pleasure of arresting the infamous Nazi foreign minister, Dr Arthur Seyss-Imquart. When the Nazi offered his hand for a cordial handshake, Speelman clapped a handcuff on it. The Nazi was later hanged at Nuremburg. (Speelman also pinched the Nazi's typewriter, which he donated to the Imperial War Museum – which appears to have mislaid it.)

Morris lived there with his wife "of independent means" Ada, their daughter, Ena, and a 15-year-old servant girl, Louise Rolle. By the 1930s a wealthy widow and her daughter resided there and then from the forties, the Balls family – Elsie, Tony and William. During the sixties the house was occupied by a Harley Street dental surgeon of South African origin who in 1921 was fined for crashing his car into an omnibus in Regent Street while driving without a licence. By the eighties, the house was the property of Leonard and Shirley Burnstein, who painstakingly redeveloped it, adding a new living room and entrance porch and cultivating the ornate ivy clad charm that Kate Moss fell in love with.

* * *

Kate's home became the HQ of what was known as the Mossy Posse, a hub of what the tabloids dubbed the Primrose Hill set (PHS). Though actually outside Primrose Hill proper, it was a venue that buzzed with PHS goings on, gossip and scandal.

The core of the PHS was an incestuous cabal of actors and TV and film producers who often appeared in or backed or scripted one another's films, and also popped in and out of one another's affairs. Added to this were rock stars and their partners, and, naturally, models. Some of these roles and functions blurred or bled into one another. The area was at its partying zenith in 1998 following an influx of Britpop glitterati like the quarrelsome Noel Gallagher and his then wife, Meg Matthews.

* * *

Geographically, the Primrose Hill area stretches leafily between a park that offers splendid views across London and sport for kite fliers, and the hip Camden Town, festooned with club and small label flyers, with its seedy pub rock venues and extensive market, famous for off-the-wall fashion and lifestyle bargains. Here is where an art student might set up a stall or hire a booth to sell one-off designs. Weekends, it's crowded with mostly young tourists and subcultural Londoners: Goths, picaresque punks, lots of shiny black garments, and tons of eyeliner. (Whereas, Portabella Road market in Notting Hill Gate is for middle aged tourists in Stetsons and tartan shorts with varicosed legs.)

The Primrose Hill community – such as it is, gathers in the coffee houses, gastro pubs and restaurants clustered around a high street that tries its best to look like a village. A hamlet where paparazzi would sometimes loiter to snap Jude Law buying his Sunday milk, or Sienna Miller's behind disappearing into a deli.

The locale has long had an artistic and bohemian ambiance. Sylvia Plath lived here with Ted Hughes at 3 Chalcot Square, and not far is the upstairs maisonette at 23 Fitzroy Road where the doomed poetess ended it all in 1963. Close by is the swanky London home of Gavin Rossdale, where his wife Gwen Stefani stays when in London.

A stroll away is Steeles Road, known for its showbiz and media celebs. Here you can check out Supernova Heights, once the palace of Noel Gallagher – "a modern day equivalent of Keith Richards' Redlands or Elvis Presley's Graceland." Noel's place was just a stagger from Jude Law and Sadie Frost's former home with its Kafkaesque mirrored windows. A house that saw a lot of Kate in all sorts of states. A house of parties and friends, almost a second home.

* * *

At this point it gets complicated, if not labyrinthine. An ethnography best done in snapshots – or diagrams – as the press loved to create, with arrows and captions listing entanglements, disputes, pregnancies, casualties and so on.

The Sun featured a double page spread on "SPEED KATING" with a portrait gallery of 16 alleged ex-lovers and the legend: "Sorry if we've missed you out! If you've been out with Kate and are not on our list please accept our apologies."

In September 2005, the *Daily Mail* ran a full-colour double-page spread of "KATE'S WEB" featuring 29 celebs snared in a spider's web with a corseted Kate at centre. Said celebs were identified in coloured caption blobs – blue for "ex-lover" and pink for "friend".

Like a psychoanalyst warning of the perils of an inward journey into the unconscious, the *Mail* warned its readers against "this dark and illicit game", admonishing, "there is only ever one winner. With Kate, it's not just about sex, it's more to do with power and control. A mind game as much as a sex game."

The *Mail* ran the stunt again, a month later in greater detail, with "NOT SO PRIM IN PRIMROSE HILL" – a collage of PHS personalities involved in what it called "debauched goings-on" linked with hand drawn arrows like a hastily done bulletin board, all helpfully annotated: "Lovers", "Married", "Threesome".

Another recurring PHS image was people on their backs, particularly on beaches, taking time off from the rigours of NW1.

This was gold for paparazzi and caption writers with a flair for flip innuendo: "NICE TOUCH [Nellee Hooper] rubs soothing sun cream into

[Kate Moss]'s shoulders; THANKS, PAL Kate shows Nellee her appreciation with a kiss; CLINGY MOSS It looks like Kate doesn't want the embrace to end; COOLING OFF PERIOD ... Kate takes a dip and, right, her friendship with Nellee Hooper is warming up while [Anna Friel] rivals her in the topless beauty stakes."

Nellee Hooper. Described by the London *Evening Standard*'s as "the capital's most formidable networker," and by an old girlfriend as "the ultimate modelizer."

Hooper cut his professional teeth in the summer of 1997 hanging out in Goa, where it is alleged he "quickly established himself [as a DJ] at the centre of drug-fuelled beach 'raves'." He went on to produce Massive Attack and Madonna, to date Bjork and Kate Moss, and holiday with Prince Andrew on a yacht. Previously, Hooper had notched up Naomi Campbell, Sophie Dahl and Petrina Khashoggi. He also had a relationship with the aspirant model, Kadamba Simmons, who was found a few years later, naked and strangled in the shower of a north London apartment at the age of 24 ....

Kadamba Simmons was also an old flame of Liam Gallagher ...

Hooper also dated Davinia Taylor, spoiled rich kid of a doting daddy, the "loo roll king" Alan Murphey, who made a £150 million fortune selling toilet paper to the masses ...

Davinia bought Supernova Heights off the Gallaghers: "I was visiting Meg and Noel one night and we were all quite drunk and Noel just said, "Do you want to buy it?" and I asked, "How much?" He said a million and I just slurred back, "All right then."

Liam Gallagher was also allegedly one of Kate's conquests. This when he had only just moved in with Patsy Kensit: "The first week Liam moved in with me, he went out and returned to this hotel with a supermodel [Kate Moss]. I went round and booted his car and everything. I'm a feisty cow you know, I really am. I can hold my own." (In fact, the paparazzi also snapped her kicking the car's owner.)

Then there was the old Etonian, Dan Macmillan – Viscount Ovenden to you and me. With a "goofy grin" and punk hairdo, Macmillan paced catwalks in Paris and New York – including an Alexander McQueen catwalk in a pair of trousers sans seat and bare bum exposed in timeless Etonian fashion. A friend explained, "Dan never really intended to be a model. He's a talented painter and has a degree in fine art. He was expected to go into the family publishing business, but he kept being stopped in the street by modelling agents."

Then there was Jade Jagger. This "celebrity daughter" was a long time intimate of Kate. Jade had run away from boarding school to live with her playboy boyfriend, Josh Astor, a self confessed coke and crack adept who'd been expelled from Eton for smoking pot. "Somebody would say here's a line of coke and I would say 'thank you very much' and that was it."

Anyway, after Macmillan left Kate, and Jade left Josh, Macmillan shacked up with Jade and they had a kid. After that, Kate slept with him again. So Jade sent Kate a necklace made from decorative stones and inscribed, "SLAG," but then two years later they made it up …

* * *

All this took place in what, for at least some of the participants, was a drugs and especially, cocaine-fuelled environment. At the time, Oasis it was joked, were "taking enough cocaine to make Concorde's nose fall off."

Like all good things, it all had to end.

Noel Gallagher's PHS epiphany came early, during the 1998 World Cup, (France won). Lying in bed with Meg, who was unconscious from party-induced exhaustion, Noel had a panic attack combined with an identity crisis.

"I was a big, fat rock star with a big, fat bank account in a huuuuge fuck-ing house in the country, with a year off, and nothing to do. So I done what comes naturally – drink and take drugs. From March till June it was intense. It was all day, every day. And then I thought, 'That's it, I can't do any more,' and I bailed out."

* * *

And five months after that, the party also stopped (or stalled) for Kate.

Nobody had expected it. Kate had appeared for Versace at the Milan Fashion Show week in October 1998, her hair dyed shocking pink, friends, Meg Matthews and Anna Friel applauding from the front row.

Then she went on yet another holiday, this time trekking "in remote areas of India with a female pal".

* * *

Trekking failed to dispel Kate's demons. She returned to London in the first week of November. She meant to celebrate her homecoming with Meg Matthews, Noel Gallagher and the Oasis record label boss, Alan McGee, in a Chinese restaurant. However, Kate arrived two hours late and stayed only 30 minutes without eating anything. During that time she was tearful. Things were not right in her life. She was deeply unhappy. She was being "used". The others became alarmed and urged her to get professional help.

Next day she booked into the Priory Clinic at Roehampton under an assumed name.[1]

* * *

Four days later at around midnight, Geoff Collman, the partner (by now the second husband) of Kate's mother, Linda, took an unexpected call.

"It's odd for Kate to ring at 12 o'clock at night, but she rang because she wanted to speak to her mother. She sounded totally distraught, just calling for her mother."

In fact, Kate sounded so distressed that Linda went into shock. After the call, she retreated to her bedroom, weeping.

* * *

On the phone, Kate repeatedly stressed both to Geoff and Linda that the trouble was alcohol and not drug related. But her insistence produced the opposite impression on Linda and Geoff. No doubt, they knew better – or feared the worst.

It is interesting too, how often Kate repeated the "H" word.

Geoff: "I [had] been talking to Kate for 30 minutes and she explained she had gone to this place, the clinic, for two weeks for a rest but promised it had nothing to do with heroin. She said, 'I promise you that' and I hope it's true. Honestly, I know Kate so well I have to believe when she says it's not heroin. She said it may be a bit of drink but whatever it is it's not heroin. Maybe I'm a bit naive and maybe I am wrong. I don't know, but she told me 'It's not heroin, I am taking no drugs at all.'"

He summarised: "She's just over-partied and thinks everyone else is using her for their fun and she's had enough of it."

That night Kate rang three times in one hour and each time Linda became more alarmed.

* * *

[1] The Priory Clinic was described by *The London Evening Standard* as "the place where the famous retreat to deal with the by-products of their high living: party fatigue, alcoholism, cocaine addiction. It is so indelibly associated with its famous clients that it has acquired its own patina of celebrity. It is considered more a luxury hotel with a rigorous spa than what it really is, a psychiatric hospital."

It may seem odd that Kate took four days to contact her mother. Even odder, perhaps, is that she never called her father at all. A snapshot of their relationship emerged when Peter gave a statement to the press shortly after the news broke: "I have been speaking to her personal assistant and she says she's fine, she's just resting and there's nothing to worry about. I last saw Kate in the summer and I spoke to her a month ago. She's always jetting about all over the place and I usually keep in touch through her PA, whom I call occasionally. She tells me what Kate's doing and what she's been up to."

* * *

Whether or not Kate had been indulging in heroin, heroin had been in the news, particularly the fashion news. In fact, "heroin chic" had become a tag for the kind of distressed fashion pictures pioneered by Corinne Day and fronted by Kate Moss. The issue of "heroin chic" had become another media discourse overlapping the anorexia etc theme.

Heroin had always been sexy. From the late forties it was associated with jazz genius through artists like Billie Holliday. The roll call of H addicts almost became the Jazz Hall of Fame: Charlie Parker, Fats Navarro, John Coltrane, Thelonious Monk, Chet Baker, Ray Charles, Stan Getz ... The Red Rodney, a trumpeter, remarked: "Heroin became the thing that made us different from the rest of the world. It was the thing that gave us membership in a unique club."

In the fifties the Beats, trying to translate the cadences and moods of jazz into poetry and prose, also took up the bad habits of the jazzers. This in turn, was an inspiration to the next generation of sixties artists, fanning out through rock and roll's proliferation of heroin related anecdotes, myths and songs: the Rolling Stones', 'Monkey' and 'Sister Morphine', James Brown's 'King Heroin', The Stranglers' 'Golden Brown' ... The list is long and distinguished. Even longer if you include indirect paeans like Lou Reed's 'Perfect Day': "You made me forget myself/I thought I was someone else,"

* * *

Where rock stars ventured, models followed.

From the sixties, the association between the two professions had become a cliché, almost a comedy turn. You can track it through the songs written about model lovers. George Harrison wrote 'Something' for his then wife Patti Boyd, who was then wooed and won by Eric Clapton who'd written an entire album about the woman. Christie Brinkley's face beautified over

500 magazine covers before she married Billy Joel and starred in the vid of the song he wrote about her, 'Uptown Girl'. Then there was Kate Moss, entranced and seduced by Pete Doherty's birthday gift of the framed lyrics of a song, 'What Katie Did'....

Models and rock stars seemed made for one another. Simon le Bon lived out several male fantasies by picking a photo of a model (Yasmin) out of a magazine, tracking her down and then bedding and wedding her. The black supermodel Iman refused a backstage pass from David Bowie, "we all know why girls like me are invited backstage, so I never went," but then changed her mind and they lived happily ever after. The prize, of course, goes to Mick Jagger, the most archetypal rocker of all, who went through Luciana Morad, Uma Thurman, Valerie Perrine, the Czech Jana Rajich and Italian Carla Bruni (that we know about) before his Texan supermodel wife, Jerry Hall, finally filed for divorce.

Where there's music there's morphine. The German model, Nico, who inspired Lou Reed and fronted Velvet Underground, habitually wrote and performed on heroin – crystallised by her album, *Heroine*. The model, Gia, inspired as a teenager by the legend of Ziggy Stardust, lived out a legendary Romantic Agony and self-immolation by addiction. Patti Hansen, co-habited with Keith Richards on Planet Smack, but then she got him back.

★   ★   ★

Not that models needed encouragement. The industry has always run on drugs. Partly as recreation, partly for stamina, partly for sound professional reasons.

Michael Gross: "As the fashion and music worlds blended, the drugs of the sixties infiltrated fashion. The alcohol and pills that did in Anne St Marie gave way to even more dangerous highs, and models, young outriders on the cutting edge, tried them all ... Drug taking wasn't limited to models, 'I was taking lots of uppers, staying up most of the night,' [the photographer] Shatzburg says, 'I didn't know pills were a drug. They kept you function-ing.'"

Gross quotes another photographer: "'I shot doubles with Iman and Janice Dickinson ... Janice would come here and if I was out of coke, she wouldn't do the shot.'"

Citing the photographer Pete Strongwater: "'We couldn't through a shoot without a major amount of drugs. People dropped coke on the table; they smoked joints. It was accepted. It was heaven. If you were bored, you called for a go-see. We fucked a lot, took a lot of drugs, and worked a lot. I'm sure the agencies knew about it. I was less than circumspect. But I never had one agent say a model couldn't come here because this was an unhealthy place to be.'"

Gross concludes: "The snorting ... [was] kept an inside secret for many years – even from insiders. *Vogue*'s Polly Mellen saw what was going on in the club's [the notorious fashion hangout, Studio 54] balcony, though. 'Two boys going at it, two girls, a girl and a boy. I saw every stage of something going on, and that scared me." It was the same at [the designer] Halston's house ... Heavy drugs'"

Stephen Fried however, thinks it was more open than that. "The modelling business knew full well how drugs and alcohol were affecting the girls. But awareness didn't mean they knew what to do about it. Several years earlier, when they still had some control over their girls, the agencies could make good on threats of threats of blackballing. But intoxicants were now so common that it seemed almost hypocritical to suggest that 'models just didn't do that or that a model's reputation could be ruined.' Some models would assert that they needed cocaine to keep up with the bookings the agency was making for them. It had reached the point where more wholesome top girls, like Kim Alexis, were being jeered at behind their backs for being too straight."

*   *   *

Fried also makes this interesting observation: "Some girls [i.e. models] were even more attractive to photographers when they were high than when they were straight: certain drugs produced certain faraway looks or stoked certain inner fires that worked for certain pictures. And certain girls had looks that were so specific, and, at that moment, essential – that it was worth risking a session in which the model couldn't perform on the chance that she could, even for a moment."

Of course, that "faraway look" is a trademark of models everywhere. It was perfected by Kate Moss. Coded "enigmatic", she has been compared to the Mona Lisa by Stephen Bailey in the *Independent*, citing descriptions of la Giaconda: "hostile superiority", "the treacherous attraction of a sick soul ... a soft look that, like the sea devours." Umberto Eco put a portrait of Kate Moss from the 1994 Pirelli Calendar as the wry summation of his *History Of Beauty*. Taking a cue from Eco, Peter Conrad reminds us that "with her wild parties and cocaine ... her fags, booze, bouts in rehab and line-up of unruly lovers ... The goddess [Kate Moss] may look delectable, but her behaviour is diabolical."

*   *   *

"None of them knows that the billboard picture of me was after getting wasted! It's a real laugh!"
- Kate Moss, quoted by *The News Of The World*

* * *

Of course, Kate Moss may have conjured her enigma without chemical aids. But then, when was she without them? She is, after all, on record as having been on something or other since the age of 12.

Rarely sighted without a fag in her fingers or her mouth – at parties, driving, in photo sessions … she has been known to consume "upwards of 80 cigarettes a day" (Malboro Lights being her favourites). "I am a chain smoker … My mum says if I see you another picture of you with a fucking Malbroro in your hand I'm gonna kill you." The web site http://smokingsides.com which documents celebrity smokers has an entry for "Kate Moss" running to 10,700 words.

As for alcohol, again she was an early starter who graduated to prodigious. "The tank" could hold her own with the most seasoned fashion boozers from her teens. In the modelling world especially, that was quite a feat. "That's what you do," she said, "You just kind of have champagne. You always have champagne before shows. Always. Even at 10 in the morning. It got to the point one time when we said, 'We're not going out without any champagne.' Terrible."

She admitted in 1999 that she hadn't been down a catwalk sober in 10 years, i.e. since she'd been 15. And, "I love a Stoli tonic. It's my new drink. I was drinking gin, and then someone told me about gin blossoms. My maths teacher used to have them – you know, when you have a red nose. The doctor said if you're going to drink, drink vodka." And she confessed to never being without her "trusty hip flask" full of vodka, to avoid being caught short on a photo shoot or flight. Always neat: "Fuck all the mixers."

As for the other stuff … Asked if she smoked marijuana: "Yeah. Who's gonna say, 'No, no, I don't now? Nobody hides it any more. It's not like a drug – people just get it out and skin up."

Until cornered by the *Mirror* in the week of Cocaine Kate, the supermodel denied she did any class A. Most people in the media thought otherwise. Indeed, given the context it would have been peculiar if she was an abstainer. Cocaine is routine in modelling circles. It gives a high and relives stress and is calorie free. You could almost say it was a professional requirement. Worthy of a tax break.

* * *

Heroin though was something else. By the end of the eighties it was starting to be produced in unprecedentedly pure forms. This meant it could be inhaled or smoked, and the idea went round that if you didn't inject you wouldn't get hooked. "China Brown" especially, was seen as a safe option. The result was a growing number of enthusiasts who later turned to needles.

"Heroin chic" coincided with a wave of heroin culture. By the nineties, heroin was newly "in", with its allure of the forbidden and the ultimate frontier. It was also available. For her last *Cosmo* shoot, Gia Carangi had to hide her arms behind her to conceal the injection scars. Later, models learnt to inject into the soles of their feet.

Following its benchmark depiction in Drugstore Cowboy, Hollywood and other filmmakers used smack as a cipher for doomed abandonment. Especially in the nineties. Movies like *Killing Zoe* and *Pulp Fiction* (both 1994), *The Basketball Diaries* (1995), and, of course, *Trainspotting* (1996), featured heroin as a glamorous flirtation with death: the necrotic stylisation of pretty people expressing the agonies of excess.

* * *

In an article on heroin chic, Carmen Vendel wrote: "Fashion models, typically underweight, are uniquely qualified to play the part of shattered, undernourished pseudo-addicts. Besides a whole slew of articles in the last few years chronicling the sad fate of glamorous models who become hooked on smack, fashion magazines have popularized a look – sickly and scruffy – in sharp contrast to the more common polished, elegant images of perfect bodies."

And speculating on the appeal of such images: "The generic loser motif brings the idols down a peg, makes the formerly "beautiful people" less than us instead of more. Perhaps that is the ultimate satisfaction of these images; they assure you that you have less to live up to."

* * *

Wrote a columnist for *Adweek*, "To many people, she [Kate Moss] represents a skeleton and death anyway." John Leo, in *US News & World Report*, added: "Moss is a very troubling figure and a prime indicator of our degraded popular culture. She is the modern female as blank, fragile stick figure. Her pictures are full of strange allusions, many of them perverse." The *New York Times* remarked that in the Moss trademark – a deadpan and hollow cheeked look with suggestions of victimisation, "some social critics see an allusion to hard drugs"

* * *

"I've been blamed for everything: used as a scapegoat for smoking, heroin, anorexia."
- Kate Moss

* * *

The rock photographer Mick Rock has certainly been around. Rock has pictured every rock and roll excess since the seventies. He's also worked and socialised with Kate Moss. Asked if he'd talked to her after the Cocaine Kate story, he replied, "I was there when the story broke", explaining:

"No, I fucking wasn't with her. No, no. No, those days of hanging out at that time of the day with a beaker up my nose are long gone. But Kate certainly gets up for it." Rock added, "She wanted to be the Keith Richards of the modelling industry, and she got there!"

He elaborated, "I remember one of the first times that I met her, I said, 'Oh yeah, in the old days,[you] couldn't have stayed up. You couldn't have hung out with us, man'. And she said, 'What do you mean? I stayed up four nights with Keith Richards!' I was like, fuck it man, even in my prime I couldn't have done that! A week with Lou Reed, maybe."

* * *

The fashion model exists to sell. Not just this or that garment or accessory or lifestyle but consumerism in general. She (and it's generally gendered that way) is the lightning rod of a consumerist version of desire: an endlessly looped, ever repeated search for novelties, the Romantic search for the blue flower, or desire for desire itself. The Model crystallises the fetishes and fantasies of the great God, Commerce, incarnating the ludic abstraction of money.

Think how many films feature as the instant of transcendence that point when bonanza shatters everyday life: the valise explodes and showers the street with $100 bills, or clicks open to reveal stacked gold bars or sachets of heroin or coke – a point which marks the beginning of the reign of nonsense: Puff Daddy in fur coats with his lady friends and bling laden crew – which is also that moment when the models finally stalk from the wings, launched onto the catwalk in a blaze of camera lights action and the pounding beat of some hot stuff …

* * *

The notion of heroin chic takes all this a stage further. The question is not whether any heroin habit is attached to any particular model (and, in any case we are not suggesting Kate herself was even dabbling in smack). What heroin chic did – before the term was coined and even after it was dropped – even now, was to represent the thrill of money pumping through the veins of fashion. A potential explosion, an imminent catastrophe: perpetual orgasm.

Heroin stands for money – trade – turnover – feverish spending – sales bonanzas – overnight fortunes – role reversals – and amazing good luck. It equally signifies fashion, which is the pulse of consumerism.

Heroin, as the ideal commodity, creates perfect consumers. As William Burroughs, the dude himself, put it, heroin is "the ultimate merchandise. No sales talk necessary. The client will crawl through a sewer and beg to buy."

No surprise then, the trade off between those ultimate icons of consumerism, models, and those ultimate consumers, junkies. Both work from wasted bodies and freak energies, they live on the margins of the tragic and the phantasmagorical – between the next frock and the next fix.

The iconography of the addict has been beautiful since the beginnings of consumer culture in the 19th century – ethereal, wanton, poignantly inaccessible, witness Millais' *Ophelia* and Wallis' *Death Of Chatterton*: elegantly doomed – near dead or just dead, gorgeous victims of all-consuming desire.

* * *

Underlying heroin chic is addiction chic. Heroin chic is about how cool it is to be strung out on the ultimate washing line. It's not the chemical that counts but its possessive attributes, its purportedly overwhelming seduction of the senses and swamping of volition.

In fact, of course, there is no such thing as heroin addiction. Or any addiction.

For all the Romantic martyrology of addictiveness, for all the reputed traumas of withdrawal – viz John Lennon's double-tracked tantrums and harmonized squealing on 'Cold Turkey', withdrawal from heroin is no worse than having flu – no more difficult to recover from. To suppose otherwise is to play the addict's game of rehabs and relapses, self reproach and all that other therapeutic cant – all grist to the mill of what the addict really desires which is this insistent focusing, this never ending talk and concern, about the addictiveness itself, as subject, object, theme and goal.

* * *

The novelist William Burroughs was the real deal: art as addiction, addiction as art. He amputated his little finger after a failed love affair, shot his wife dead and filled a trunk with hallucinations in a Paris hotel. All that became his "lifestyle" – a life spent being wasted in a natty suit – tie – trilby: he was the first model for Heroin Chic – cadaverous and elegant with eyes of burning vacancy.

Feted by the equally cadaverous Andy Warhol and Mick Jagger, then hailed as an inspiration by the anorexic-like David (Ziggy) Bowie, and after that the world: Debbie Harry, R.E.M., Nirvana, Laurie Anderson and Kurt Cobain … then U2's music vid, *Last Night On Earth* …

At the age of 80 the skeletal novelist starred in an ad campaign for Nike's new Air Max 2 ("Air Max Squared") shoes. The trade press hailed this as "'Tech' spot delivers senior beat author to athletic shoe marketing arena." Judy Smith for Nike explained, "When he came onto the scene, what he was doing in literature was the equivalent of what Nike has done in the athletic world in terms of pushing the limits and taking risks and doing things differently …

"And we like his voice."

* * *

Kate stayed at the Priory for five weeks. During that time the media roared with innuendo. Storm tried to play it down, "Kate's burned out. She wanted to re-evaluate her life, and so she put herself in the situation where she's be able to do that."

Kate explained: "It was just a buildup, really. I was definitely living fast. It was 'Sleep? Why? Why not go on? There's too much to do. There're too many places to go.' I was working, I was travelling a lot. I was playing and I didn't stop. It got to the point where it wasn't so much fun anymore. It all became unbalanced, so one day I just said, "I can't do this anymore. I've had enough." It was getting ridiculous. I was not very happy. I was doing things that weren't good for me. So I checked into the Churchill Priory clinic. It was the best thing I've done for ages. I needed to check in and ask 'What's going on?' I had tried to stop certain things before; I had tried to get focused on other things. But I always ended up back in the same place, and it wasn't making me happy. I needed to get the focus back, and ask, 'What do I want?' Going on holiday wasn't doing it. That's not real life. I needed to do it in London. Then people found out, and the newspapers went at it and …"

* * *

She told *The Face* she'd enjoyed rehab and even went back to visit people there. But was her stay so happy? She described it as "kind of like being at boarding school." Her stay was also marked by a bizarre incident – a fire in her room. At the time, the explanation was that a candle accidentally ignited a scarf her mother had given her that happened to hanging in her room near some candles that were helping her to meditate …

Three fire engines arrived, but the flames were already extinguished. Some time later, Doherty claimed in an interview that Kate's version to him was more along the lines that being so frustrated by how naff and tiresome it all was she had perhaps inadvertently set fire to her bed (by smoking? in frustration?) and shortly after discharged herself.

★ ★ ★

Johnny Depp had not forgotten his ex. As a get well present he sent a new £50,000 BMW with a note, "Enjoy the ride".

But otherwise he was gone. Of the period just before going into rehab she'd said, "It is quite amazing what I didn't feel after a while. I didn't really want to feel things, probably…."

The burst of drink and drugs and all that sex had been to anesthetize her against the pain of losing him.

★ ★ ★

However distasteful the experience and publicity, the Priory helped. Her metabolism was corrected and her outlook brightened. For a time she continued with therapy sessions as an outpatient.

Otherwise she took up her life where she'd left off.

★ ★ ★

For a time she dated the *Spacehog* star, Antony Langdon. According to Langdon they had something good going. But perhaps Langdon wanted too much too quickly.

They'd met in New York in Summer 1999 and began a relationship in early September. Three weeks later they were sharing a tent, watching the unique lunar eclipse of that year from Cornwall. Langdon apparently proposed in the tent. She didn't say no. A friend reported, "She was swept off her feet – all starry-eyed." They then spent a week together in Ibiza, where Langdon bought Kate a £10,000 emerald "friendship" ring made by her friend, Jade Jagger – who lived on the island. It seems they even made plans for a wedding and pre-booked "a plush villa in the island's trendy Santa Eulalia resort" for the happy event.

But back in New York the mists of romance cleared. The wedding was called off.

An English friend of Kate's offered this analysis, "She is still very angry with [Depp] at the hurt he caused her and the way the split happened. But there is no doubt, none at all, that when Kate looks for a man, she looks for a man like Johnny. She says the problem is that she can't find one who matches up to him. He is a complex, powerful guy. He is strong and creative and not cowed or impressed by Kate's success. And he is much older. Kate herself says that his edginess is what drew her to him – but, also, what caused the relationship to end. What they shared went deep which is why the split hurt her so much. She says he was her one and only true love and that she struggles to make sense of the way she felt for him and still feels about him."

There were other men. The press loved to picture her "inseparable" or "cavorting" or (even better) "frolicking" with someone, preferably, for that double whammy headline, another celeb.

* * *

That year Klein dumped Kate Moss as the face of CK. It was rumoured her spell at the Priory had tarnished her for him. But just as likely that after almost six years, he was after fresh meat. Which he discovered in Russia.

At the unveiling of the Calvin Klein collection on February, instead of Kate Moss, the assembled punters and pundits saw the 18-year-old Musovite and medical student, Colette Pechekhonova, "a fragile-looking 5-foot-10 blond with faraway eyes and the grace of a ballet dancer."

Klein gushed: "It's hard to believe she's so perfect. She's got beauty, she's got style, she used to be a dancer, she's got intuition, she works like a soldier, she understands the clothes and, what's most important, she's got a brain." He volunteered, "When she's not here she's studying."

Storm refused to comment. And a spokesman for Klein denied the contractual lapse was to do with Kate's behavioural lapse. "Her contract came to a natural conclusion, and at that time we were looking in other directions for the next season. This is totally unconnected with her recent revelations."

Klein hinted he would continue to use Kate in advertising. "No one can replace Kate," he lied through his perfect teeth. (Rebecca Lowthorpe in *The Independent*: "the first thing I notice about Calvin Klein is his teeth: pristine white, impeccably straight. Like all those Hollywood film stars, Calvin Klein boasts a mouth full of cosmetic dentistry par excellence. His teeth reflect his quest for perfection in his clothes – beautifully formed, clean and utterly desirable …")

As usual, Klein was ahead of the game – he saw the Russians coming. Five years later they'd arrived, led by Natalia Vodianova, Carmen Kass, and Karolina Kurkova. By 2005, Kates's replacement was the Russian rags to riches fairy story, Natalia Vodianova. Kate's erstwhile champion, Fabien Baron enthused, "It was when [Calvin] saw her in person that he clicked, because you come across this type of girl rarely. I remember when we first brought Kate Moss to Calvin. It was the same thing."

★ ★ ★

Meanwhile, Kate was not short of work. As Klein's show opened she was in Miami, doing a shoot for *Vogue*. Shortly after, she flew to Paris to appear on the catwalk for Donatella Versace, along with Naomi Campbell and Amber Valletta. Donatella Versace swooned, "Kate deserved the highest marks for this extraordinary appearance."

Donatella of course, was under some strain. This was her first show since her brother Gianni's gruesome murder by the deranged Andrew Cunanan.

Cunanan had shot the designer twice, in the face and neck. At the time, Gianni had been returning home after purchasing *Vogue* and other magazines from the News Café. It seems he was wearing shorts "with $1,200.00 in the pocket", sandals and a dark shirt. Witnesses who saw Cunanan leave the scene reported he was "walking like a duck."

The incident may have preyed on his sister's mind as her show was generally deemed flat and over showy: "more special effects than clothes."

★ ★ ★

Donatella had also organised a birthday celebration for her "favourite model's" 25th.

It was held at the Ritz with an appropriately star studded cast. Kate was relaxed, though some tongues wagged she'd put on weight. She wore "a strapless red and black top and micro mini from the Versace ready-to-wear set and six-inch spike heels."

As fireworks exploded, Kate blew out 25 candles on a diamond shaped cake presented by Naomi Campbell, Eva Herzigova and Catherine Zeta-Jones. Between sips of mineral water Kate reported, "I have had the most fantastic birthday. It is so brilliant everyone has turned up from all over the place." Then she slipped away to the trendy Les Bains nightclub to dance till dawn.

★ ★ ★

Apart from the disappointment about Klein, her career soon picked up. Burberry in particular, wanted her cool factor – which if anything, had been enhanced by the romance of rehab.

Desperate to revamp out of its beige taint: check patterns for creaky Sloanes, Burberry's new boss, Rose Marie Bravo, paid handsomely to blend the brand with Kate Moss (as well as Madonna).

This was a sign that Kate's selling power was now extrinsic to the brand. And more potent. Rather than the brand lending its aura to the model, the model now distinguished the brand. The lifestyle being sold was not Burberry's as worn by Kate Moss. Rather, Burberry was being redefined by Kate Moss.

* * *

In line with her new status as a talking point, Kate gave an unusually personal round of interviews with *Vogue*, *Interview* and *The Face*. These shed partial light on her bad habits. But though she freely admitted the alcohol, she was guarded about anything else.

To *The Face* she admitted: "I never wanted to go into rehab. I never, ever wanted to be in the position where I couldn't have a drink. Which is probably the first sign of it: 'No, I never want to not be able to have a drink.' You moderate things so you don't have to get to that point. But I couldn't keep myself in check anymore. Couldn't do it. I kind of lost the plot really there a little bit."

And: "It's like when you do shows, the first thing they give you before you go out on the runway is champagne. I'm not saying that it makes a difference. I was drinking when I was fourteen or fifteen, when was still living in Croydon I was down at the pub getting drunk. I don't think it's anything to do with my work. There's as much pressure in this industry as any other high-pressure industry."

As for Depp, her analysis now was that: "He was away a lot of the time, and I'd go shopping, that ladies-who-lunch crap, faff around. It was so boring – the most lonely, shallow place. I was going insane, I'm not normally a depressed person, but I brooded, got really sad – and we grew apart. And now he's got his life and I've got mine."

* * *

She also revived an old project, something she'd been publicly mooting on and off since she was 15: motherhood.

Before, I was never really around babies and stuff, but now everyone seems to be having a baby, loads of my friends. I'm broody, anyway. I love kids, but it kind of makes me think about it a lot more. If I haven't met Mr Right in a few years, I'm going to do it anyway. Definitely."

★ ★ ★

"I'm going to do it anyway." And the vehicle she chose for "it" was the nicest man. Not anything like Depp at all, not mercurial or multi-talented, and lacking Depp's saturnine good looks. Rather, this man was pretty, tremulous, sweet looking, almost dopey – diffident, in that British way.

Step forward, Jefferson Winston Hack.

But not quite yet. For in between Tarka – remember him? – and the others, after Langdon the *Spacehog* man and other dalliances, there was Jesse Wood, son of Rolling Stones' Ronnie.

At the time both Jessie and Kate were on the rebound. After a four year affair, Jesse had been dumped by the blue-blooded heiress and model for Pretty Polly, Jasmine Guinness. Jasmine had caught Jesse having "a foolish fling" with another model. Rued Jesse, "Jasmine was the love of my life and I blew it. She hates me now. That infidelity was the one thing I've ever regretted doing. It fucked me up, fucked her up and tore us apart."

Kate and Jesse vacationed in Phucket (I'm not making this up) in Thailand, and then returned to spend New Year at Ronnie's 13-bedroom mansion in Kingston-upon-Thames – where Jesse also lived.

Maybe Jesse picked up a few tricks from dad, because his partying with Kate was reported to be "hard". So hard that at the end of February, Kate went off on her own to Barbados, apparently to "recover". Then, just as the couple were preparing to jet off in March for a spell in Dubai, Kate suddenly "collapsed" and was rushed to hospital.

The official explanation was a kidney infection. Storm was unusually forthcoming, "Kate doesn't know where the infection's come from. They can develop from chills and women's problems – but it has nothing to do with her lifestyle."

Sarah Doukas commented: "I've just spoken to her and she's doing fine. She's got a straightforward kidney infection because she didn't take her full course of antibiotics and it's come back with a vengeance. It's no big deal but we all know that if you don't finish your anti-biotics you must be mad. The poor thing had to go into hospital because she was in agony.

She's not trying to hide anything and is booked under her own name. Overall, she's in superb health."

Kate's New York agent, Paul Rowland, was equally reassuring: "I spoke with her [yesterday], and she was getting her hair coloured in her room. She's going blond."

Released a few days later she was said to be "recovering at home". Not for long. Within two days she was partying at the Met Bar in Park Lane, looking, as well as newly blonde, "pretty pale and tired". In early April she lent glamour to the Dublin premiere of Nora, a movie based around James Joyce's muse and lover, where, accompanied by Jesse and Sadie Frost, Kate stole the paparazzi show in a "a red polo neck jumper". Come May and Fashion Week, Kate and Jessie, accompanied by Jerry Hall, Elizabeth Jagger and Jude Law, partied for the opening of the new Embankment club, Roc.

But by the middle of that month, in the words of the Stone's song, 'It's All Over Now', it was all over: Kate had told Jesse the "spark" was gone.

"But now she's here and there, with every man in town ..." It's All Over Now, The Rolling Stones.

* * *

Let a prostitute be whoso stands before a door and winks or parks herself in the fornix near a makeussin wall (sinsin! sinsin!) and the curate one who brings strong waters (gingin! gingin!), but also, and dinna forget, that there is many asleeps between someathome's first and moreinausland's last and that the beautiful presence of waiting kates will until life's (!) be more than enough to make any milkmike in the language of sweet tarts.

- James Joyce, Finnigan's Wake, 1939

* * *

The Sun next innuendoed that Kate had been caught "playing the oboe" "(Unfortunately, Kate's symphony was interrupted before she reached the finale)," with Elastica drummer Justin Welch at a Blur party. *The Express* sniggered, "Kate Moss and Rhys Ifans have been practising their skills at mouth-to-mouth resuscitation in the Bohemian surroundings of London's Notting Hill Arts Club."

Things got more solemn after she posed for the "controversial" artists, Jake and Dinos Chapman, who drew her for a *Vogue* feature. Miseryguts Jake and merrymaking Kate became an unlikely item. They holidayed in Ibiza and Kate got predictably topless, which made tabloid splashes and filled dull hours at the Groucho Club. Jake: "Our work does have a social function, it gives the chattering classes something to talk about."

Maybe Jake's famously tough guy poses thrilled and terrified Kate as much as they do the art fops who sometimes mutter he should get stuffed–like his mannequins. Jake and Kate became "inseparable". Then they separated.

Three months after she had jacked in Jake, Kate was said to be "head over heels in love" with Angus Fairhurst who was, the tabs obligingly explained, "the best friend of controversial artist Damien Hirst." Angus also made "videos of himself dressed up as a gorilla."

* * *

Jefferson Hack was born in 1971 in Montevideo, Uruguay, His father, Douglas, was a salesman for tobacco companies. His mother, Teresa, was Swiss-German. They met in South America and called their first son after the band, Jefferson Airplane (allegedly). As a child, Hack travelled the world from South America to Singapore to Brussels.

When he was nine the family settled in Ramsgate, Kent, where the parents still live. Jefferson attended a local school and then Pangbourne College, a British public school. He then became a student at The London College of Printing, a prestigious art college with a strong tradition of media disciplines. Here he met the young Scottish photographer Rankin (John Rankin Waddell). The two started the magazine *Dazed And Confused*, after the Led Zepplin track, with a loan from Rankin's father while still at college. By the time they left it was already creating a buzz.

Dazed, as it became truncated, was a brew of fashion, music and art, with an emphasis on experimental. Boasting Alexander McQueen as a roving fashion editor, it initially focused on the Young British Artists (YBAs) and Britpop.

Hack explained, "The format was inspired by *Interview* magazine as it was in the early Eighties, when it was a fan-based title about movies, before it became part of the publicity trip."

And "The title is meant to be anti-hip and accessory. We wanted to reflect the whole style tribe thing that had got all mixed up – dance, soul, reading books. We felt style magazines were too much about dictating a lifestyle for people to buy into: how to be groovier, for pounds 2.50."

Dazed existed through advertising and sponsoring arrangements with companies like Black Bush Whiskey, Levi's and Stella Artois – all in it for the street factor. *Dazed* also set up its own art gallery, staged club nights and live events, and produced a book and compilation CDs. Hack: "Our style has always been to do as many different things as we can, working across as many different platforms as possible."

Hack has never courted publicity on his own account and is prone to wind up journalists who get nosy. A former colleague recalled, "I worked with Jefferson on an arts initiative for about a month. When I met him, I thought that he was incredibly charismatic and had an incredibly cool name, especially for a journalist. By the time we said goodbye, I didn't know much more."

In the opinion of a rival editor: "He is very good at what he does. He plays this part of being the trendy, friendly guy from Britain, and he plays it very well. It's a charisma thing. I've seen him at fashion shows in New York, sitting next to Winona Ryder, saying hello to Puff Daddy. Personally I think the magazine itself is crap, but it has got a great image and he is responsible for that."

* * *

Kate Moss first met the "elfin, sparrow-chested" editor when he interviewed her for the February 1999 issue of *Dazed*. Rankin had already photographed an arty tit and bum cover of Kate, with her in black suspenders and stockings. Legend has it that Jefferson's opening was, "you smell of pee." Maybe that got to the Purley dosser.

One of the questions he asked the model was, "There's been a lot of different men mentioned in your life recently, but no one permanent relationship. Is there no one out there good enough for you?"

* * *

That summer Kate tried to reinvent herself. She told Storm she was giving up modelling – or at least taking a break.

"I wasn't happy with the way my life was going. I quit because I thought, I fucking hate it. It's mind-numbing, repeating yourself like Groundhog Day. I didn't want to have to say, 'I'm a model' ever again."

She took summer off, and in an even more radical gesture, had her hair – already cut from its celebrated long brown tresses to a blonde bob, shorn in a "Mia Farrow look, the ultra short all-over crop."

Some interpreted that as nihilistic, even self destructive, pointing up a connection with the awful fate of the similarly styled actress, Jean Seberg. Kate also had her dyed platinum blonde: the typically brazen, don't give a fuck signal of harpies and good time girls.

Then it was off to Ibiza yet again, this time with Stella McCartney and Meg Matthews.

* * *

But the reinvention and new gamin look was possibly also because she was falling in love.

Jefferson Hack had a knack of befriending the people he interviewed or worked with. Bjork and the Chapman brothers, for example. So it was with Kate Moss. Since that interview they'd kept in touch.

It wasn't difficult, as they moved in the same circles and shared the same friends. Hack was however, more level headed than many of her friends – and possibly one of the few not keen on drugs – not because he thought them wicked, rather, uncool.

Kate called him "the sweetest man I've ever met. Definitely."

Kate and Jefferson came out as lovers at the Berlin Film Festival's premiere of Enemy at the Gates, which starred Jude Law as an improbable WW2 Russian sniper (and Bob Hoskins as a farcical Nikita Khrushchev). Kate's new haircut caused almost as much excitement as the confirmation that she and Jefferson were official. After that (perhaps ominously) they became "inseparable".

But here there was a real connection. When Kate turned up at a party given by Bryan Adams at his Chelsea riverside pad wearing a raincoat "and not much else", Adams was love-struck and tried to get between her and Jefferson. A friend confided, "Kate is all Bryan talks about these days. They had a lot of fun at his party. He knows she is taken, but would like to build their friendship." The rock star deluged the model with calls. She held out.

Part of Jefferson's allure was his culture. He could educate her, but maybe in a sweeter way than Depp. Hack knew fashion as well as he knew music and the art scene. He was all about mixing and matching.

This was a period when Kate moved from socialising to collaborating with the YBA crowd. She also began collecting their work, though perhaps not very attentively. Tracey Emin for example, had made a neon sign spelling out, "Moss Kin" and offered it to the model. It was valued at £100,000. Kate neglected to collect the artwork for two years despite reminders from Emin. It was then discovered dumped in a Spitafields skip.

* * *

In May 2000, British Vogue sponsored a bunch of YBAs to mess around with the idea of Kate Moss as muse. The results were of their time and place. As the organiser of the project, Justine Picardie, put it: "These are artists who understand celebrity – who have become celebrities themselves."

Jake and Dinos Chapman got Kate to draw her own portrait, which they

Kate in 1992: "People had told me that I ought to try it, but I would never have gone to a modelling agency and said, 'I want to model'. Never." (Vic Singh/Rex Features)

Kate in Paris in 1993; above: a tax exile in Pigalle; below: in the engine room of fashion
(Geoff Wilkinson/Rex Features)

Marky Mark's well-filled underpants advertised the Calvin Klein brand together with a topless Kate Moss in 1993. But there was little electricity off the set. Kate: "He liked girls with big butts and big tits and shit and I didn't really fit into that category." *(LFI)*

With Mario Sorrenti in New York, 1993, the photographer and lover who lifted Corinne Day's look for Calvin Klein's Obsession campaign. Kate: "We fought the whole time. Obsession is the way to describe our relationship." *(PVA/Rex Features)*

With photographer Corinne Day in 1993. Day's exotic passions and drug-fuelled creativity created the look that became Kate Moss. *(bigpicturesphoto.com)*

With Naomi Campbell in 1993. The two supermodels enjoyed an especially intense friendship and travelled the world together. They also visited Cuba, where they were entertained by the bearded dictator, Fidel Castro. Unbeknownst to them, Castro had bugged their bedrooms. He apparently liked what he heard. *(Richard Young/Rex Features)*

Nick Moss' unusual and short-lived career as a model was scorned by his sister. "When she's bitchy, she's very bitchy. That's always been in her blood." *(Mirrorpix)*

Calvin Klein. Klein's sponsorship made Kate Moss a supermodel. Clever Calvin refashioned fashion in the image of branding. His approach was later taken up by Tom Ford. Klein and Ford shuffle and deal fame and luck and image. More familiar with percentages than scissors, they are cultural investment bankers as much as entrepreneurs. Kate Moss was a monster this image-obsessed fashion industry created without really thinking it through. *(W. Coupon SIPA/Rex Features)*

Kate: "In photographs it doesn't matter, but on the runway I think clothes look better on taller women. It must be a bit weird for them, everyone saying this [the waif] is the new look when they've got the perfect face, the perfect body, the perfect everything, and somebody who's not at all perfect comes along and starts taking all their jobs." *(Steve Wood/Rex Features)*

Johnny Depp was the love of her life. His "bad boy" image entranced her and his brilliance overwhelmed her. But in the end, maybe he tired of the Eliza Doolittle factor. *(Richard Young/Rex Features)*

In her 1995 picture book *Kate*, she mused, "the more visible they make me, the more invisible I become". *(LFI)*

Fashion week '97 with one of her jetset celeb party friends, Jade Jagger. Their friendship was temporarily interrupted when Kate slept with Jade's man. Jade sent her a necklace made from decorative stones and inscribed, "SLAG". *(NI Syndication)*

Some began asking who was the bigger hell raiser – Johnny or Kate?
(Sipa Press/Rex Features)

Among her detractors, the *US News & World Report* grumbled that "Moss is a very troubling figure and a prime indicator of our degraded popular culture. She is the modern female as blank, fragile stick figure. Her pictures are full of strange allusions, many of them perverse."
(Erik C Pendzich/Rex Features)

Depp with the woman who had his babies, Vanessa Paradis. In many ways, the multi-talented Paradis was everything Kate herself had dreamed of becoming.
(Alex Berliner/Rex Features)

That classic Kate Moss pose, drink and ciggy to hand, teasing the paparazzi lens.
(Richard Young/Rex Features)

Noel Gallagher eventually tired of Primrose Hill Set shenanigans, cruelly dubbing the scene "the whores on the hill", and advising his wife Meg Matthews to keep away from it all.
(Richard Young/Rex Features)

At a Versace party in 1999, with Mum and Donatella Versace.
(Richard Young/Rex Features)

At an aftershow party in 1999 with Jo and Ronnie Wood, Marianne Faithful
and Anita Pallenberg.
(Richard Young/Rex Features)

then surrounded with brightly scrawled cartoon heads. This was amusingly titled a portrait by "The Three Stooges". Tracy Emin opted for a wobbly nude sketch in felt tip, perhaps emphasising the model's fragility. Gary Hume sketched Kate from photos, then projected the images on her body and photographed the result. He announced that his aim was, to "complete a circle of looking". For her bit, Sam Taylor Wood photographed Moss as Madonna in a veil in church and in tears, while Sarah Morris went for pop art with Kate in a bathing suit with fizzy drink recomposed in squares of colour.

Marq Quinn was more interesting, playing a layered game of deception, permanence and surrogacy. Quinn first cast Kate's body into an ice sculpture dressed in Alexander McQueen. This was designed to melt over four months. Quinn explained: "It's a perfect metaphor for our consumption of [her] beauty – as the ice evaporates, it will be released into the art gallery, and people will literally breathe [Kate] in." The press was outraged. "There's something eucharistic about it," Quinn added.

Tom Lubbock got the point of it all, fulminating in *The Independent*: "Fashion and Britart are simply in the same business. And that business is pure fame."

* * *

In the autumn after her exasperated break with fashion, Storm persuaded Kate back onto the catwalk. A flurry of contracts followed. Kate Moss in the news meant Storm in business.

She became the face of the new Chanel perfume, Mademoiselle Chanel: "glossy pixie haircut … smoky eyes," (and Coco turning in her grave) … she also became the face of Rimmel cosmetics – looking like a spectacular accident – something between all tarted up and only just got up … she starred in ads for Gucci and for Burberry – for the latter as a London dolly bird with a "What's up, guv?" stare, fresh out of *Alfie* …

This Kate Moss had a hard, almost brutal allure. Sarah Doukas reported, "I think she's metamorphosed. She's gone the next step. This [Chanel] campaign represents something different: she looks more grownup, more sophisticated, more knowing, more together."

From poor waif to rich bitch.

* * *

Moss's millions had now been clocked by villains operating in the St John's Wood area.

In November, thieves broke into her home while Kate was away on one of her holidays – this one in America. According to the police, it was a "very professional job". The thieves were in and out in no time and left no mess and no prints. Their haul was estimated at £300,000.

Most of this was accounted for by jewellery, but also missing were £50,000 worth of travellers cheques. Kate was distraught. Most of the jewellery was insured, but some was irreplaceable. This included "a diamond ring which was a family heirloom", and a £20,000 necklace that was the first gift Depp gave her after they became lovers. Kate remained in America until a new alarm and surveillance system had been installed.

* * *

Her broodineess had not gone, and now there was a man on hand who might be the one to seed her. She told friends that she and Jefferson were trying to conceive. Jefferson told his parents, Douglas and Teresa Hack, the same.

By May 2001 Kate was telling friends that if she didn't become pregnant in the next six months, she would "start on a course of fertility therapy."

* * *

July saw Kate at one of the celebrity galas that had become a staple of her life. This was a rock concert come fashion show, "Frock and Roll", put on in Barcelona to raise funds for the Nelson Mandela Foundation for Children.

Mandela was a favourite of Naomi Campbell's, "I'm proud of working with Mr Mandela. I'm proud to know someone like him. I'm proud he took me in. And he's always told me to hold my head up high and use who you are to help others." The admiration was reciprocated – the 83 year old hero anointed the supermodel his spiritual "granddaughter".

This gala was Cambell's initiative and supported by fellow models, Kate Moss, Helena Christensen and Elle McPherson. Celeb musicians included Bono and Wyclef Jean. Mick Jagger and Macy Gray cancelled at the last moment.

But only 3,000 people turned up to the Palau St. Jordi, which held up to 17,000. Bravely, Mandela pronounced himself "happy" at the turnout. The Spanish newspaper, *El Pais* commented the gala was a "little caprice of a few famous people who were so full of ego that they did not call off the event in the face of evidence that the people of Barcelona were not impressed."

Unexpected drama came when Kate and Alexander McQueen had a

public spat. McQueen had whispered something to Kate during the fashion show finale that was not to the model's liking. She took umbrage and pushed him away. When the designer tried to "kiss and make up", Kate stormed off. An observer reported, "Everyone was totally stunned. Models are pretty temperamental but there has to be a major drama for one to flounce off. McQueen thought Kate was only joking and that she'd come back – but she didn't." (They soon made up.)

* * *

That September, Kate had her second lucky escape from a car crash. As in the first, back in Sanderstead days with Clark, she was a passenger.

Though she'd only recently passed her driving test that May, her black Range Rover was being driven by a chauffeur as she was on her way to Southend for a *Vogue* photoshoot. Just after 11am, her Range Rover smashed into a Rover Montego on the A13 just outside Orsett.

The collision was violent. Both cars rolled down an embankment. Kate's car smashed through trees and bushes and stopped in a six foot ditch the right way up. She was trapped for half an hour until a fire crew forced open the doors. Treated by paramedics she was helicoptered to Basildon hospital complaining of pains in her back and neck. A hospital official confirmed she'd suffered "quite a nasty injury", but nothing permanent. The chauffeur escaped with minor neck injuries.

The occupants of the Montego were also lucky. They were an elderly couple in their eighties, Edith and Bert Hills. Their car had landed upside down and for a moment Edith lost consciousness. Bert panicked, "I didn't know if Edith was dead or alive. Then I heard her groaning softly." They too, were treated for minor injuries.

The crash started a media show. The hospital was besieged by paparazzi scenting blood. To get Kate out unseen, she was covered in a blanket and led by hospital staff through a tunnel into the mortuary and then through a fire exit. A hospital worker commented, "I couldn't believe the lengths Kate's entourage went to avoid being photographed. I thought that's what she did for a living. It seems crazy that the hospital had to go to all these lengths to prevent photographs being taken of a model."

* * *

In December that year Kate met the painter Lucien Freud. Kate had expressed admiration for the veteran portraitist in an interview which Freud had read. He rang and invited her to lunch at Clarke's restaurant in

Kensington, near his home. It was reported: "They were both intrigued by each other; they got on like a house on fire." [1]

Kate began hanging out at Freud's house and eventually he suggested a series of portraits. She was delighted: he was one of her heroes. She even "danced animatedly with him at a party given by his daughter Bella Freud." Freud professed himself "enthralled" by the model.

Freud was a notorious womaniser, though more known for sang froid than hot blood. An ex-lover, the writer Joan Wyndham, recorded he was "icy in bed. I made love to an intriguing mind and a finely chiselled face. But no more."

Even so, as the *Daily Mail* tutted: "There is no painter alive today with a reputation as sinister or sexual as his, as a long line of female sitters before Moss can testify…. Over the years, many of his female subjects have become his lovers and stories are forever being retold in the bars and clubs in Soho that he used to frequent of the times he has been pursued by irate husbands and outraged fathers."

Jefferson, of course, was too cool to be irate. While Freud's own partner, Emily Bearn, was the same age as Kate, there was no evidence Britain's premier supermodel was shagging "Britain's greatest living painter".

* * *

The grizzled and grumpy septugarean was an unlikely cupid. But not long after meeting him, Kate discovered she was at last pregnant.

Jefferson's mother, Teresa, recalled, "We were thrilled when Jefferson phoned us one day and said: 'You're going to be grandparents.' He was so very excited. He couldn't wait to become a father. I said to him: 'This is wonderful, as long as you make her happy and you love her.' He said: 'I do love her. We are really happy.'" Teresa also recalled how they all met for dinner at the Savoy to celebrate before going to see the musical, Chicago.

"They'd gone to the hospital that day for the first scan and Kate couldn't wait to show the pictures to me. It was still meant to be a secret, so we went off to the Ladies so she could show me in private. She was so happy she was giggling and laughing. Then, when we got back to the table, she couldn't contain herself and said 'Oh Douglas, you haven't seen the scan pictures,' and started showing them round the table quite openly."

* * *

[1] NB. As an art student Freud famously set his art college ablaze with a misplaced fag.

Freud had already begun painting Kate. He'd even destroyed one attempt as it didn't meet his standards. The sessions lasted several months. They generally began with a meal at the trendy Locanda Locatelli restaurant. Then, artist and model would retire to the privacy of Feud's studio for protracted sittings into the early hours. This perfectionism meant that by the time he'd finished, his subject was now swollen with Lila Grace Moss Hack (no hyphens). The finished canvas went for almost £4 million. (Freud had previously painted a pregnant Jerry Hall for the 1998 Large Interior, Notting Hill, even though on a whim, he erased the supermodel's head and substituted that of his assistant, David Dawson.)

Pregnant superstars were then all the rage. In 1991, Demi Moore had exposed the bump of her second child on the cover of *Vanity Fair*. Then a 32-year-old Cindy Crawford "did a Demi" for *W* magazine in 1999. Mel G of the Spice Girls had also shown off her pregnancy in a Sunday tabloid, and Jerry Hall displayed what Mick had been up to in *Playboy*. This was generally seen as an affirmative device: female stars celebrating and empowering themselves – a departure from seeing pregnancy as something grotesque, even a deformation.

The challenge was in some ways superficial. Postpartum, these same women worked out and dieted manically to obliterate or conceal all traces of pregnancy. As a cultural historian writing about high art models suggested, "Whether protruding during pregnancy or sagging afterward, the female belly presents a stubborn problem to artists of the modern …" (Marie Lathers, *Bodies Of Art*, 2001).

* * *

By March, the Internet was chattering about Kate's pregnancy. A more reliable source was the happy couple themselves, who confirmed towards the end of the month. The stories then switched to whether the parents to be would marry.

Hack stoically denied he'd been repeatedly turned down. Kate declared she had no intention of getting married, adding, "Every two weeks someone says we are planning a wedding but it's not true. I wish people would stop going on about it." Meanwhile she took advice from mother of four, Sadie Frost, who was also pregnant – their pregnancies were almost simultaneous and Frost gave birth to a boy, Rudy, three weeks before Kate.

Conventional wisdom and medical advice were less congenial and Kate found it hard to stop either drinking or smoking when pregnant. Although friends like Tracie Emin loyally protested Kate had stopped or "cut down", paparazzi often snapped her in that classic Kate Moss pose: fag in one hand, glass in the other.

*   *   *

On September 28th, Kate lunched with Sadie Frost and Jude Law at the Lemonia restaurant, Primrose Hill. The paparazzi were on the prowl and captured the style icon looking comfortable in a sweater, green army jacket, and leggings,

After an hour, trusty Jefferson appeared, driving Kate's Range Rover with its blacked out windows. Sadie and Kate boarded and were driven to the nearby private hospital, St John and Elizabeth. Kate and Sadie ran ahead, leaving Jefferson with the luggage.

Lila was born the day after.

*   *   *

Jefferson and Sadie Frost were with Kate when Lila was born in the "birthing pool". There were no complications and it was a natural birth. Said Kate, "I had simply the best birth, I had candles and everything. A bottle of Cristal champagne. I had the best time."

Teresa Hack recalled: "The next day when we went to see them, they were so happy and proud. People were coming in and out of the room with flowers and champagne and Kate couldn't stop smiling. She was tactile and loving with Lila."

It took the couple two weeks to settle on their daughter's name. By that time a live-in nanny had been installed in the room next to Lila.

Within weeks Kate was back at work. And back to partying.

The Primrose Hill ethos was back with a vengeance – in the words of Spinal Tap, "having a good time all the time."

She was equally in a hurry to erase the pregnancy from her body. Normally, Kate weighed around 7st 7lb. During her pregnancy she put on 2st 7lb, and grew from size 8 to size 12. While pregnant she wolfed chips and burgers, quipping afterwards: "I liked being fat for a change." But then she booked the trainer David Marshall for an £1,800 course which included "a regime of 22 exercises combining Pilates, yoga, weight training and specific toning exercises." Ten weeks later, she was showing off the results on yet another beach, "wearing only a microscopic pair of bikini bottoms."

*   *   *

About now, cracks in her relationship with Hack began appearing. Several people commented she increasingly treated him as a butler or chauffer. Her attitude was sometimes dismissive. She even laughed when friends described him as "the sperm donor."

At Stella McCartney's wedding in Scotland to Alasdhair Willis in August 2003, it was noticed that Kate and Jefferson seemed unhappy with one another's company.

* * *

Hack's parents realised something was awry quite soon.

Douglas Hack: "She was demanding. She'd want to go out every night of the week and then fly off to Mustique at the drop of a hat. And Jefferson just couldn't do that – he had a business to run. He is his own man: he wants to be a success in his own right and not live off Kate's millions. He used to say to us: 'It's all right for Kate, she's made her millions. I've still got to make mine.'

"It was financially draining for Jefferson because he told me Kate never pays for anything. So, if she said 'Let's go to Mustique', he'd have to foot the bill, and let me tell you, it wasn't exactly cheap. Even now [2005] he pays half for everything."

When the Hacks visited Kate and Jefferson at her London home for Christmas 2003, Teresa noticed that: "Kate was polite and friendly, but there was an atmosphere which was not entirely comfortable. It was as if she didn't really want us there. She was getting ready to go out with friends to a birthday party while we stayed behind and had a roast lunch with Jefferson and Lila. Kate couldn't make up her mind what to wear and kept coming down to show off different outfits. Jefferson seemed exasperated. Douglas said: 'Don't ask me, I haven't a clue.' A month later, Jefferson told us he was moving out of Kate's house. We weren't entirely surprised."

* * *

The PHS however, was on the verge of disintegration.

Already, several members had defected. Some, like Noel Gallagher denounced the goings on and distanced themselves both physically – by moving out of the area, or mentally, by cutting former PHSers.

At the centre of the PHS spider's web were Jude Law and Sadie Frost. They were the mummy and daddy of the PHS. Kate, equally central, was the "wicked" auntie. When Jude and Sadie's marriage started to break up so did the PHS.

This particular marital breakdown was long and painful. Frost cited Law's "unreasonable behaviour". This, she claimed, had exacerbated her post-natal depression so much she'd sought medical help. Law tried to salvage things, at one point by organising a "make or break" Christmas holiday in Thailand.

To his bewildered disappointment Frost insisted that Kate come along too. Commented an observer, "He barely even got a chance to talk to Sadie, and it was from that point that he knew that he wanted out of the marriage." Adding, "Of course, they had lots of other problems, but I think he felt that Kate's presence did not help."

The romantic holiday duly turned into yet another Kate Moss party, the kind of party the ex smack addict and virtuoso partier, Bobby Gillespie, had been shocked by when he "went on holiday with Jude and Sadie, Kate Moss, all of those, and everyone was off their faces and there were really scary times."

★　★　★

And then came the curious case of the pill on the floor.

This incident occurred at a party given by the girlfriend of Danny Goffy, drummer for Supergrass. The party was held at Soho House, a private member's club owned by the millionaire husband of Channel Five newsreader, Kirsty Young.

This was the club where it seems, the novelist James Hawes may have been inducted into a sophisticated London drug scene. Hawes recounted his experience in the novel, *White Powder, Green Light* – described as "a satire of the coke-fuelled, ego-driven media hell that is the Soho film world." In PR speak, Soho House was a "celebrity haven". Its members included Madonna, Prince Edward, Robbie Williams and Kylie Minogue. Hawes dubbed it the "chapel of the lost souls".

The party was for Goffy's young son, Alfie. Sadie Frost took her two-year-old daughter, Iris. According to Frost, the event was "all mummies and grannies and cups of tea," plus a banquet of "children's food, such as sausages and chips." This diet was supplemented when Iris – as two year olds do – picked something up off the floor and put it in her mouth. According to Frost, she was alerted by "my best friend Zoe [who] spotted Iris spitting something out of her mouth".

She continued: "I could have ignored it. But thankfully my instinct told me to go straight over and take a closer look. On the end of her tongue was a small grey tablet with a line through it. It had partially dissolved in her mouth but there was enough left for me to grab it."

Frost said she then tasted the tablet thinking it might be something like Paracetamol. Then she realised what it might be: an ecstasy pill. Realising that Iris had taken "about a quarter of the pill" she ran with the child for a taxi and whisked her into the AE unit at University College Hospital.

"Although Iris wasn't really aware of what was going on, she was shaken – especially as she could see I was worried. 'Mummy, mummy, I'm sorry,' she said, and I told her not to apologise and that we just had to go and see the doctor."

The doctors gave the child a charcoal drink to absorb any chemicals. Luckily perhaps, the drink made her vomit. The doctors also noted that Iris appeared to be "intoxicated". The following day the police confirmed that the substance was, indeed, ecstasy.

In the aftermath, Frost was understandably defensive. "Jude and I aren't some rock 'n' roll couple … I still can't believe all this happened … I'm not a bad mum; nobody was taking drugs that afternoon. If I had seen anyone taking ecstasy or anything else I would have been out of the door immediately."

* * *

Jude Law was not impressed. In fact, he went apeshit. Maybe this was the final straw, a confirmation that the PHS and all it stood for might destroy his family as well as his marriage.

What he did next was symbolic. Kate and Sadie had hatched the idea that their new babies would be christened simultaneously. But Law decided differently. In August that year he also stopped his three children from returning to England from America, where they had been on holiday. Their mother, who was expecting to take them to Lila's christening reportedly, "rushed home to greet her children and found no one there. She screamed, 'Where are my babies?' When told Jude had refused to let them home they had a row on the phone." But Jude was adamant. He refused to allow his children to go to "an unsuitable party".

* * *

At this time Kate and Jefferson were renting a cottage in the Gloucestershire village of Fyfield.

The 300-year-old Walnut Tree Cottage was owned by retired merchant banker, Sir Rowland (Radley and Trinity College Cambridge) and the Norwegian born, Lady Isa Whitehead. The Whiteheads are nothing if not posh, and Isa was suspicious when the lettings agency told them Kate Moss wanted to rent the place. Sir Rowland – who lists "poetry and rural indolence" under "Hobbies" in *Who's Who* – travelled to London to check her out.

"She was bubbly. She never stopped talking. She was quite fun. She'd just come off a plane from America and was wearing a T-shirt. She wasn't made up – in fact, I don't think she makes up much. I was looking at a model, a well-known model, a model who was friendly and appealing. I felt that probably it would be quite interesting for her to be in this house. With hindsight, you can say a lot of things,' but I agreed."

He also met Jefferson Hack and decided he was "a nice sort of bloke". The tenancy started soon after. Jefferson celebrated his 30th at the cottage with a tasteful gathering.

That December there was a flood in the cottage. The Moss Hacks had left for a holiday in Thailand without filling the oil tanks, causing pipes to burst. Minor damage was done to furniture. A settlement was reached and the tenancy continued.

The Whiteheads say that, though subsequent reports of noisy parties started to filter through from neighbours, "We were away for much of the time."

Then came Lila's christening party.

It went on for almost three days and nights and cost an estimated £40,000. A marquee was set up in the field behind the cottage. Bouncers patrolled the land.

Sir Rowland: "There was a lot of noise, a lot of mess, a lot of people – nearly 100 coming in and out of the house. The septic tank overflowed and they left dozens of black rubbish bags of food lining the lane afterwards, which the foxes and crows got into, encouraging rats from the farm."

Marianne Faithful, a fairly recent addition to the Mossy Posse had been especially lively, and was spotted "walking around with a gin bottle weaving through the village."

By the time nine-month-old Lila was driven to St Peter's church in the nearby village of Southrop, to be christened by Canon Tony Ross, many guests were already the worse for wear. Which explains why they mostly turned up at the 12th century church in shades.

Sir Rowland: "There was a second christening that day, and they were a bit put out that they had to share the service with someone else – someone who lives here, for goodness sake."

"Suddenly all these people piled into church wearing dark glasses, skirts that went up and tops that went down. They were, by all accounts, the most extraordinary people in dark glasses and funny clothes. Lady Penelope Robson, the organist, said you could almost feel the stench before they came in … [a] sweet, cloying smell.

"Ms Moss arrived in one of these big cars that backed up to the church porch so she didn't have to walk the 30 yards along the path to the church. When the wardens offered around the collection bags, most of them thought they were being offered a sweet. We're told some of them had huge wedges of notes, and others offered to pay by card."

One of the guests described Kate as wearing, "a pale-yellow or white kind of 50s-style dress, you know, with a strapless bodice and then a chiffon skirt, to just below the knee ... like a real lady dress." Lila was "a bride in a cream dress with a tight bodice and floaty skirt, which showed off her figure."

Sadie Frost played godmother. (Jude Law was originally meant to be god-father but that arrangement changed.) Lila was baptised with holy water from a Norman font decorated with several arches. Under each arch is "the armed figure of a Virtue trampling its opposing Vice underfoot and stabbing it with a sword or spear." Marianne Faithful thrilled, "It was a wonderful service." Another guest observed: "Lila was superbly behaved."

Not so the grownups. After the service they partied till 5am. They slept that off till next afternoon. Then began again. Several of the guests got so smashed they stumbled around the village shouting incoherently. Some collapsed in neighbouring gardens and slumbered. A woman opposite Walnut Tree Cottage reported, "Lady Whitehead, I could tell you so many things, but I can't, it was so awful what I saw."

Another neighbour complained: "We had music going non-stop, engines revving and funny bodies all over the place."

* * *

That was nothing to what the Rowlands found after the Moss Hacks had vacated the place. Walnut Tree Cottage had been wrecked.

Lady Whitehead: "We came in here the day after she left, and we were devastated because each room was worse than the next. It happened to be my birthday as well. Everything was so demeaned, so kicked about. The chandelier in the dining room had been pulled from the ceiling and dumped in the hall with a football in it. The mirrors had been taken off the walls and left face up on the tables – why would someone do that? [Indeed.]

"The bedrooms were filthy. In the spare room, they'd put the beds together. The beds were in pieces and the headboards pulled off. One can only imagine what they'd been doing. The poker from the downstairs fire-place was also propped against a bedroom wall. Why would you want a poker in the bedroom?" [Indeed, indeed.]

She continued: "The bedclothes were really filthy – I wouldn't touch them. We got these chaps to put them in dustbin bags. Throughout the house the walls had a layer of I don't know what on them. And the whole house had this sweet, horrible, cloying smell."

* * *

Kate and Jefferson drifted apart rather than split. There was Lila to consider and Jefferson wanted to be a real, rather than absentee dad. He also made sure his parents got to know the kid, spending time with her at their seaside home. There were periodic speculations about a reconciliation but by now Kate's course was firmly and irrevocably set on an existence not amenable to marriage.

More couplings ensued. Jack Nicholson was mentioned, but seems unlikely. Primal Scream rocker Bobby Gillespie was more likely, but then it turned out they were never lovers. They had become close friends however, and even duetted on a song called 'Some Velvet Morning'.

* * *

That was not the first sign of Kate's fascination with rock music. She'd always cultivated the friendship of musicians and long wanted to become something in the pop world. Of all the supermodels, she featured in most music videos: Johnny Cash's 'Delia's Gone' – slammed by MTV for its "gratuitous violence", Primal Scream's 'Kowalski' – where she plays a "stiletto-heeled assassin [who] summarily offs the entire band" – MTV again objected, Elton John's 'The Way You Look Tonight', White Stripes' 'I Just Don't Know What To Do With Myself' – "writhing around in her undies and pole dancing", which was however, tastefully directed by Sophie Coppola so no one objected. Kate also acted as a foil to the "Minnesota love god" Har Har Superstar.

Another sign of her infatuation with music was her fascination with Marianne Faithfull.

* * *

"I like old music. Jimi Hendrix, Lou Reed, Janis Joplin and people like that. If I had a wish, I would love to be able to sing and scream like those girls do. I can't, though."
- Kate Moss

* * *

Marianne Faithfull was Kate's rock and roll mother, her link to the excitements and excesses she imagined she'd missed out on. The convent girl who became the nude in a fur coat in the Stone's drug bust at Keith Richards

Redlands mansion: "NUDE GIRL IN MERRY MOOD AT DRUG PARTY!" The cute pop singer who resurfaced as a tough rock performer. The accomplished smack aficionado intimate with the best guilty parties. In her biography, Faithfull recalled the flash she got after reading Burrough's *Naked Lunch* while on vacation with her then lover, Mick Jagger: "This was something I was going to have to pursue. I would become a junkie … a junkie on the street."

And so she did, down every mean alley she found, sharing needles with the philosopher of smack, the Beat writer Alex Trocchi, sharing dealers with the cream of rock artists like Eric Clapton. She also empathised with the founding member of the Baader-Meinhof Gang, Ulrike Meinhof, and wrote a song, 'Broken English', in homage to the terrorist: "I identified with Ulrike Meinhof. The same blocked emotions that turn some people into junkies turn others into terrorists … 'I won't have it! I won't stand for it! This is totally unacceptable!' … A form of idealism that leads down different paths."

Kate was right to be impressed with Faithfull – she is a fascinating woman. But her devotion was overkill. It was noticed that they were – that word again, "inseparable". At gallery openings, rock venues, clubs, Kate and Marianne formed a duo dubbed by the press, "the odd couple". They were said to be "joined at the hip and the wallet". That last jibe being a reference to Kate's generosity to her new friend. Kate lavished Marianne with first class airfares to join her on holiday in Jamaica, and she bought her friend couture accessories and pricey jewellery.

* * *

Faithfull had plenty of stories to tell. She'd lived through "partying" and survived the brink. But while the student always finds the teacher, the student may not always heed the lesson. Rather than Marianne's survival and rejection of her shamanic journey to the end of the night, it was Marianne's "previous" that fascinated Kate.[1]

In particular, it seems that Faithfull influenced the supermodel in search of a destiny to frame that destiny as luxurious excess. Here, the template was Scott Fitzgerald's novel *The Beautiful And The Damned*. It became one of Kate's favourite texts, a touchstone for her manic frivolity, a paradigm of creative auto-destruction.

---

[1] In the same way, Kate was also a close friend of that other rock chick and Stones leftover, Anita Pallenberg.

The opportunities destroyed by the characters in that book filled Kate with admiration and awe – and emulation. An addictive person, addicted to nicotine, "partying", travel – and, perhaps above all, to love, Kate sought to satisfy her addictions through a nihilistic potlatch: the sacrificial self-destruction of her fashion capital – endangering her looks and continually courting exposure, in a reckless and extravagant bonfire of whatever got in the way of her pleasure. But the addict is always addicted to addiction itself. Whatever the satiation there is always a craving for more – for the next fix, and the next … There is no salvation. No redemption. And as for rehab, tell it to the birds – or Pete Doherty.

★   ★   ★

And I'd lie as quiet as a moss. And one time you'd rush upon me, darkly roaring, like a great black shadow with a sheeny stare to perce me rawly …
– James Joyce, *Finnigan's Wake*, 1939

ACT FOUR:

The Doherty and the Damned

"You photographed Kate Moss without noticing that her hands were so badly taken care of, her nails were actually black." - Reader's letter, *Vogue*

Kate's 30th birthday party was designed as such a potlatch. It was themed on the Scott Fitzgerald book, *The Beautiful And The Damned*. Jefferson Hack took charge of the overall arrangements, while the decor and mood was fine-tuned by the professional party organiser, Fran Cutler of 2 Active Ltd[1] and the designers responsible for Alexander McQueen's surreal catwalk extravaganzas. Guests were instructed to show up in suitably decadent and period costume.

But the underlying theme of the event was money and what money

[1] 2 Active was founded on the address books of Fran Cutler and her business partner, Meg Matthews. As well as suggesting ideas for decoration etc., it will circulate your party details to trendsetters or get A or B or C listers (depending on your budget) to show their faces at your event. Instrumental in setting this up with Cutler was Ossie Kilkenny who started his career as U2's financial advisor and is now a music and media mogul with many tentacles. Kilkenny also put together the first business plan for Sarah Doukas' Storm Agency.

means: Kate as a Marie Antoinette of conspicuous consumption. And there was not one party, but four.

Kate started celebrating at midday, lunching at the Mandarin Oriental hotel in Knightsbridge, in a "stunning yellow dress and Bet Lynch-style leopard-print Mac." Here, she and a group of intimates reportedly downed several thousand pounds worth of champagne.

After this, they set off for the deluxe Mayfair hotel, Claridge's. Two suites on the seventh floor had been booked at great expense. One suite was decorated in red, the other white. The guests now dressed and made up twenties style. Kate was got up in a flowing midnight blue sequinned dress, with matching scarf and eye shadow, her hair a studied mass of curls. She looked tanned from a recent Jamaican holiday. She also wore "a £300,000 necklace in the shape of the figure 30 made from 30 cut diamonds" – a gift from Louis Vuitton.

There were other gifts, about £1 million worth. Exclaimed one guest, "You'd think it was a royal wedding, the amount of stuff that was being delivered. There were Tiffany bags, Cartier, De Beers, Bulgari and a load of D&G stuff." Ralph Lauren and Calvin Klein also sent samples of their wares. Then there were the mischievous undies and a diamond-encrusted whip from Agent Provocateur. And a more self-effacing gift from Jefferson Hack: a star named "Kate" with a telescope to view it through.

At the reception, 130 guests danced or helped themselves to 30 kinds of fish, "specially flown in on Friday from the Caribbean, the Pacific and the Indian Ocean and costing £60,000." They were served by – naturally, 30 waiters (some of whom, it was thrilled, were moonlighting from Buckingham Palace), while "30 cases of vintage Cristal champagne at £100 a bottle were downed with 30lb of Beluga caviar costing £500,000."

Then, at about 9.30, everyone moved on to the third party.

This was held in the adjacent West End houses of artist Sam Taylor-Wood, and Serena Rees and Joseph Corre – founders of the fetish lingerie brand, Agent Provocateur. One house was themed "Beautiful" the other "Damned". The homes were connected by a private courtyard, so guests could wander between them. The design included a staircase strewn with pink flowers and moodily flickering candles. The obligatory red roses were artistically strewn through rooms that were also decorated with erotic photos of women in fetish and SM gear.

Relentlessly focused on the 30 concept, 30 bouncers kept paparazzi at bay, only admitting people who knew the passwords, "Big 3-0". On arrival, guests were presented by liveried waiters with fragrant and pricey blooms "from Israel, the Caribbean and South Africa". There were of course lots of

A-listers – this was a "star studded" "glittering occasion". Media reports recited the guest list like a mantra: Naomi Campbell, Grace Jones, Alexander McQueen, Stella McCartney, Chrissie Hynde, Ronnie Wood (and his wife, Jo and daughter, Leah), Rhys Ifans … [1]

Kate "frolicked" with a troupe of "scantily-clad beauties". Jefferson seemed lost and ill at ease in his white suit, spending much time chatting with Kate's mother and brother or fretting over arrangements. Meg Matthews – "Her fake tan was peeling off and she was glassy-eyed" – nattered to Fran Cutler. A gang of beautiful young things tried new dance moves, "leaping onto the floor, rolling over and then springing back up in apparent tiger impersonations."

As Jools Holland bashed the ivories, "Kate entranced everyone as she ran through numbers from 'Summertime' to 'Great Balls Of Fire'." Knocking back "bottle after bottle of Cristal champagne" she slurred at one point that she felt more damned than beautiful. Jefferson gamely stepped in, "That's rubbish. You're beautiful." At midnight, the guests assembled as two topless male models carted a three-foot high profiterole cake into the dance room. Kate blew out her 30 candles and made a wish and everyone clapped.

Less happy were the Westminster Council noise prevention officers who turned up around 1.45am and told the party to quieten down. Kate and about 50 others decided to return to Claridges where they resumed festivities …

* * *

And we get to that point in the evening, where the Sky documentary *Kate Moss: Fashion Victim?* resorted to sly "reconstructions". A point about which the Mossy Posse, today, get coy. However, several journalists had infiltrated the party. One of them was Katie Nichol, who was eventually able to reveal what she'd seen in a *Mail on Sunday* exposé.

Noticing that Kate had been absent from her own party for some time Nichol asked where she was. A guest indicated the master bedroom. Nichol described how: "I peered into the dimly-lit, smokefilled room where … Kate Moss had been hiding for the past hour. A tangle of bodies writhed on the king-size bed.

"Above the sound of the Rolling Stones record playing quietly in the background, I could just hear a soft murmur and an occasional ripple of laughter.

[1] The family minded Madonna and Guy Ritchie who'd been expected, failed to show. The pregnant Gwyneth Paltrow and her teetotal partner Chris Martin looked around with disdain and left early.

"As the doors opened to Kate's bedroom ... Sadie Frost, was immediately visible. Her red dress was hitched up around her waist as she straddled a fellow guest.

"Although I couldn't see her companion's face, one thing was for sure it wasn't her toyboy lover Jackson Scott. He was sitting on the bed next to her.

"Sadie blocked my full view of the others. All I could see were limbs entwined in abandonment.

"Standing in the corner of the room was Jefferson Hack ... talking into his mobile phone and gazing at the incredible scene before him with a look on his face that said he'd witnessed this all before."

* * *

At one point, a model emerged from the bedroom and asked groggily if anyone had any condoms. As word spread of what was going on, people went to look. Some joined in. Ronnie Wood took a peek, thought better of it, and emerged guffawing. At four in the morning, Kate emerged, swaying unsteadily before running barefoot to the dance floor.

A little later, noticing the TV pundit Janet Street Porter lounging on a bed in a second bedroom she shrieked recognition and jumped onto the bed, shrilling, "Janet is my intellectual friend. You're such a fucking intellectual." Another model then joined them and Street Porter was inadvertently pushed off the bed. She fell on the floor on her back and lay helplessly, wiggling legs in the air like an upturned beetle, giggling like a schoolgirl. Kate yelled delightedly, "Janet Street-Porter's on the fucking floor."

Katie Nichol also watched as Kate, "armed with a magnum of champagne and her Marlboro Lights", "collared" a male guest and "pulled" him into a bathroom. The door was locked: "Another private soiree. This one lasted 45 minutes."

* * *

The 50 or so paparazzi waiting outside were thrilled when, as the revellers began to stagger out in the early hours, Sadie Frost appeared like tabloid manna or a scene from a Russ Meyer flick: catatonic and with her ample left tit squeezed out of her red flapper-style dress. A lightning storm of flashbulbs created an icon. Another storm erupted next day, when Jude Law saw the mother of his children cruelly exposed in the papers.

* * *

In April 2004, Kate had begun a relationship with a new boy to the Primrose Hill crowd, the rugged actor Daniel Craig, AKA Mr Potato Head (soon to be canonised as James Bond). This was just after Jefferson Hack finally moved out of Kate's St Johns Wood home.

It was groundhog day again – the usual suspects, "sources" and "close friends", said the usual things: Kate and Daniel were "inseparable"; "the sexual chemistry between them is so potent that you'd be blind not to see it"; "There is a real spark between them"; he is "just what Kate's looking for at the moment"; and "It is serious, and they both know it."

They travelled to New York and spent days "holed up" in a $ (fabulous price) a night hotel room/suite, and then to Goa where they "soaked up the sun" together, and Kate "looked a picture of happiness".

* * *

Their first semi-official sortie as a couple was in June, at one of those funny celebrity events where celebrities bid for one another's tat for a good cause. Not unusually, the cause was an AIDS charity. The theme was black – suitable for Kate, who had by now taken to calling herself, Dracula.

The Earls Court event was sponsored by American Express who were "celebrating" that their Centurion credit had lasted five years. Alexander McQueen threw his design genius behind the gala, and made it as black as possible, black being the "signature colour" of this credit card. McQueen also organised a "greatest hits" catwalk show.

The venue was swathed in black, the VIP guests turned up in black, the waiters served Guinness and squid-ink sushi and chocolate truffle lollipops. An auctioneer from Christies then flogged a pair of Madonna's black fishnet tights for £1,200 as well as a (presumably underexposed) signed snap of Kate Moss by Sam Taylor Wood (£8,500), a pair of black leather trousers donated by Christina Aguilera, a Galliano black dress, and a pair of Elton John's black sunglasses.

The catwalk show was just as black, "staged in a black version of the mirrored padded cell McQueen has used previously". One highlight was the black Naomi Campbell "strutting in a black pirate coat over snakeskin bra and knickers". Another was Kate's debut as a dancer, accompanied by Michael Clarke. First, Kate walked on stage in "a stunning floor-length skull-print dress" and began waving her arms around. Then Clarke pranced into view and, raising the model's arms above her head, brusquely swung her over his shoulder. An onlooker gasped, "It was an amazing spectacle."

* * *

When Kate and Craig fizzled out towards the end of June, Johnny Knoxville, the American comic actor, born with the comical name of Philip

John Clapp, was rumoured. The pair were "caught smooching" in the VIP enclosure of a Franz Ferdinand gig in New York. Said an observer, "Franz Ferdinand put on a great performance but it seems Johnny and Kate weren't too interested. They were all over each other and they didn't seem to mind sharing the limelight with the band on stage." But then it seemed that this too, was a no-no as Kate got back with Daniel for a "last ditch attempt" to save their love. They went off to the Balearic island of Formentera and were "spotted cycling down dirt tracks to the beach".

That Christmas, Kate and Jefferson spent Christmas together with their child as a family. Then Kate threw a New Year's party at a remote Scottish castle and didn't invite Jefferson. So Kate saw her year of nemesis, 2005, in with, among others, Rhys Ifans, Davinia Taylor, Danny Goffey and Mick Jones. "Kate had a wild night. The castle was a great location for a party and there was dancing and drinking into the early hours."

* * *

That was the year of the Tsunami. Kate had planned to travel to Phucket in the New Year with Sadie Frost and entourage, but that plan was changed.

One of Kate's close friends had been engulfed by the tragedy. Samantha Archer Fayet, a booking agent at the Paris Marilyn modelling agency, had been holidaying in a beach hut with her six-month-old baby, Ruby Rose and husband, Patrice. When the water hit, Patrice recalled, "The waves got bigger and bigger and more powerful. I was holding both Sam and Ruby but it was too hard, too hard." It seems Samantha's last phone call was to Kate, to wish her a happy Christmas.

Undeterred by the catastrophe, Kate arranged a week's holiday at the £6,000-a-week villa, Frenchman's Lookout on Tortola in the Virgin Islands. With her was Miranda Davis, the wife of Mick Jones, ex Clashman, and now Pete Doherty's record producer.

* * *

For Middleage, – that wandered
And found it hidden here,
And, pausing, gazed and pondered
Knowing a mystery near –
A dream, its childhood squandered,
Or lost, gone many a year.
- Madison Julus Cawein, *The House Of Moss*, 1913

* * *

2004 had also been when Kate decided to put down proper English roots. This meant a permanent place in the countryside, a stake in the green and pleasant land – the destiny of all pop culture rebels, with in the offing a place in the flower roster of the village church, attendance at charitable events, and eventually maybe, a damehood …

Kate had fallen for a corner of Gloucestershire that many other celebrities have favoured. This was the cluster of Cotswold villages and towns around the upper reaches of the Thames, between Swindon and Oxford. A pretty and prosperous locality with royal connections, where she and Jefferson had rented the cottage they'd wrecked. The nearest town was Lechlade.

Lechlade is one of those "unspoilt" country towns which nestles by the Thames: olde teashoppes, cute pubs with window seats, and that mix of retired gentlefolk and stockbrokers playing squire. There are also the locals, weather-beaten tenants of council homes and habitués of the social security system, best observed in the bar and gardens of the pub just below the bridge that leads into the town – from which bare-chested lads jump into the Thames to the cheers of gnarled and otherwise surly drinkers.

Kate eventually settled on a picturesque village which (perhaps unknown to her) had several singular and appropriate connotations.

The village had originally marked a site sacred to druids, whose priests gathered mistletoe from its oak groves. Mistletoe was a revered plant for druids, who gathered the stuff with a convoluted ceremony involving the sacrifice of two white bulls. With its suggestively forking and paired branches and white berries oozing sticky white juice, the plant also featured in the orgiastic fertility rites of pre-Christian Celts – a pale memory of which lingers in the custom of kissing under the mistletoe.[1]

Equally, the site had been a place for worshipping Freya, the Nordic goddess of love, beauty and fertility, a deity who recalls our own Kate Moss.

---

[1] Druids are also associated with that other Kate Moss location, Primrose Hill. The poet William Blake, inspired by Druidic lore to dream of Albion, claimed he was struck by a vision of the "Spiritual Sun," the true light of the imagination, on Primrose Hill. The 18th century Druid revivalists claimed the hill as a sacred vantage point and in 1792, the Welsh druidist and opium addict, fantasist and forger, Iolo Morganwg, launched a revived druidism with his Primrose Hill proclamation of the Gorsedd of Bards of the Islands of Britain. Ever since, the site has been favoured for druidic ceremonies, its view making it "a prime location from which to 'charm' London."

"Aphrodite's amorous escapades pale by comparison with those of Freya, whose unbridled sexuality was legendary … none could resist her. To make matters even worse, like the Greek goddess Aphrodite, she possessed apparel that made her irresistible to men … a magical necklace [aka the "necklace of desire"] … Moreover, "The goddess Freya's passions were abundant, vigorous, and unrestrained. Clothed or not, she is usually shown in sensual poses." (www.goddessgift.com)

After these exciting beginnings the village turned into a peaceful enough agricultural hamlet, hardly even disturbed by the enclosures of the 18th century.

However, on July 22nd 1893, it suffered a very dark day indeed.

* * *

James Lopworth, a 27-year-old gardener, then lived with his parents in a cottage next to the schoolhouse. Lapworth was a paedophile. He had been "intimate" with seven-year-old Beatrice Alice James and possibly also with five-year-old Emily Ethel Judd. Both girls lived in the village and their parents counted Lopworth a friend.

On the evening of the 22nd, Emily's father, Henry, realised his daughter was missing and began a search. He discovered her body in the nearby river Leach. There were no marks on her and people assumed it was a tragic accident.

But that same evening, Beatrice's parents reported that their daughter too, was missing. When Beatrice was found two days later, in the words of the attending surgeon: "The head was almost severed from the body and there was distinct evidence of attempted violation." Lapworth declared his innocence and explained the abundant blood stains found on his clothes and handkerchief by saying he'd tripped while tipsy on the steps of the Temperance Hotel in Lechlade, "and broken his concertina". He was eventually hanged.

After that trauma, the village vanished into comfortable obscurity. For the next century or so, until the arrival of Kate Moss, the biggest local excitement was when Ruth Enid Cress, the housekeeper at the Farmhouse in 1935, was knocked off her bicycle and robbed by a 20-year-old under gardener, Henry Keene.

* * *

Real estate psychogeography is a legitimate tool of the assiduous snooper, especially revealing when it comes to monied celebrities. Such people have the need and means to express their personalities through their habitations.

Their homes are also sometimes more revealing of their desires and hesitations and neuroses than they might imagine.

* * *

If you take the M4 out towards Lechlade from London, you will soon pass junction 12 towards Theale, which leads to the paranoically secluded estate of that other Kate with a vegetative surname that is equally a synonym for what the Victorians used to call "the female part": Kate Bush.

Just as you couldn't imagine two people more different in personality or lifestyle than Kates Moss and Bush, so are their country estates opposed.

Kate Bush lives on an island. This is an artificial island created from a moathouse complex, blocked off by a canal as well as high walls and thick hedges, supplemented by rush screens impregnated with vegetation and abundant barbed wire. Security cameras survey the passer by, while signs warn in red, a mite hysterically: "PRIVATE – KEEP OUT CCTV PRO-TECTED GUARD DOGS LOOSE." The exterior also has a scotophobic aspect, simulating ugliness to repel the observer, like that unpleasantly tex-tured stucco the British plaster over their semis, or the dense polyester foliage of net curtains, which all says: "look away." And there is no village near the Bush estate, just a straggle of houses and a small encampment of barge dwellers.

The Kate Moss idyll is very different. Set in the heart of a village not far from its 13th century church, her mansion complex is a rambling and picturesque series of outbuildings clustered around the main house which was probably first built in the 17th century. From a distance it has the look of a working farm, and indeed, the grounds and several adjoining sheds and buildings are used for agriculture. Its sprawling and open aspect is especially noticeable from the back, where a series of linked gardens suggest an enormous and deluxe version of the garden at Church Way. These some-what ambiguous borders perhaps reflect Kate's own hazy and relaxed boundaries.

* * *

The vendors from whom Kate acquired the property have deep roots in the area and can trace their line from William the Conqueror. They are part of an aristocratic clan dripping with Debrett references that has long domi-nated the village.

Kate's mansion was valued in December 2002 at £1.5 million. It was sold it to the excitable supermodel two years later, for £1 million more, a tidy Norman profit. In addition, Kate bought adjoining land, flat empty fields suitable for cultivating vegetables, for £2.5 million. Her country estate therefore cost £5 million.

* * *

An indicative local contrast to Kate's domain is Liz Hurley's estate which is 15 or so minutes drive away at Ampney Knowle. Hurley's £3.3 million mansion looks enormous and is set on a rise with exposed lawns all around so that interlopers can be picked off, and also so you can admire its size and importance. Hurley's is therefore a blunt public statement of her status – whereas Kate's is hard to fathom all at once – its many layers unfold discretely, almost secretly.

Hurley's mansion moreover, is reached by a half mile drive from electronically operated gates with swivelling surveillance cameras, and past a wary housekeeper's dwelling. And if you should take a closer look by trekking up the public footpath that approaches and then skirts the estate, and if you linger with a telescopic lens wondering what that whitish shape is in the upstairs window (Hugh reading the riot act?), you might become (like me and my photographer) suddenly aware that the housekeeper has emerged and is watching you through a pair of binoculars. And after that, he jumps in his Land Rover and comes patrolling.

Liz has thought of everything, Kate about nothing – which after all, is admirable and endearing. And while one might judge from the real estate that Hurley's taste is arch and pretentious – Toad Hall in Ruritania, Kate's is romantic and crumbly, rather hippyfied, sentimental, suggestively vulnerable.

* * *

Kate got the keys to her new paradise just in time to prepare for her 31st birthday, and less than a month before she met Pete Doherty at a Charlatans gig at the Shepherds Bush Empire, on December 8, 2004. Pete was already on her case – he was a fan. He had the posters and had read the stories. He also knew her penchant for wild men of rock and roll.

The Charlatans were performing with one of the original wild men, Kate's close friend, Ronnie Wood. This concert was marred at first by technical cockups and at one point, Wood addressed the audience: "As it's being fucking filmed, we're going to have to start the whole thing again." He added, "You all don't mind staying for a bit longer do you? We can play all day so we can play all night." Said problems were fixed, and the band and Wood rocked away.

Pete meanwhile, had his own technical problem: how to chat up a supermodel? She was surrounded by her usual entourage, Tracey Emin, Stella McCartney, and Sadie Frost. Jefferson Hack was also present. Pete got one of his friends to introduce him. Kate gave him a cheery hello, and then ignored him. Some in the entourage sniggered – who the fuck was Pete Doherty?

*   *   *

Pete Doherty was born March 1979, in Hexham, Northumberland. Both his parents were in the military. His father, Peter John Doherty, was a sergeant in the Royal Signals and previously a member of the Parachute Regiment. Pete's mother, Jacqueline Michels, was a lance corporal in a Nursing corps.

Pete's paternal grandfather was Timothy Peter Doherty, a railway carriage cleaner. The grandmother was Doris Winifred Ford. They married in February 1951. The Irish – Doherty – connection comes from granddad Timothy, who was born in June 1922, in Lower Grange, near Cheekpoint, Waterford. He was the son of John Doherty, a fisherman, and Josephine McCormack. It seems the family lived as fishing folk – today, Cheekpoint is a tourist-friendly fishing hamlet.

Pete's maternal line is more exotic, and maybe part Jewish-French, guessing from the names: Paris Michels (grandfather), Moise (from Moses) Michels (great grandfather), and the great grandmother, Chana Peress (Peres or Peress being possibly Jewish Sephardic).

The military background of Pete's parents meant travel – the boy was shunted around various garrisons in Ulster, Germany, Cyprus and the UK. But he shone at school, gaining straight A's for all his 11 GCSEs and 4 A levels, (General Studies, English Literature, History and Economics.) When 16, Pete won a poetry competition organised by the British Council and as a result toured Russia. So far so good …

He was then accepted to read English at the university of London (he sometimes claims Oxford). But at this point he tired of being straight and turned the offer down. Instead, he hung out with a bohemian clique at Filthy McNasty's Whiskey Café near Kings Cross, where he worked as a barman and also dossed. Then he met Carl Barat and moved into a North London flat with him. The result was The Libertines.

Doherty and Barat began writing songs and performing together. They paid their dues in the Indie way through pub rock venues etc and were signed by Rough Trade in 2002. Their first album, *Up The Bracket*, was lionised by *New Musical Express*. That propelled it up the charts and widened The Libertine's fan base.

The band added to their growing fame by cultivating a violent and drug fuelled image – lots of fights and fiascos at gigs, and blatant drug taking.

Pete's life mirrored his image. His relationships were fraught and episodic. He fathered two children and left the mothers – and the kids, to work things out for themselves. He rowed with his band, estranged his allies and played sometimes manipulative games with fans.

A rift appeared between him and Barat, "All our dreams came true," explained Pete, "We played every night for about a year and a half. Started getting press. And then some of the reasons that I had needed him and he had needed me disappeared. Suddenly, he was the sexiest man in rock, so he didn't need me to tell him he was good any more. And I didn't need him to pull girls, so we lost each other. They said it was the drugs but it wasn't, because it wasn't that he ever took less drugs than me."

But most of Doherty's problems did stem from chronic drug taking.

* * *

His trumpeted addiction was a career move, inspired by the Romantic poets and artists. Many of these 19th century transgressives cultivated their craft with everything from opium to hashish to laughing gas to absinthe (the artist Fuseli would eat raw meat just before going to bed to give himself the nightmares he then painted).

Doherty had been having his own nightmares since childhood, "Colours and numbers crawling up in your skin, and stretching you and crushing you … these are the things that were haunting me since I was a kid. Hallucinations … Long before I took drugs."

Doherty experimented with weed and then graduated to opium, before taking his masters in heroin.

"The first time I had heroin, I was 21. Walking round the streets of Whitechapel, smoking brown and thinking I was cool. As it got into my bloodstream, I noticed it exaggerated parts of me that were already there – solitude and loneliness. Then I started getting all these creative thoughts."

He later described his addiction as, "It's like you are in love with some-one. You never stop loving them." But there were also the lost times, like when he woke up in the early hours, "Under a taxi with no clothes on, and I ended up knocking a cyclist out and nicking his bike."

Pete's heroin and crack-spurred antics got increasingly out of order. Alarmed, the band booted him out. To feed his habit he had resorted to petty theft, as formerly he had dabbled in male prostitution. "There was no shame, because I kind of knew that they were just lonely pissed-up old queens. And 20 quid was a lot of money!" He was then arrested armed with a flick knife, and just escaped jail. In July 2003 he burgled his friend and ex band mate Barat's Marylebone flat, lifting among other saleable items, an antique guitar and a laptop.

"I turned up at Carl's flat to speak to him and I saw that all the flight cases were outside the flat, which I thought was a bit strange. I heard a noise inside the flat and I knocked on the door and said, 'Let me in,' but got no answer. So I kicked the door down and found out that they had all gone to Japan without me. So I put his telly in the boot of my car. And the Flying Squad came and caught me."

* * *

Sentenced to six months in prison, with three of those months suspended, Doherty was then tearfully reconciled with Barat. Tears turned to vinegar as Doherty rejoined the band and jacked up his drug intake. At one point, bouncers were employed at recording sessions to keep the two rockers from one another's throats.

The manic drug taking went with manic sex. Doherty soon realised his pulling power as a rock star. His predilection for groupies and sometimes predatory approach to fans, as well as his creative sexuality, resulted in scenes of notable wantonness.

Doherty also retained the bisexuality he'd had since childhood, "I was dressing up in Brownie uniforms when I was young. I went pretending to be my sister's cousin – I got the uniform and everything." His ex girlfriend Katie Lewis lamented: "It broke my heart the day I walked in on Pete in the shower delicately soaping down another naked man, a groupie he'd met that night. I felt sick."

Meanwhile, Doherty had assembled a collection of ringers and dealers who followed the scent of his notoriety.

* * *

Doherty has several times played the classic addict's rigmarole of remorse-penance-rehab-relapse. On one such occasion, he scarpered from the Thamkrabok Buddhist Monastery in Thailand where he'd gone to be purged.

"I am not strong enough for this treatment, I wanted to go home so badly. I was crying in the night and the afternoon. I had a breakdown."

Successfully advertising on his web site for £1,000 to get him home, he waited for the cash to arrive in a seedy hotel which "offered room service of heroin with my bacon and eggs. I told them I had no money but they said I could have it on a tab. I notched up a £280 bill in three days. If I'd done the same amount in England, it would have cost me thousands."

Eventually, Barat could not bring himself to forgive anymore. As for Doherty, he said, "In the end, I just got better conversations out of the needle than I did from Carl."

They parted company and Doherty started another band, Babyshambles. This outfit embarked on a chaotic but effective touring programme. Fans would never know whether Doherty or the band would turn up at advertised venues. Or he might phone a few fans at home and invite them round his flat for an impromptu strum, cash at the door.

Said a tour manager, Matt Bates, "Peter doesn't mind playing to one person or 10,000. The little shows are where he really comes into his own. He will do a gig, get his guitar from the tour bus and sit in the street and do a second gig for his fans. There isn't another rock star in the world who would do that."

And while his recordings are uneven and sometimes slapdash, as one critic said, "when he is at his best, he simply opens his heart and invites you in."

* * *

Doherty resembled Johnny Depp in his vagrant intellectual curiosity and mock malevolence. But Doherty's is a very English-suburban brand of rock demonology (just as Kate Moss' profligacy is more Tropic of Ruislip than Hellfire Caves). It melds The Clash (four suburban lads in search of an inner city), the acerbic vignettes of Ray Davies' The Kinks, and the kitchen sink pisstakes of Jarvis Cocker. Also suburban is Doherty's fascination with the glum drollery of fifties comedian, Anthony Hancock, the Poootererque citizen of East Cheam. And Doherty's appropriation of Blakean folklore – the Books of Albion and all that jazz – was earnest, evoking school visits to Tate Britain rather than rambles through New Jerusalem.

* * *

An ingénue in other areas, too. Despite his A levels in History and Economics, Doherty spouts radical chic. Interviewed by the Trotskyite *Socialist Worker*, he suggested: "You have to replace capitalism because that's the only thing it understands. It's like a disease or a fungus. You can't tidy up the flower bed and restrain it a bit – you've got to dig it out from the roots and replace it, otherwise it will keep growing. That's the nature of capitalism.

"As far fetched as it seems, it can happen the way it's always happened in history, and that's through a radical turnaround.

"Who really would have thought in Russia in 1917 that that would happen? They were coffee shop philosophers who ended up in charge of the most incredible revolution human history has seen. (And which killed over four million under Lenin and 20 million under Stalin – outshining that other coffee shop philosopher, Adolf Hitler.)

But at least he had the wit to fuck up at the grotesque flummery of Live 8.

* * *

Doherty's musical successes, his flair for music, performance and self advertisement, his charisma, and his exotic drug fetish, had given him cachet and renown. But that was all relatively low key, mostly confined to his young audience and cognoscenti. His approaching liaison with Kate Moss however, would propel him into tabloid heaven.

* * *

After Lila's birth, Kate's career resumed. In July 2004 she signed to continue as the face of Coco Mademoiselle perfume. This was at the insistence of Chanel's artistic director, Jacques Helleu – and the teeth of rumours that Kate's gathering notoriety as a party girl had given the fashion house pause for thought. Kate had also recently become the face of the Cacharel perfume, Anais Anais, "recommended for romantic use." And at the same time she was fronting campaigns for Burberry, Missoni, Rimmel, Stella McCartney and Louis Vuitton.

Some commentators thought she seemed set for the longevity of Elle Macpherson or Lauren Hutton. But the Worth Global Style Network muttered she was "spreading herself too thinly" (no pun was presumably intended). She was in any case by now "the most sought-after model in the world."

Jefferson Hack's father Douglas, had once half jokingly asked his son whether Kate might present prizes at his local yacht club. Jefferson replied: "Dad, Kate gets asked to do hundreds of things a week. She doesn't do anything for less than £25,000."

* * *

Kate's financial arrangements seem to have been based abroad until 1996, when she is named as director of Tilly Church Ltd with her father, Peter Moss. In 1998, Burn Ltd was also incorporated, with Kate as sole director.

Both companies were dissolved in 2003. Her present company, Skate Enterprises Ltd was established in 2001. Kate and her father are sole directors – though Peter is not a shareholder and doesn't draw a salary. Simon Chambers, the brother of Sarah Doukas and co-owner of Kate's agency Storm, is named as company secretary.

The last available, 2004, return states that "The company is controlled by K. Moss, who owns 100% of the share capital." Turnover in 2004 was £1,257,513, and pre tax profits £1,099,275. Kate's director's salary was £130,935 (down from £404,299 the previous year). The company listed three employees, with combined wages of £162,550 (down from £437,262 in 2003).

Limited companies like this are mostly used to filter earnings and limit UK tax liability. They give little indication of the real wealth of the people involved. One indication however, is the renowned *Sunday Times* Rich List. In April 2004, this ranked Kate joint 24th in the league of 100 richest young people. It was estimated that between 2000 and 2003 she earned around £9 million and that her fortune was about £14 million. However, also in April 2004, *The Sun* suggested Kate was worth more like £30 million.

What is incontrovertible is that as a brand, as a business, she is the business. The way her Name was made and maintained through hype and promotion and the oxygen of headlines, went along with a concentration and fusion of symbol and capital, rendered as a beautiful spectacle: increasingly the direction of fashion through its increasing fixation with branding and celebrity.

As witness the rise and rise of Calvin Klein and Tom Ford. Klein and Ford shuffle and deal fame and luck and image. They owe more to Andy Warhol and Jeff Koons than Coco Chanel or even Jean Paul Gaultier. More familiar with percentages than scissors they are cultural investment bankers as much as entrepreneurs.

Kate Moss was a monster this image-obsessed fashion industry created without really thinking it through. Luckily for the industry, Kate and the other supermodels never realised their unassailability. In any case, they were fixated on their personal affairs, dealing in power only via tantrums or conceits rather than applying it to the motor and motive points of the industry. They were also mediated – contained, by their agencies. But in the end, when it came to disciplining or dumping her, Kate Moss proved a bigger brand than any label she represented.

* * *

Kate's 31st was held at her new country home. This time, the theme was a rock and roll Circus. That came from the 1968 film of a gig organised by The Rolling Stones, which featured performances by, among others, Eric Clapton, The Who, John Lennon, Jethro Tull, and Kate's new friend Marianne Faithfull.

Jagger had envisaged the event as a multimedia extravaganza and came up with the idea of a circus as a metaphor for the madness that was rock and roll. So the original gig was held under what looked like a disreputable big top. While the Stones withheld release of the film until 1996, the concert became part of the legend of 1968 – that magic year of revolutions and riot.

Kate transformed the large barn attached to her house into a venue complete with stage and bar area. The same logo that had appeared in the original décor and promo was placed on the outside of the barn and over the stage area.

*   *   *

Maybe it was an omen that on her way to the party, Kate's mother was involved in a car crash. Linda suffered shock and an injured arm. In panic, as she staggered from her wrecked Nissan Figaro, Linda called Kate on her mobile. She was brought to Kate's home and an ambulance summoned. The ambulance personnel treated Linda at the house. Kate insisted the party would go on.

Kate also ensured that her daughter would not be around to witness the party. The two-year old was packed off with her nanny for the night.

*   *   *

The pricey cars started arriving down the driveway, eerily lit for occasion with long candles. Sadie Frost turned up with her boyfriend, the somewhat younger flamenco guitarist, Jackson Scott – a tryst fixed by Kate to take Sadie's mind off Jude, who'd recently taken up with the blonde actress and Kate Moss lookalike, Sienna Miller, 13 years younger than the mother of his children.

Davinia Taylor, the loo roll princess also rolled up as did the R.E.M. star Michael Stipe, the actress Samantha Morton, and Travis singer Fran Healy. From behind a hedge, a journalist noted the arrival of "An exotic beauty wearing a blonde wig beneath a black Cossack hat", and wondered who she was.

In general, this party was celebrity lite. Several Names, perhaps alarmed by last year's carry-on, had made their excuses. Their place was taken by makeup artists, stylists and young models.

The guests congregated and Kate appeared, got up in yellow hotpants and a jewelled bra top. The waiters offered a choice of Krug or Cristal champagne. Also on offer were canapés and caviar and lollipops. Other options for ingesting pleasure were also on offer, as was later revealed.

For musical entertainment, Kate had got Primal Scream, ex Clash Mick Jones and Paul Simonon to play a medley of Rolling Stones numbers. Kate duetted with the singer Pearl Lowe, on Leader of the Pack.

★　★　★

Another musician too, had turned up.

Pete Doherty presented Kate with a framed copy of the lyrics to his song, What Katy Did, handwritten on an envelope. The song was about a girl who cannot shake her drug habit. The present seemed to delight the super-model, "She was thrilled with it, she thought it was really romantic." Doherty also performed the number: "There's a lesson I have learnt/If you play with fire you will get burnt."

In fact, the song was originally written for Doherty's former girlfriend Katie Holmes. Doherty had turned that teenager on to crack and heroin. Their relationship had been tempestuous and violent, "Once we were both high on crack and heroin and had a blazing row at my flat. He got a razor blade and started slashing at my arm. We both ended up going to hospital for stitches. I have huge scars for life."

★　★　★

Doherty stole the show that night. The party girl was all over him and guests were surprised that the couple spent the evening necking and on one another's laps. At one point they disappeared for over an hour into Kate's en-suite bedroom.

The party went on till around 5am, when people started to make for one of the bedrooms or crash on sofas or carpets. The premises were heavy with tobacco smoke. Outside, the journalists and paparazzi waiting in cars dozed off.

★　★　★

Kate had booked a table for 30 for the next day, at the Swan pub in the neighbouring town of Southrop. The revellers were supposed to congregate there for Sunday lunch. At the last minute the pub got a call cancelling the booking. Instead, later that afternoon, Kate and Pete got in a car and headed for London. They stopped at her house, then set off for a nearby pub.

Soon after, Kate introduced Pete to her parents as her new lover. They were appalled. Doherty complained, "Ever since, they've called me the crackhead."

Now the real rock and roll circus started.

★ ★ ★

Kate Moss and Pete Doherty as an item sparked media hysteria. Doherty had already raised enough eyebrows on his own – his winning the *NME* nomination as cool icon of the year for 2004 was controversial. Now he was attached to the coolest woman in the world. Two weeks later Doherty told a startled nation on TV: "We got each other's initials tattooed in little hearts. I have a K in a heart." He added, "I'm kicking drugs for her, too." (Later he elaborated, I've got a little K tattoo on my arse, she's just got a little P there. And it doesn't stand for Pirelli.") He also announced, "I believe her when she says she loves me and I know I mean it when I say I love her."

Sadie Frost thought it would all end in tears: "Pete's not the sort of guy you would wish for your best friend. Kate has had a history of partying hard and the idea of the two of them together would be a terrible idea."

By January 30th, the *Sunday Mirror* was gasping about its featured "chilling photographs", showing Pete "smoking a fix of heroin": "Heating foil with a lighter, the 25-year-old former Libertines frontman eagerly 'chases the dragon' as he inhales the drug in a North London recording studio.

"The sordid scenes were captured on video on the day the self-confessed heroin and crack cocaine addict failed to appear in court for possessing a knife, claiming to be unwell.

"The pictures will strike new terror into the heart of Kate's worried friends and family, including ex-love Jefferson Hack."

★ ★ ★

The video in question was a documentary about Doherty by Max Carlish that had been seven months time in the making.

Carlish commented: "Taking heroin is integral to Pete's music-making. Two or three times he would come out of the studio and smoke heroin just like having a cigarette. No one batted an eyelid …"

He added: "Pete is tempting heroin to kill him, but believes he can beat it. He's constantly daring himself and others to go further … I hope that when he sees the pictures he will realise that he needs help."

★ ★ ★

Far from seeking help, Doherty was enraged at what he saw as a betrayal. He tracked the Judas down to a hotel, where he allegedly broke his nose, blacked both his eyes, and then made off with the film-maker's mobile phone, spare cash and Barclaycard.

Carlish recounted later, "I was in a hotel with Pete and everything was going fine until he started demanding loads of cash. He wanted thousands and I knew he was going to go out and spend it on heroin. He was desperate for a fix. I said no and he went berserk, punching me."

Doherty was especially peeved that the exposé would diminish him in Kate's eyes. And indeed, the press reported that Kate, who was in New York at the time, had now had second thoughts ...

This put into play a staple of the ensuing media game. Reports that Kate had dumped Pete on account of a photo-incident-rumour were followed by counter reports that after all she had not, or that they were "back together" as well as sightings-images-anecdotes of them "canoodling," or "partying," etc. Associated themes were: "Can Love Save Pete?" and "Will Pete Destroy Kate?"

Whatever the opinion of the pundit pondering these questions, it made for lots of copy at £x per word.

Another popular implication was that wicked Doherty was leading innocent Kate astray. But the subtext here was that what was natural to the goose was perverse in the gander. Red rags – or green lights, for feminist inclined journos to rally to a sister's support, and notch up yet more words slagging male hypocrisy.

It wasn't long before practically anything went, so long as it fuelled the fire, and the public was more than welcome to join in. In *The Daily Star*, reader Mark Baker, from Nottingham, sneered: "How can Kate Moss, one of the world's most beautiful women, agree to marry Pete Doherty, who looks about 12? I love the fact that she's only got a P tattoo rather than his full name, like he asked for."

* * *

There now followed a black comedy of Doherty arrested, bailed, charged, jailed ... going into rehab ... falling again ...

In February he was jailed briefly for the Carlish affair, "It was hell. At night the noise was horrible. My cell stank of vomit, I felt the walls closing in. I thought I was going to die. I felt like crying but the thought of Kate on the outside kept me going. I'm determined to kick the habit for good for the sake of my relationship with her."

He also recalled, "I was completely green and out of my depth, and you are banged up 23 hours a day. You only get a telly if you are a paedophile.

But there is a library, which was great. I wrote a diary. And I read *Crime and Punishment*, which is an unbelievable book."

Kate was quoted that he must give up drugs for her sake (!). Pete publicly vowed he would give up for everybody's sake. Pete's mum was quoted that he had promised to give up for her sake. As for Pete's dad, "My dad told me I'd broken my mum's heart. He said I represented everything he hated about humanity. That really got to me. But after five minutes, five days maybe, I cut myself off from him completely. We hadn't spoken for years anyway."

Later that month he went into rehab and was reported "close to tears" talking to Kate on the phone while the doctors plotted a medical fix by giving him the "opiate blocker", Naltrexone – an expensive treatment partly funded by *The Sun* newspaper, "to help him beat drugs – and to highlight the dangers to young music fans." Kate urged him to have an implant in his stomach, a device which released the drug continually. "You must get [this done] I can't have you around if you're this out of control because it's going to get me into trouble."

Then he was at large again, and scoring again: here we go again. "It's fucking weird. One minute I'm in a prison tracksuit queuing for chicken and rice and the next I'm clobbered out in Dior."

*　*　*

Startling pictures of the rock star appeared, looking abnormally beautiful in a debauched genre: "Pete Doherty is drenched in sweat, his eyeballs are rolling and it looks like he's about to throw up. He is totally out of it." In contrast, Kate, was pictured glowing and grinning, as she hobnobbed at a fashion show in Paris with Sir Elton John and Yoko Ono.

Nevertheless, they were now, "the hottest couple in showbiz". Their trials front page stuff. As usual in Britain, where the tabs went everyone followed. The previous December, viewers of the austere *Newsnight* programme on BBC2 had been startled to see Doherty hailed a "hugely talented songwriter and poet" and given a major profile and interview by the presenter Kirsty Wark.

Equally impressed was *The Observer* in October 2005, heralding a "World Exclusive; Pete Doherty's Diaries", plus "sensational backstage photographs". This featured snippets from his Books of Albion, which despite an allusion to "senses deranged", read more like the dippy comedian Arthur Askey than the seer Arthur Rimbaud splattered with doodles and shortcuts to the heartfelt like "heart" "betraying my heart" "you have my heart" and "in my heart". But the main selling point as touted on *The Observer*'s front page was Kate's "contribution", a photo with a bubble out of her mouth –

written by "the model" herself: "spend two hours staring at a fucking [heroin] spoon."

No one wanted to miss out on the new Basquiat.

$$\star \quad \star \quad \star$$

Where there's muck there's brass. *The Independent* headlined, PUBLISHERS SCRAMBLE TO SIGN TROUBLED ROCKER PETE DOHERTY. Indeed, publishers had discovered the headline champ was also a poet, and moreover, had a stash of unpublished treasure. Matthew Hollis, poetry editor at Faber, home of TS Eliot, a poet who never got high on anything except Anglicanism and dry sherry, confided: "Literary publishers are open minded and respond to the quality of the work. The fact that someone is known primarily as a musician does not inhibit them from being taken seriously as a poet." But Pete was averse to contracts, and prone to giving work away on his web site – where he also made a lot of his private life available.

$$\star \quad \star \quad \star$$

Posing was more congenial. With a supermodel girlfriend, why not? Style and fashion magazines were hurrying to snag him for their covers, the more liminally wasted the better. Doherty became a popular cover boy, his mussed hair and rolled-up eyes in Imitation of Christ. And he had dandyish flair: flagrantly cool in neo mod nattiness. He was also physically striking, about six foot four, with starkly pale skin and richly black, round eyes: "full of sadness, and innocence and wonder."

A heroin chic icon for real, beautiful and self destructive, wreaking a trail of spectacular waste – a perfect cipher for fashionability.[1] He posed for the Saville Row tailor Richard James, "a handmade two-piece bespoke suit will cost around £1,800 plus VAT and a three-piece suit from £2,185 plus VAT", and in a photospread for *Esquire* in April. By October, there was an entire glossy coffee table tome, Hedi Slimane's *London: Birth Of A Style*, which while not exclusively about Doherty, was a kind of shrine to his style and influence. Slimane was a Paris based designer working for Dior and

---

[1] This was not the first time errant rock stars had posed for fashion. In 1996, Jimmy Pursey, ugly as sin and skinny as a rake, chief bootboy and broken toothed smack addict of the ancient Oi band, Sham 69, was skulking catwalks for Katherine Hamnett and Comme des Garcon. Less surprising perhaps, was that far from bad boy, Jefferson Hack signed up to face Saville Row tailors, Gieves and Hawkes, with a campaign photographed by David Bailey

fascinated by the British singer. He pictured Doherty's look as a "slim-line aesthetic, a cross between sleek and slacker, mod and 1980s punk." In an interview, Slimane declared that Doherty was, "a poet and one of the most important performers of our time".

* * *

Meanwhile, the blitz of headlines was unrelenting: HE SNORTED COCAINE THEN MADE LOVE TO ME IN THE TOILETS, KATE MOSS IS EITHER MAD OR DERANGED, I'LL KILL MYSELF: DOHERTY THREAT AS HE FACES 6TH NIGHT LOCKED UP, I'LL KICK DRUGS HABIT FOR KATE, SAYS ROCK STAR, MUTILATION, ORGIES, DRUGS: INSIDE PETE DOHERTY'S DEBAUCHED WORLD – this last effort from the *Sunday Mirror* claiming: "Wearing a tatty T-shirt daubed with Leave The Boy Alone, Doherty is barely able to stand after smoking heroin.

"[These] shocking pictures will horrify Kate's worried friends and family as they show pasty-faced Pete, 25, revelling in his role as a perverse Pied Piper – attracting girls to a run-down Bethnal Green flat in East London and seducing them.

The article continued that: "The singer and his 'muses' [groupies] would indulge in drug taking, casual sex and self-mutilation – with Doherty slashing his chest. These astonishing snaps also show, for the first time, another secret passion Pete indulged in while 'chasing the dragon' – cross-dressing.

"Dressed in a black bra, a fishnet top, mini-skirt and black tights, young girls barely out of their teens gravitate to him. They would often 'play act' for him – sometimes brandishing kitchen knives and then cavorting half-naked on his dirty bed while he mutilated himself. To them, Pete is like a god.

"A former friend said: 'Pete draws the girls in like moths to a flame.' Groupies spent days with Pete at his home – some taking drugs and some having sex. Others would take part in lesbian romps to please the singer.

"He always has girls there. I'm told they're still coming round – even since he's been with Kate Moss."

* * *

In mid-February there was a respite when someone noticed Kate's tits seemed to have got bigger: "experts were last night puzzling over how she achieved her latest growth spurt. *Sun* Fashion Editor Erica Davies said: 'It may just be a clever trick of the eye.'"

Then, bored with her tits they went for the jugular. Surely such a love could not last, it was founded on sand, the two were continually rowing …

CRACKHEAD PETE ROWS WITH KATE ... Kate Moss and her drug addict lover Pete Doherty had a bust-up during a boozy bender yesterday.

KATE FIGHT WITH HER JUNKIE EX ... Angry Kate Moss flew into a rage at her junkie ex Pete Doherty yesterday as friendly pub chat turned into a blazing row. He fled after she screamed: 'Go away, leave me alone!' in front of astonished drinkers at [a] North London local."

In *The Sun*, Tony Parsons informed us that "Kate's trousers are getting tighter as Pete's actions become more desperate. The girl has clearly moved on."

But then it seemed that wasn't true, and Tony was talking through his trousers. These were lover's tiffs overtheorised by an anxious media.

Even the hysterical arguments and physical fights witnessed by insiders, were part of the dynamic of the relationship – what held them together.

Once, after Doherty had accused Kate of flirting with a studio technician called Mike, he grabbed a pair of scissors and lopped off a hank of her hair. An observer described how: "She went berserk and was shouting abuse at him. She fled the studios in tears. It was strange thing for Pete to do – it was definitely a power thing. He snipped off her hair and she submitted to it, though she wasn't happy. It showed a little bit of his dark side."

The same source commented, "They are like two immature teenagers, constantly bickering with each other. They just row over silly, petty little things. If he uses the wrong tone of voice, she'll snap back at him. It's really immature. It's like, 'I saw you flirting with so and so last night,' and the other will reply, 'I might have been' and the first one will say, 'Really, were you?' and then it will all just kick off."

He added, "They are always slapping and hitting each other. Pete started smashing computers and she started smashing guitars. They've both swapped now. She's smashed the computers and he's smashed the guitars. I think they simply do it to wind each other up."

They needed the tension and drama. That was their spark. After all, if they wanted slippers and coco, Kate would have stayed with Jefferson Hack, and Pete gone home to his mum.

They even played at it to taunt the paparazzi. Once, returning from a holiday in Ibiza (where else?) they gleefully staged a "roadside row" on the way back from Gatwick airport, when "Pete leapt out of the model's Mercedes with his guitar and bag in moving traffic ... [and] flagged down a taxi," leaving Kate in the car. Only to rendezvous at her house.

In fact, Kate and Pete were "inseparable" – and this time the term was justified. When he went to record at the remote Twin Peaks studio in the Brecon Beacons, Kate followed him – to the desperation of his manager, who had hoped to keep his protégé clean for the sessions. Kate brought a smile and some gifts to the studio.

* * *

In mid-April Pete moved his belongings into Kate's country home. Here was the clearest indication yet, that they thought of themselves as a permanent item. The mansion was after all, the closest Kate had come to creating a real family home. While she'd spent several thousand pounds when Lila was born, building a nursery area at her London house, the entire country estate was selected and designed with Lila, and possibly other children, in mind.

Pete even got his own wing of the estate to be creative in, not in the main house, but in a detached outbuilding a few paces away, which had two connecting rooms. This he christened, "the potting shed". Here, Doherty moved in the bulk of his books and notebooks, cassettes and videos, and Tony Hancock memorabilia. And here he hung his numerous shirts on a rack and set up his guitar and amp and the Apple Mac he worked on. Parking his battered but elegant Jaguar outside, Pete was now set up to become Lord of the Manor. Kate confided to a friend that she loved mothering him, "I haven't gone as far as cooking. But I've been running around after m'lord."

* * *

She also loved fucking him. Theirs was an intensely erotic partnership: two lookers who loved to screw and the time the means and the drugs to go for it, "a veritable laboratory of pheromones and other substances".

Remarked an observer, "They are a tactile, touchy feely couple. They kiss all the time. When Kate wants some attention, she will sit on his lap and kiss him." Or she might impetuously drag him away for some "private time." Pete's manager also noted that after beginning his affair with Kate, Pete became less attentive to the band. A Babyshambles insider revealed, "When he hooked up with Kate, it got to the stage he wasn't showing up for anything. He missed shows, but she won't wake him up in the morning."

It was obsession all over again. But unlike Sorrenti, Doherty didn't know when – or how – to stop. And Kate was not inclined to tell him.

Isabel Lynne, analysing her own penchant for obsessive love in *The Guardian*, wrote: "I look at recent pictures of Kate Moss and Pete Doherty and I see a woman gripped by something that I understand … Pete inspires that kind of love in Kate – that's obvious. She loves his madness and his badness; she loves the way he made her feel that the two of them were united against everyone else, against all the things that convention and society demanded of them. So what if it lost her some modelling contracts? She and Pete lived life only on their own breakneck terms. In loving each other, they had found pure and truthful love, even if it alienated her from the things that formed the substance and stuffing of life: her family, her friends, her work . . ."

This was the amour fou lauded by the surrealists as the only truly revolutionary act, the most powerful – because irrational and taboo smashing, addiction of all.

* * *

There were not many men Kate could admire, but rock stars were her weakness. To the point that she became a notorious fixture backstage. She was humiliatingly rejected by the Franz Ferdinand star, Alex Kapranos, who turfed her out of his dressing room saying that he wanted to concentrate on his music. She was also spurned by Kasabian singer, Serge Pizzorno, and by Sam Endicott, lead singer with The Bravery who, ignoring a note she'd sent him backstage, sneaked out of the venue without alerting her.

But Doherty was available – a man who fashioned himself as the very archetype of rock stardom. Endorsed by that other wild man and ex Primrose Hill Setter, Liam Gallagher, "There is only one British hero right now, Pete Doherty. He lives the rock 'n' roll life. He has understood everything about that side of things. He doesn't give a monkey's about anything; he does exactly what he wants to do. I admire his decadence. I completely recognise myself in him."

But he was also a romantic, who used his way with words to charm and woo. An early lover recalled how he would make up stories about the swans in St James Park for her, and read her his love poems. And how "He cried after we first had sex as he said he was so happy. The next morning he was running around like a little boy making me toast and tea and prancing around the flat in his dressing gown and slippers. He told me he hadn't slept with many girls and that he felt inexperienced." She added, "Pete had a nice body, but he wasn't toned. It was his mind and his boyish face I was more attracted to."

That boyishness and sweetness, mixed with the craziness and debauchery was what Kate craved. And what she chose.

People often misunderstood or underrated the element of choice. As if she was an ingénue corrupted. Paul Vallely in *The Independent* thought that, "In Doherty's slipstream, Moss has been pulled into a classic vortex of drugs and rock'n'roll."You could reverse that equation and it would be as true and as false.

★   ★   ★

More than any other question you heard, especially from women bemused by their relationship, was: "what does she see in him?" Kate's friends and family wondered the same. Warnings were uttered. Even her normally compliant mother, Linda, fretted out loud. Despite all the good advice – or more likely, because of it, the relationship developed and intensified.

This was the most worthwhile thing for her since Depp. Doherty moreover, was a Depp whose background chimed with hers: the siren from Sanderstead found reality in the arms of the wrecker from Hexham who had references she was comfortable with: an ex choirboy who once authored a QPR fanzine, *All Quiet On The Western Avenue*, who grew up with *Neighbours* and Madness, who knew the jokes about Cliff Richard and Sam Fox.

Doherty was "mad, bad, and dangerous to know" – a phrase coined for Byron. And like Lord Byron, Doherty was a rootless wanderer, reckless hedonist, drugged seer, dashing and chameleon, into dangerous substances and dangerous ideas and dangerous liaisons. All Doherty lacked was a club foot and a peerage, but then he had a disabling drug habit and a rock and roll pedigree back to Depp's hero, Iggy Pop.

★   ★   ★

So they got married. Not really. A pretend marriage at Glastonbury that June.

Kate was in her element at this festival. She loved the mystic vibe, the crowds, the boozing and bopping. And that year, Shane McGowan was there to notch up the hellraising.

An observer of the group recorded: "Pete, Shane, Victoria [McGowan's girlfriend] and Kate took up residence in the bar at the Clarence before Pete was due to play the ball. Because the ball goes on until 5am and Pete was the headline act, they had plenty of time to kill before he went on stage. Unfortunately for Pete he couldn't quite keep up with Shane's legendary drinking habits which caused a bit of friction within his own band."

By the time he went on stage, Doherty was so out of it he forgot the words to one song and then hurled a beer can into the audience. This began an argy bargy on stage, whereupon the lead guitarist stormed off and refused to return. Undeterred, Doherty picked up a guitar and completed the set, cheered on by Kate and Co from the side of the stage.

Kate and Pete afterwards betrothed themselves at the Glastonbury festival attraction, The Chapel of Love and Loathing in Lost Vagueness, which conducts spoof weddings and divorces behind its corrugated iron door. The marriage, only "valid" on the Glastonbury grounds and for one day, delighted Pete. Kate later underlined her commitment by writing "I love you baby" over her body with a biro pen. Then they celebrated at a party given by the fashion company, Diesel. Unusually forthcoming, Kate confided, "I love him very much. He's a really great guy and we get on so well. Everything is just perfect. I'm really happy with everything and I want to be with him."

★   ★   ★

This was also the Glastonbury of the famous "hotpants"[1] that Kate so stylishly wore. These pants, the object of much admiration for their boho flair, which feature in dozens, maybe hundreds of paparazzi shots, and became her trademark look, revived in the Virgin mobile ads, deserve consideration.

★   ★   ★

The Sun announced that "Glastonbury, 2005, will be remembered as the year of mud, Kate Moss's hotpants and Coldplay's touching tribute to Kylie Minogue." These hotpants were, in reality, buttoned male underpants. The garment suited Kate's relaxed look and set off her legs. Their provenance also highlighted her louche bricoleur's flair: a cheekily androgynous appropriation of the old man's lingerie.

Kate wore these pants trudging the Glastonbury mud in wellies, arm in arm with Pete that summer. *The Birmingham Post*, and several other observers, mistook – or transformed, them into "tiny tweed hot pants", which sounds more refined than plain grey underpants – though from a distance or photo they might pass for couture.

The Mirror, closer up, noticed she'd worn the same "grubby pants" for

---

[1] Luckily, the alleged pants were saved by a quirk of fate, by a party who wants to be anonymous. There is of course, no certificate of provenance and I only have it on the word of that party – and the situation they were presented to me – that they are authentic. However, I believe them to be so. They were presented with a discarded corset, which I also analysed, but we should dwell here on the pants, which provide a richer source of material than the corset.

several days. "Yesterday the 31-year-old model went to the newsagent to stock up on fags and chewing gum in the same pair of micro-hot pants she'd worn all weekend." London's *Evening Standard* had "Kate Moss apparently modelling incontinence pants." (The *Standard* gets the prize.)

★ ★ ★

These were not designer briefs. They were cheap and cheerfully mass produced. The label read: "Medium, 33-35in, 84-89cm, 77% Cotton, 23% Polyester, Style No 807754.[2] There was no logo or other manufacturer identification. Was the maker tag removed to avoid an endorsement issue?

Their condition corresponded with the *Mirror* observation that they'd been worn over several days. Their general condition, and what Gary my photographer thought were "skidmarks", suggested, pace Jefferson Hack's opening line to his future lover, that our Kate may be a bit of a crusty.

But the most striking feature of the pants was that at some point the buttoned crotch had been shredded – razored or scissored or otherwise sliced, into strips. For what reason? Was this an erotic ritual? Had Doherty been so impatient to get inside her pants that he ripped them open? Or had Edward Scissorhands passed by as Kate slumbered? Or maybe it was a fashion experiment, a deconstruction ...

But these Glastonbury pants, or the traces of the supermodel's body they had absorbed, may have enabled me to have samples of her mitochondrial DNA extracted. Analysed at a Cambridge laboratory, this mtDNA might have revealed that Kate's mother clan – or haplogroup – is H, and she is therefore descended from the female genetic tree whose common ancestral mother has been named "Helena". Helena lived in the Pyrenees area about 20,000 years ago. As the ice age retreated, her descendents began trekking into Europe and the Helena clan eventually reached Germany and then moved to Norway and Scotland – and eventually south to Sanderstead. A map of matching mtDNA clusters could indicate that Kate's mtDNA ancestors extend as far as Russia, but are mostly clustered in Scotland, Normandy and Western Germany.[3]

★ ★ ★

[2] Googling the product number reveals only that this is also the product number assigned by marine specialists, Stem to Stern, to a "MER10-807754 [SCREW @5], priced at $0.50."

[3] Information from Genetic Ancestor (Roots for Real), with thanks to Gilly Booth and Dr. Peter Forster.

161

Not long after Glastonbury, came a forewarning of what was soon to come. Maybe it was Pete's paranoia, but he alleged that "I found a bug and a hidden camera in my home." He added, "I'm investigating."

Certainly, by that time, the Kate and Pete saga had become so irresistible, such a provider of what paparazzi call "money shots," that the media was up for anything. This anything was helped by the fact that Pete himself would borrow money from paparazzi and would also – for a fee – fix up scenes for them to stumble across.

Thus the many happy accidents when camera snoopers knew in advance just when Kate and Pete would turn up at a club or at Kate's home. At these assignations Pete would often photogenically entwine himself with his lover, or grasp her hand meaningfully, or they might pause for a lingering snog. Pete even sold phone cam pictures he'd taken of them amorously mucking about to the tabloids – which resulted in a row with Kate.

It also seems that at an early point some paparazzi – a foreign group possibly – had rigged the garden in St John's Wood, and possibly the interior too, with remote controlled surveillance cams. A nondescript white van with its back window curtained was sometimes parked nearby. Inside this van was a paparazzi spotter, with a laptop wirelessly connected to the cams. When things looked like they could get attention-grabbing another white van would appear, this one rather smarter. A man with a camera would then emerge just at the right time …

* * *

In early June, Kate received a "fashion Oscar" from the Council of Fashion Designers of America (CFDA). The award recognised her contribution to couture and street style, especially her espousal of boho chic: "Kate was doing it [before Sienna Miller]. The way she dresses shapes what women buy and how they want to look." Speaking for the CFDA, Peter Arnold said, "It [boho] happened after Kate started us all thinking in her spontaneous way. She's not just about looking great on the red carpet. Kate is about looking great on her way to the supermarket while at the same time looking as if she didn't give whatever she is wearing any thought."

The Americans also enthused about how unspoilt she was, how she had kept her personality private and her private life a mystery, and about her "cockney accent" – actually an affectation of "Sarf London" – a conscious shift from the Home Counties drawl of her father.

Women's Wear Daily lambasted the awards for dire repartee and poor speeches. "Catherine Deneuve, who presented *Elle's* Gilles Bensimon with the Eugenia Sheppard Award, proved that a great actress does not make a great public speaker. Deneuve, not one to ad-lib, struggled to read the teleprompter and seemed lost at one point. "I am sorry, Gilles," she said. "I could have done better, but I am confused."

However, the reporter conceded that, "Kate Moss, for her part, offered one of the evening's most succinct speeches. Leaning on the podium and grasping her statue, she whispered: 'I'd like to thank the CFDA for this award, and all the people I have had the chance to work with.' Then she was off."

She was also, according to *Vanity Fair*, off her face: "The only flaw in the evening was that when Moss got to the podium to accept the award she was so wasted, according to one designer, she could barely say "C.F.D.A." Which may have accounted for the succinctness of her address.

* * *

Kate had worn "a nude-coloured strapless corset dress with a black lace overlay" to the glittering gala, which glittered all the more for being under-written by Swarovski, the crystal people, who'd commissioned a design "to incorporate their glamorous crystals into a dramatic 'Magic Mirror' that had a live video-feed of the red carpet arrivals beamed into Astor Hall."

As well as a cocktail reception there was dinner in the Celeste Bartos Forum of the venue (The New York Public Library), cheffed by Balthazar of Paris. Come evening, the venue transformed into a "modern-day 'supper club' with Tony Okungbowa, the energetic DJ from 'The Ellen Degeneres Show.'" Plus lots of other stuff.

All a bit different from what Pete and Kate usually rocked to.

* * *

Doherty's next big outing was the Live 8 concert. The handsome young bisexual had caught the eye of Sir Elton John and was invited to duet. Again, Pete proved the worse for wear at this festival of the celebritariat. The boy turned up demolished and "could hardly open his eyes". Lurching on stage with what appeared to be a cigarette lighter in his mouth he forgot the words to T-Rex's 'Children Of The Revolution' and was booed by the crowd.

Not only did Doherty sully Sir Bob's Big Day, he had the nerve to blame Bob's daughter Peaches. He alleged the pretty young thing had put him off his stride by squeezing his bum backstage. Maybe there was a subliminal message to Geldof somewhere in the allegation: arses, charity, daughters of the revolution …

* * *

Pete was more at ease appearing with Kate in July at the Paris launch for the Dior Men's Spring/Summer Collection for 2006, designed by the same Heidi Slimane who celebrated Doherty chic in, *London: Birth Of A Style*.

Kate arrived in a slinky black dress and chatted with Sir Elton and his future husband, David Furnish – the Live 8 fiasco forgiven. Slimane had organized two Eurostar carriages to fetch over Kate and Doherty and a considerable entourage. Slimane dedicated his catwalk show to "Doherty, London and the Mods." His models paraded on the runway in "pork pie hats, white shirts, skinny trousers and black skinny ties."

Not everyone was awed. The veteran fashion critic Suzy Menckes, grumbled in the *International Herald Tribune* that: "Leaving aside Kate Moss and her wild rock star boy friend Pete Doherty, it was difficult to think of any likely coupling between the skinny back-to-the-Mods boys at Dior Homme and any typically stylish woman. Least of all did this assertive music scene male from designer Hedi Slimane seem to have any connection with the grand romance of the Dior couture show on the following day."

Later, at a party in Monmartre, Doherty and Babyshambles sang 'Happy Birthday' to celebrate the rebirth of London style. The party mood was spoiled for Doherty however, when Kate began dancing with Jefferson Hack, who'd also been invited.

Pete began sulking jealously and the couple made a spectacle of themselves on the returning Eurostar. Kate threw a glass of champagne over Doherty and in the ensuing fracas his T-shirt was ripped and his hands were cut. An observer noted, "It just erupted out of nowhere. Kate stormed out of the carriage and then Pete disappeared with blood all over his face." When they disembarked at Waterloo Station, Kate pursued her lover along the platform, yelling, "wanker!"

This particular row had a knock on effect on Doherty's career. So intense and time consuming was it, raging through the chunell and up to Kate's doorstep, that he forgot he was supposed to be opening with Babyshambles at an Oasis gig that night, to kick off a UK tour. Oasis, themselves legendary for dodging appearances, were not amused and scratched Babyshambles from the menu, replacing them with The Zutons.

* * *

Doherty was now a legend with international reach and hidden depths. On July 30th, the *Hindustan Times* reported that, "Pete Doherty has vowed to become a born-again Christian after he sought life-coaching from his

British soccer hero, Dennis Bailey." They quoted our Pete, "I had been to Sunday school, and that, but when I wrote to him [Bailey, not God] he wrote back and told me I should be looking at the Bible, and I opened it up to the Book of Genesis."

*   *   *

The illumination didn't last long. The next sensation was KATE'S JUNKIE LOVER SLASHES HIMSELF WITH BROKEN GLASS, referring to scenes recorded by a "startled" TV camera crew making a documentary about the singer, *Who The Fuck Is Pete Doherty?*

"It was very disturbing," said a film-maker. "Pete was in a highly agitated state and frenziedly attacked the cameraman several times. Then he dragged a shard of smashed beer bottle deeply down the middle of his chest and started to play with the river of blood that flowed down. It seemed to calm him down. Like it was a relief." A newspaper report called it, "a shocking act of self-mutilation that reveals a man on the brink of madness." The Samaritans protested it might incite young people to self-harm. The scenes were later cut from the film.

*   *   *

It was only rock and roll, but we liked it. As with the next sensation, when following another row with Kate – it was the Eurostar ruckus rumbling on – Doherty smashed his guitar up and set fire to his own bed, but not while he was in it. This "cry for help" was answered by the supermodel, and they were soon together again, "canoodling" at her country home and strolling in Primrose Hill Park, with Pete tucking into a bag of chips.

*   *   *

August saw Kate in full frontal display in *i-D* magazine, celebrating the mag's 25th anniversary. Meanwhile, Doherty and a friend got arrested and fined for trying to smuggle class A drugs (1.7g of crack cocaine and 1.5g of heroin) into Norway at the start of a tour. "It will not go to court as they accepted their fines but it will be registered as a criminal offence in Norway," said an irate Norwegian. By now the clock was ticking. More partying followed. Kate's career continued to flourish …

The Rio de Janeiro-based jeweller, H. Stern, used her as their new face, to shift their image from *Breakfast At Tiffany's* to "a more urban, fashion-savvy" consumer. The campaign had been shot that June by Rankin. It featured "a gilded, sinewy Moss in a shadowed background dripping in multiple rings, bracelets and long gold and crystal necklaces from the company's Golden Stones and Stars collections."

"She's an opinion leader," pronounced Stern's CEO. "She will attract people who aren't currently our customers and she brings edginess to the campaign."

★ ★ ★

The partying continued, as did the rows. Caught with a flat tire one night Doherty asked two passers by to change his wheel, and while they laboured opened his heart. "It's a nightmare because I'm always trying to please her but I keep making mistakes. And then we'll be arguing about something or other. But she's a lovely girl, she's the one for me. No matter what people say, we're gonna be together."

More parties. Kate and Pete turned up at one and cuddled in a corner all night, giggling and sharing a pipe. Or they snogged in the street en route to a night in, with Pete heaving a six pack of Stella. Said an onlooker, "It may be a stormy relationship but they were all over each other."

Late August, H Stern, pleased with results so far, announced fresh images forthcoming from Rankin. These were to "showcase Kate Moss with a sparkling golden skin, as if she were a jewel herself."

★ ★ ★

Then Kate flew off without Pete for a holiday in – you guessed it, Ibiza. Here, it was observed that she indulged in a marathon session of "partying" that went on for 18 hours non stop. She was snapped taking pot shots at tin cans with an air rifle while "cackling with laughter" and "nursing a gin and lemon". Then back to London. Tick tock …

Nowadays the chatter tended to focus on how, with such a lifestyle she managed to look so good. What was her secret? Maybe it was the 40 litres of bottled Evian water she was having delivered every day to her London home, presumably to bathe in. (NB: The well known story about Kate and Johnny Depp filling a bath with champagne in a London hotel, only to have the plug pulled by a chambermaid who thought it was just dirty bath water, was denied by Kate as absurd.) Meanwhile, Pete was holding his own in the headline stakes by throwing beer over his ex-girlfriend, Katie Lewis at the Reading Festival, and 24 hours later, headbutting his ex-bandmate Johnny Burrell (Razorlight), at the Leeds festival.

In early September, a few hours after "partying with junkie boyfriend Pete Doherty, Sadie Frost and Jade Jagger" Kate was up in the morning doing a shoot in St John's Square. "You'd never have guessed she'd had a big party the night before. She looked flawless. Whoever applied her slap is highly skilled."

★ ★ ★

Then Kate went home to her country house. She chilled out and had pizzas sent round. She told Dolly, her housekeeper, that she would be away for some time. Then drove back to London.

When she packed that day and got into her Range Rover she would have been surprised to know it would be the last time she would see her idyllic country home for many months.

★ ★ ★

That September, it was announced that Doherty and Kate had recorded a duet, 'La Belle Et La Bete' ('Beauty And The Beast') which would be given away free in a forthcoming edition of French *Vogue* which Kate had been asked to guest edit. It looked like her dreams of rock stardom might come to something. Then, on the evening of 6th September Kate went, as usual, to the Babyshambles session at Metroplis Studios in Chiswick, where Doherty was recording his new Babyshambles album. The gang was all there …

ACT FIVE:

The Media Blitzkrieg

"It's all fake. I'm all fake."
- Kate Moss, after a stylist accidentally dislodged a hair extension

"A lot of what the British tabloids print is just fiction, you know."
- Kate Moss

"The press! They pump you up and make this whole big deal of you, and as soon as you're up there they pull you down. Yet it still hurts if they say horrible things about you, even if it's lies. Fame definitely takes away your freedom."
- Kate Moss

Earlier that year, Kate Moss had done a pretty silly thing. She sued the *Sunday Mirror*. This was over an article, KATE IN COCAINE COMA. It alleged that at the 2001 Nelson Mandela charity event in Barcelona, Kate had taken so much cocaine she'd passed out in a drug induced coma. She won "substantial" but undisclosed damages and a public apology from the *Sunday Mirror*. However, this appears to have been the writ that broke the fragile pact observed by the media around Kate's appetite for the fast lane.

She was maybe emboldened by her litigation record. Back in 1994, she had a writ issued against Perrier UK, because they used an editorial picture of her on the catwalk at Bella Freud's 1993 show. Dressed in a pink fringed black bikini, Kate was swigging a bottle of Vittel water. The image was used as implied endorsement of Vittel. The 20-year-old's pique over this came possibly from Storm. It seems the agency had arranged for Kate to judge a modelling contest, Face of '94, underwritten by the rival beverage, Highland Spring. Following tongue in cheek reporting of the incident, Kate averted a possible conflict by failing to show.[1]

In 1997, Storm, along with Kate's new lawyer Gerrard Tyrrell, of Harbottle & Lewis, weighed in against an "unauthorised" poster campaign by satellite TV station, UK Living – "TV with a mind of its own". The posters wondered, "Wouldn't it be great if Kate Moss were fat?" They were meant to foreground a debate about the unrepresentative shape and size of models in general. Alerted to Kate's displeasure, Lisa Howell, the managing director of UK Living said: "We are sorry if Kate Moss is upset about this poster. We never meant to offend her but do think it is important to continue the debate about having more models that reflect the different size of women." The key point here, was whether the image was in the public domain. There was also the question of public interest.

Then, in 2001, Kate won an action for libel against the *Daily Mail* for an article published in 1999, alleging she'd turned up to a photoshoot incapacitated by drink or drugs. Acting for the supermodel, Gerrard Tyrrell thundered in the High Court that the allegation was "false and completely unfounded". The *Mail* accepted they'd been wrong and "apologized unreservedly for any distress and injury caused to Moss". An "undisclosed sum" was paid. When the settlement was announced, Kate was at the Cannes film festival, exciting the paparazzi in "a white three-quarter length fur style coat and green high-heeled shoes."

★   ★   ★

Gerrard Tyrrell's costume was more sombre. He was by that time reckoned the leading libel specialist at Harbottle & Lewis, a law firm specialising in celeb sports and pop clients like Robbie Williams and Sir Richard Branson.

Tyrrell also had Establishment pedigree. His work for the Queen's Golden Jubilee celebrations led to membership of the Royal Victorian Order for "personal services to the Sovereign". This entitled him to wear a medal (in shape, reminiscent of the German iron cross) with a blue ribbon edged white and red. (Not quite as sartorial as higher ranking members, who sported mantles that, in their asymmetric cut, piercing colour and

---

[1] That case followed a rash of similar controversies over the use of images of the golfer, Nick Faldo, footballer, Vinny Jones, and Baroness Thatcher.

layered flounces had the fruity sophistication of mid period Vivienne Westwood.) Tyrrell also acts for Prince Charles, and is sometimes described as Charles' "personal solicitor".

Harbottle & Lewis have been involved in many high profile cases, and with enviable success. One such was a dispute over the authorship of the BBC TV children's series *Bill And Ben*.

A core issue here, revolved around the provenance of the celebrated catchword, "flobbadob". One of the disputants claimed rights to the series by declaring that "flobbadob" "was invented by him and his brother to describe the sound they made when they broke wind in the bath." During the case, Tyrrell sent a letter to *The Independent On Sunday* explaining: "The only similarity with [his client] Freda Lingstrom's creations were the names Bill and Ben. The stories do not involve flowerpot men, a garden, a gardener, weed, made-up language or anything else that anyone would associate with the flowerpot men ... The word flobbodob [sic]... does not appear."

The word "cocaine" however, figured hugely in what the *Sunday Mirror* had trumpeted as an exposé. They were essentially suggesting what was axiomatic in media circles, that Kate, like many other models, was a habitual user of the drug. But the *Mirror* got the details of this incident wrong, and that did for them. Even so, one of Kate's wiser friends, the Hong Kong businessman David Tang, one of those in her circle immune to "partying", had urged her not to take that legal action. Perhaps he foresaw trouble. Whether Tyrrell or Sarah Doukas also had misgivings on Kate's behalf is not known. Maybe they did not know, or had been misinformed, about the context.

* * *

It was evident by 2004, and especially after her 30th birthday party, that Kate's high wire act between public "edginess" and private delirium might result in a prat fall. This possibility well antedated Doherty. The contradictions she navigated were remarkable. You needed to be a juggler to keep all those roles in the air, one moment a corporate "face" filling a city's billboards, the next lining up candy cane with a dexterity that earned her the nickname of "the conjurer", then swanking around celebrity galas, then glaring at paparazzi as she filled her car with petrol, the next moment signing off the accounts of Skate Enterprises – and all the while conducting so many intricate and interwoven relationships.

These contradictions were evoked in a typically fatuous outburst from Tracey Emin, "Kate was holding every bloody thing together until that stupid film came out". But only just. And for how long? With Doherty, a new and eventually calamitous set of factors appeared. But the feud with the *Mirror* was begun in an already explosive environment.

* * *

In general, Kate had benefited from a perception among journalists that she was off limits – not so much because of her formidable legal eagle or her millions, but because she was "a nice girl" – a breezy and likeable wench, who was, after all, no more debauched than many a Fleet Street Jasper Milvain.

Writing in *The Times*, India Knight pointed out that: "The most astonishing thing about the whole Kate Moss debacle is that there is one reason and one reason only that explains why the veritable avalanche of stories about Moss's various impressive addictions didn't surface earlier. Everyone even tangentially involved in London's fashion/media/showbiz circles knew for years about the sex, the drugs, and the general wildness, which were euphemistically referred to as 'partying', but nobody blabbed. This is unusual."

Knight speculated the reason for this was simply, "Because she's beautiful and wears nice clothes."

In other words, almost everyone had an affable crush on her. Kate Moss was Barbara Windsor and Vera Lynn and even Kate Bush. A national treasure.

* * *

What's more, Kate rarely played the celeb game with the grotesquery of say, Victoria Beckham, whose Simian smirk alerted us to her fame as often as possible. Nor did she cultivate anything like the omnipresent garrulity of Madonna, who'd been stalking the planet and intruding on our privacy with unsolicited intimacies for over 20 years – assisted by a global PR apparatus that stalkers can only fantasise about. Indeed, Kate famously said, "I don't do interviews," and she rarely did. It was a source of wonder that most people had never heard her voice (for the record, it's more squeaky budgie than Twiggy's "demented parrot".)

Apart from the Fidel Castro farce and appearing as a finger clicker in a Make Poverty History ad, Kate also steered clear of the infiltration of politics by celebrity. You could hardly imagine her angsting like Angelina Jolie about the fate of orphans, or jetting to summits like Saints Bono and Geldof. Ibiza was more her scene, and she got high on Charlie rather than the Almighty.

But on the other hand, she knew what she was for – not to model garments but to be famous in them. And when it suited her she let morsels drop. And though she turned down *Hello!* and *OK!* she was preparing a turnaround in the December issue of French *Vogue* – till she went awol as guest editor on account of jetting to rehab, and the contents had to be trimmed.

Fashionweek daily.com cited *Vogue* editor-in-chief Carine Roitfeld: "Kate has always been very discreet. She never talks about herself or shows photos of her house, daughter, or car." The piece continued, "Which is precisely why this issue was to be so groundbreaking: Moss was set to give everything to the magazine. They, in turn, would be getting the exclusive into Moss' life."

* * *

The one-time editor of the *Daily Mirror*, Piers Morgan, defined celebrity as the public exploitation of one's private life. This, he suggested, made such exploiters fair game for curiosity and investigation.

At the time Morgan was fronting a rather limp *Mirror* campaign "against" celebrity. This involved outing Naomi Campbell as a cokehead in a case that then rebounded on the *Mirror*. Morgan may have stayed up all night polishing his riposte: "This is a very good day for lying drug-abusing prima donnas who want to have their cake with the media, and the right to then shamelessly guzzle it with their Cristal champagne."

But there were not many such excitements. Maybe because Morgan himself – as witness his autobiography, *The Insider*, is an accomplished groupie who never fails to be delighted if his hand touches the hand that once touched … What's more, Morgan – like many other red blooded red toppers, had a thing about Kate Moss. According to *Vanity Fair*, even Gerrard Tyrrell affirmed that Kate had always enjoyed a "pretty frank relationship with the *Daily Mirror*".

After Morgan was ejected from his editorial seat with max velocity following the fake Iraq atrocity pictures debacle, he was replaced by Richard Wallace. Wallace's remit was to halt a dire sales decline. A traditional show biz reporter, he cut down on Morgan's anti Iraq war stories, and junked the anti celeb angle. That meant the *Mirror* was hungrier than ever for celeb goodies. Commented a colleague, "Richard's just a straightforward newsman. He's got a good eye for a story. He's got a tendency towards the light and trite and frothy – the kind of stuff that sells newspapers." And Wallace held no candle for Kate Moss.

* * *

The Doherty carnival had created a chink in Kate's armour. It was easier to penetrate the circle of cash starved druggies around Doherty than the millionaire altitudes and attitudes of Primrose Hill. Wallace assigned one of his best reporters, Stephen Moyes, to the case.

Moyes had already covered several drug/celeb stories, including the substance shenanigans surrounding the lachrymose TV presenter Michael Barrymore, and "the cocaine-fuelled sex sessions with hooker Caroline Martin" of the hapless TV compere, Angus Deaton. For the Kate Moss case, Moyes went undercover, hanging out with the Babyshambles crew: dealers, groupies, musicians … offering money, and then more money …

★   ★   ★

At the time, Doherty was recording the Babyshambles album, *Down In Albion*. This was a suitably shambolic operation, requiring incessant comings and goings in the studio, unexpected noises off, and sudden exhaustion.

The master of ceremonies was Mick Jones, whose "shockingly unfinished" production exploited the studio ambiance. Explaining the album's abrupt finale, Jones described Doherty: "He goes off into another room, still singing. He's wandered off looking for something – I think it was a lighter – and you hear him fall over a music stand. So we left it in, and that's how the album ends. In fact, he stayed there for about an hour. Someone gave him a guitar and we carried on recording."

This method created bad blood between Jones and Doherty's long suffering manager, James Mullord. Mullord recalled how, "I said, 'Mick, clearly you like a very raw and natural production style, whereas your albums, as a member of The Clash, other than the first one, were nicely and relatively well produced and refined. How did you resolve that at the time?' He just looked at me and walked off and the next day said, 'How the fuck do you dare question me? Who do you think you are?' I said, 'Mick, I'm just asking a question …'"

Meanwhile, probably unknown to Stephen Moyes, Mullord had bought audio surveillance equipment two weeks before the sting. It's not known whether he also bought surveillance cams. Nor is it clear whether any surveillance equipment was actually rigged up by him.

By his own account, Mullord had become frustrated and alarmed at the dealing and associated conduct during the sessions. Perhaps he wanted photographic proof that his own hands were clean. In any event, Mullord has always denied he had anything to do with the incriminating footage. There is nothing to suggest that he is not telling the truth.[1]

* * *

Moyes' patience paid off when he was approached – apparently by one of the two alleged dealers who serviced the sessions, with the infamous phone cam video. Whoever it was took the footage, and the *Mirror* has always been coy on that, he got rich quick. It's been rumoured the images fetched £750,000. (Another tabloid source affirms it was nearer a million, and that the *Mirror* recouped its outlay in a week.)

* * *

"The light of the public darkens everything."
- Martin Heidegger

* * *

The story broke on the 15th September, and Kate Moss came crashing down. *The Mirror*'s entire front page screeched "COCAINE KATE… Supermodel Kate Moss snorts line after line. Exclusive. More amazing pictures inside …"

The pictures on that cover and across four inside pages were indeed, amazing. They instantly redefined Kate Moss. They repositioned fashion and made a monkey of fashion photography. They flaunted what was formerly forbidden. They had that furtive and glassy look of the true exposé: a secret vice spectacularly gone public. They encapsulated what Jean Baudrillard called the Ob-cene: "where there is no more spectacle, no more scene, when all becomes transparence and immediate visibility, when everything is exposed to the harsh and inexorable light of information and communication" – a primal scene witnessed through the media's totalitarian lucidity.

---

[1] This theme of surveillance in the Babyshambles camp is an intriguing one. It also seems that Doherty, as well as extensively recording his life in diary and note form, sometimes covertly recorded his gigs and other activities. For example, I've heard a cassette recording apparently made by him of the aftermath of a Babyshambles concert in Brighton. This 90 minute tape seems to have been made with a concealed tape recorder. It features Doherty and friends driving to a beach to meet people who engage in an ambiguous transaction with the Babyshambles party. Pete and Co also have a takeaway in the car and several protracted conversations. We also hear several phone calls being made, one by Doherty, apparently to Kate Moss. I'm unable to say whether this recording is an accidental one-off.

Better than that, what the pictures depicted was downright illegal. Here was the supermodel, fresh from her victory in the courts, giggling and chattering as she dexterously chopped lines of coke with a credit card on a plastic CD cover ... handing the stuff out to members of the entourage ... snorting the arguably enormous quantity of five lines in 40 minutes through a rolled up fiver ...

These images of Kate Moss completed a perverse circle from Corinne Day's first pictures. They were as intrusive and raw. They stripped her privacy as once Day and Sorrenti had dispensed with her modesty. The collective gaze that once lacerated her flesh now scored her in her lair.

Here was Kate, luscious in hotpants, long legs curved into snazzy boots, with a look of studious facility as her fingers went at the business – a complacent composure, as if she'd done this so often she now daydreamed with that seraphic smirk smokers have when the flame touches the fag and they draw ... or like mum pouring tea and passing round a tray of meringues ... "one lump or two?" Only on the tape Kate is asking who wants a line and calling over to Mick Jones to come and get his sniff.

* * *

The hunt for the definitive fashion scenario ends here. Forget moody tundra, orgies in incinerated apartments or scenes of violent crime: police tape – Beretta – Vuitton handbag ... This was the real scene of a real crime, enacted by a real supermodel, gaped at by the world. What is the supermodel endorsing here? What is the product?

It is Kate Moss: sassy savvy naughty ... what a cool bitch, what a fucking nerve, and look at those legs!

* * *

The video also recalls Warhol in its unscripted prattle and abject aesthetic – emphasised by the wild framing. But the garish unreality of Warhol's partying universe is superseded – his Polaroid mug shots and pixellated screenprints, the studied longueurs of Couch or Chelsea Girls, are fussy by comparison. They suggest distance and refinement, the art dealer rather than the cocaine dealer.

Equally, the pixilation in the Cocaine Kate pictures is so extreme it is almost the subject itself: we see through a fog of congealed inhibition, which increases our pleasure and intrigue. Here is the nightmare imagined by David Blunkett, the blind Home Secretary who criminalised voyeurism.

Only in Britain could scopophobia stumble into legislation. But just as British was the prurience that hatched and then relished this visible catastrophe of Kate Moss through a disintegrating fuzz – the contrary of Helmut Newton's hard-edged hardcore, but more vicious and unsettling, because there was no artistic agenda, only this white noise looping: desire for desire itself.

* * *

The only other celebrity pictures that have the eerie potency of Cocaine Kate are ones that were once genuinely forbidden, the ultimate paparazzi snaps of the ultimate celebrity: Diana bleeding to death in the wreckage of that Mercedes in a tunnel underneath the streets of Paris, images censored for seven years. Until, of course, they surfaced and CBS screened them on prime time TV.

Because the other lesson of such images – or the strategy that underlies them, a lesson Kate and her entourage should have thought about, is that the logic of celebrity obsession – where paparazzi and stalkers commune through voyeurism – is to exceed all boundaries, to erode all limits and exploit all constraints. Until the next outrage …

* * *

The images that flashed round the globe from the 15th September certainly weren't from a fixed surveillance cam. Rather they were taken by someone moving erratically around the studio. That seems to rule out Mullord who was not there at the time.

The manager however, was instantly blamed by Doherty's entourage, with Jones' wife Miranda Davis – according to Mullord, accusing him by text message while he was in Paris: "I would never lower myself to the likes of you! Looser! [sic]" "Don't think you will enjoy Paris." "You should be ashamed of yourself you even double crossed mick! And Pete! Cant help but think u r capable of anything …" When Mullord protested innocence, a fourth message shot back: "… he who doth protest too much … i rest my case!"

* * *

The Mirror had held on to the pictures for a week before publishing them – no doubt there were contractual niceties. When they hit, Kate was in New York with Pete.

Her reaction seems to have been confused. She was woken early that morning and warned by Storm of the gravity of what was implied. Doukas recalled, "I called Kate immediately. She was gutted, absolutely devastated. I read it over the phone to her and the avalanche started almost immediately."

But a source close to her mother says that Kate told Linda she was not particularly bothered. Some of the press too, reported her first instinct was glee – these images might make her even more famous and kickstart a pop career. And anyway, who cared? – everyone took the stuff. Doherty also took it lightly, "Everyone knows you do it anyway." Kate seemed most exercised by the "betrayal" and intent on finding the culprit – which was, of course, beside the point.

Next day, when approached by a *Mirror* reporter, she was rattled but defiant. She shouted, "Fuck off! Fuck off! Fuck off! Fuck off! Just fuck off!"

She'd gone to New York to model in a session for the November issue of *W* magazine, shot by Mario Sorrenti. When the ex-lovers tried for a *tête-à-tête* in SoHo's Omen restaurant, Sorrenti was astounded by the vigour of the press pack: "It was like rats over the garbage. She got pushed and shoved. So did I."

★   ★   ★

The press frenzy now also turned on the brands she represented. For every brand that might ditch her there would be oodles of copy, fresh opportunities to couple the magic formula "Kate Moss" with "disgrace" "cocaine" "Chanel"…

Most of the brands seemed nonplussed. Bizarrely perhaps, given what they must have known about Kate's not exactly private life, they were unprepared. They dithered and prevaricated.

But the *Mirror* scoop had opened the vaults of the tabloids, in which many a juicy tale had been lurking, untold, sometimes for years. It was open season on Kate Moss.

★   ★   ★

On the 16th, *The Sun*'s front page attacked with "KATE'S £200 A DAY COKE HABIT. Inside, the story was headed, "KATE Moss is blowing £200 every day on cocaine – snorting the drug morning, noon and night."

It quoted "a pal": "She'll get up at 6am and she'll do a line before she goes and does a job." *The Sun* ranted that the supermodel: "regularly swills the drug down with champagne and vodka and once stayed awake for THREE DAYS on a mega binge in Ibiza."

A picture showed a distressed looking Kate. An inset featured: "Mum fury over Pete," "Linda Moss … rolled her eyes in fury at the mere mention of Doherty's name. Asked if she thought he was bad news, she snapped, 'Tell me about it!'"

There was more bad news that day when *The Mirror* followed up its story with a transcript of the video. This included a dialogue that shed new light on the Mossy posse. As Kate was snorting through a rolled up banknote, she remarked that two of her acquaintances had been sectioned, "One of them for ever." She then revealed that one of them had tried to rape his sister while high on skunk. She continued, "then they put him in a home and then he did rape two girls." She commented how "awful" that was, since he was "only 17," and confided, "I've known him since he was six. He used to come and deal with his sister."

★ ★ ★

Two days later, the *News Of The World* delivered a coup de grace. COCAINE KATE'S 3-IN-BED LESBIAN ORGIES.

Inside, the allegations sprawled across four pages: SHE HAD SADIE, THEN SADIE AND JUDE, THEN SADIE AND DAVINIA. THEN DAVINIA ALL ON HER OWN.

These allegations, of course, were published when Kate was not around to refute them. But the subeditors rammed home the lesson for that Sunday with how Kate variously COAXED, ROMPED, BEDDED, FORCED, POUNCED and HELD various members of the Primrose Hill Set in a variety of sexual activities, including that tabloid prayer, "Three in a Bed". Other choice headings went: "Shock dossier on secret life as lipstick lesbian", "We uncover truth about insane sex binges", "NO LIMITS … NO SHAME."

★ ★ ★

That did it for H&M. H&M (Hennes & Mauritz) is a Swedish fashion giant with over 1,100 stores in 22 countries. Its executive chairman is billionaire Stefan Peterson. Peterson is a dour man and a patriot, "a stereotypically reserved Swede".

The company is enthusiastic on corporate responsibility. It has to be. A major shareholder in the company is the Lutheran church of Sweden, which had already flexed its muscle to force the company to employ more women executives. H&M had also nailed its anti drug stance to the door by sponsoring the drug prevention charity, Mentor, whose president is Sweden's queen, Slyvia. This demure lady, twitchy about her commoner origins and allegations about the ex-Nazi party past of her father, worked on Mentor with Princess Anni-Frid Reuss-Lyngstad, aka not the blonde girl in Abba, which performed 'Dancing Queen' at Sylvia's royal wedding …

178

Given such wholesomeness, what's surprising is how long H&M took to cancel Kate's £1.2 million contract. It seems a tearful phone call from Kate stayed their hand. They announced, "she has assured us it will not happen again and we are willing to give her a second chance." Kate had promised to be a good girl. She'd even signed an undertaking to remain (or become?) "healthy, wholesome, and sound". End of quote. Then the Swedes changed their mind. End of contract.

It was a bitter parting for Kate. She'd had a long and sentimental association with the company. Johnny Depp had preceded her there, in 1999, smouldering in stubble for H&M knitwear. In 2002, Kate had done H&M proud in a shoot by Christophe Kutner promoting the company's foray into a high fashion market, posing, as *The Independent* enthused, "in a lavender mini-dress, shagadelic sheepskin coat and H&M's high-heeled take on vintage Vivienne Westwood suede pirate boots". The paper continued, "With minimal make-up and a bubble perm, Moss looks like one of those cheeky little painted putti that float on the ceiling of the Sistine Chapel. Heavenly!"

Not so heavenly now. Yet H&M were no strangers to provocation. They'd selected Depp as well as his ex, for their "edge" – their hints of disreputable glamour. Nor were they averse to controversy. In 1989 they featured Kara Young, cute and curvy in undies, captioned, "What the au pair will be wearing this winter." They then logged 78 complaints. Their next campaign showed lingerie-clad Elle MacPherson with a sexy simper and a caption that went: "Last time we ran an ad for Swedish lingerie, 78 women complained. No men." More complaints, another withdrawn ad, a bonanza in the stores. In 1991 they were also obliged to withdraw roadside posters of Cindy Crawford which transport officials had deemed "a form of visual pollution". Then there was Pamela Anderson crouched on all fours, pouting for it in high heels. Another tempest: "Much of Pamela Anderson's beauty has been created on the operating table," etc. So they were not shy about the sex. But lesbian threesomes were something else. An "edge" too far.

As for the drugs, it would be surprising if they hadn't known. Sweden is maybe a weird place, but it's not in outer space. What's more, like all her other sponsors, what H&M valued in Kate's endorsement was her allure of a life lived for real on the margins – how could they now claim to regret that reality or sterilize those margins?

★ ★ ★

In the UK, the *Daily Mail* got busy with what suits them best, the moral high ground. Cannily realising H&M's Achilles' heel was its appeal to young teenagers who needed their parent's dosh to buy the gear, the *Mail* went for the parents.

Hammering the "role model" aspect and castigating Kate Moss associated brands as "These greedy profiteers", Marcelle D'Argy Smith raged that they "are making it clear that they don't give a damn about their customers. By using Miss Moss as the public face of their clothes and cosmetics, they are saying to the young women and teenagers who buy the stuff: 'It's okay to live like this, the world doesn't mind at all if you snort cocaine as long as you look good in clothes and can retain a pretty face.' Where on earth are their ethics and their morals?" D'Argy Smith concluded, "There have been acres of publicity and Miss Moss has apologised. So it's all okay. She has said: 'I'm sorry' very prettily and she's ready to sign 'good behaviour' contracts. And, of course, she's never ever going to do anything like that again. Yeah, if you believe that you'll believe anything."

★　★　★

You didn't need to be a fly on the wall to realise someone had set off a banger in the fashion anthill. The Queen ant was wounded. The soldiers panicked. On September 21, Chanel announced they'd no longer be renewing Kate's contract to represent Coco Mademoiselle perfume. A few hours later, Burberry, eliding Kate's appearance in nine of their 18 campaigns since 1998, also threw in the Mac: "Kate has always been a fantastic model and highly professional for Burberry. We are saddened by her current circumstances and hope she overcomes her problems as soon as possible. We wish Kate all the best." Then H Stern decided that despite dripping with their jewellery Kate herself should be dropped …

And yet, as this sveltely belted face of Burberry disappeared from bus stops all over London, it remained at some key sales points, until the press started asking why – as if Burberry couldn't quite bring itself to relinquish her. And indeed, nor could it. Burberry-Kate was soon back, her demise rescinded like an especially popular character in a soap opera, which of course she was. Two months later, Burberry's creative director Christopher Bailey was claiming, "There has been so much nonsense in the press about Burberry dropping Kate. 'Is Kate still part of our family?' Absolutely."

Others stood by their model from the go. French *Vogue* declared her guest editorship would go ahead in December. The Rimmel execs never flinched. They knew she was all the more perfect for the brand. While they claimed to find the Mirror pix "shocking", they suavely pointed out that Kate was "a very stylish, very individualistic representation of London today, which is what the brand is all about." And also what the broad was all about.

★ ★ ★

Meanwhile the press onslaught continued. On September 18th the *News Of The World* reported allegations from the fashion PA Rebecca White. White alleged that she'd partied with Kate Moss over 60 times in many cities over many years and had "not once" seen her when she wasn't "doing drugs or booze". White catalogued Kate's allegedly prodigious consumption of vodka, champagne, cocaine and Es. White also claimed that on a flight from New York to Paris, both Kate and Naomi Campbell took Es with champagne and proceeded to create havoc in first class by "playing loud music, jumping on the seats and generally being crazy".

★ ★ ★

The scandal had coincided with the beginning of fashion week when Kate had been expected to model for Frost-French, co-owned by Sadie Frost. In the event, of course, she didn't. But imagine the buzz. There was more talk about Kate Moss than anything else.

The London *Evening Standard* scooped Fashion Week itself by sending reporters with cotton swabs into the loos at a number of key parties thrown by Versace, McQueen and Topshop. Analysed by a laboratory, they all revealed traces of cocaine. As did "a party to raise awareness of Aids".

The *Standard* stated, "In many cases the tests only proved what anybody entering the cubicles could see. Trails of white powder crisscrossed the enamel surfaces of every cistern, while groups of friends openly discussed their 'stash' as they queued in the long line waiting for the previous group to emerge sniffing from the lavatory." In another venue, "lines of white powder covered lavatory seats, cisterns and shelves. In the women's lavatories, an advertising executive and a barrister, both in their thirties, discussed-their appearance before going into the cubicle for 'a quick sharpener'. One partygoer, asked to sum up the atmosphere, said: 'Nothing special. They are all models. They are all dim. They are all on charlie.'"

★ ★ ★

The day after that, *The Sun* headlined another "world exclusive: KATE'S ON CRACK." This alleged that Kate was partial to "two hits" of crack a week. Inside, a story signed off by no less than five reporters, quoted an

181

alleged eye witness, named as Wesley Hunt, describing two of Kate's country house parties.

Hunt alleged that "There were lines of coke everywhere" and there was even "a special snorting room" at the house: "a small lounge with cushions everywhere and a glass-covered table and a music system." Hunt reported this room as littered with "£10 and £20 notes all over the place [with] about an ounce of coke stuck on the table. Hunt also alleged he saw Kate taking cocaine as well as "smoking crack from a Coca-Cola can. She was also taking Es – two or three at a time."

Another claim made by Hunt was that a full blown orgy involving hetero and lesbian sex was going on at the house: "There were clothes everywhere and people having sex and everyone was popping pills like sweets." He described Kate parading bare breasted as if on a catwalk while singing Bob Marley's 'One Love'. At a subsequent party Hunt declared that after taking assorted drugs at a frenetic rate Kate had called out, "Anyone want a good fuck tonight? Who wants to come to the bedroom for a good fuck?"

* * *

Then, when you thought it couldn't get more lurid, came an equestrian angle from the *Mirror*: "HORSE DRUG KATE … KETAMINE KATE; MODEL WENT CRAZY AFTER SNORTING DRUG FOR HORSES".

This story alleged that Kate had been seen snorting the horse tranquilliser, Ketamine. A model recounted how she'd met Kate at a party, "She seemed quite hyper. She was moving her jaw in a weird way and her eyes were huge. I could tell straight away that she was on something."

Kate then apparently placed a large white plate of Ketamine under the grill in the kitchen, explaining that warming up the drug made it fluffy and easier to snort. The observer claimed, "She was quite greedy about it. She was like a machine. Once she had snorted the line, she wiped her nose and started jumping around the room like a mad woman. She wouldn't stop talking. She was going on about Special K, saying how great it was. She said she had done a lot of it."

Several other papers picked up on this latest surprise. In the *Sunday Times*, India Knight analysed the context, drawing on her experience of fashion circles: "If it's not coke, it may be ketamine. Or crystal meth. Or all three. Everyone drinks. Everyone smokes. Everyone is anorexic-skinny and thinks it's cool."

* * *

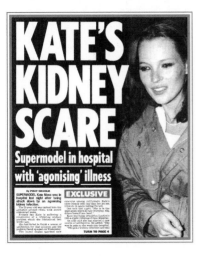

Her British agency, Storm, was unusually forthcoming, "Kate doesn't know where the [kidney] infection's come from. They can develop from chills and women's problems - but it has nothing to do with her lifestyle." Her US agent commented: "I spoke with her [yesterday], and she was getting her hair coloured in her room. She's going blond." *(Mirrorpix)*

Back in circulation, Kate resumes her "partying" lifestyle with a vengeance. *(Mirrorpix)*

Step forward Jefferson Winston Hack. As waif-like and ethereal looking as Kate, Hack became the father of her child. But could he satisfy a woman who by now had given herself the moniker, "Dracula"? Kate's adoption of a "Jean Seberg" cropped hairstyle was seen by some as ominous. *(Steve Wood/Rex Features)*

Kate found it hard to stop either drinking or smoking while pregnant with Lila Grace Moss Hack. The ever vigilant paparazzi snapped her sneaking to the corner shop for a packet of Marlboro Lights. During her pregnancy in 2002 Kate put on 2st 7lb, and grew from size 8 to size 12. She also wolfed chips and burgers, quipping afterwards: "I liked being fat for a change." *(LFI)*

Lucien Freud's painting of a nude and pregnant Kate Moss. Curled before the master's forensic eye, luxuriant and expansive, mistress of her desires, the proprietor of significant investments and a pile in the country, and gazing at us with sardonic ennui…
(Ray Tang/Rex Features)

The paparazzi gaze. An agency picture of Kate arriving at Sadie Frost's house in Steeles Road, Primrose Hill, 2003. The keyword-caption reads: "UNRECOGNISABLE BACK REAR BEIGE DRESS SHOWING KNICKERS PANTS BOTTOM BARE LEGS BUMPY CELLULITE?? BRUISE BRUISED BRUISES." *(Stephen Butler/Rex Features)*

Snapped by a long-distance lens on yet another beach. So often we see her killing time, and especially on beaches, at the edge of everyday life…
(Kore Press/Rex Features)

Filmed from closer up by Jefferson in January 2003, holidaying as a family with Lila. Despite Jefferson Hack's evident charms, the relationship was soon in trouble. Jefferson's father commented that, "It was financially draining for Jefferson because he told me Kate never pays for anything. So, if she said 'Let's go to Mustique', he'd have to foot the bill, and let me tell you, it wasn't exactly cheap."
(bigpicturesphoto.com)

The relationships of the Primrose Hill Set were complicated, if not labyrinthine. An ethnography best done in snapshots - or diagrams, as the press loved to create, with arrows and captions listing entanglements, disputes, pregnancies, casualties and so on. Here is one example of many. *(bigpicturesphoto.com/NI Syndication/The Sun)*

Kate's 30th birthday party on the January 16, 2004 was styled after Scott Fitzgerald's novel of decadence and debauchery, *The Beautiful And The Damned*. But the underlying theme of the event was money and what money means: Kate as a Marie Antoinette of conspicuous consumption. And there was not one party, but four. The evening developed into a notorious orgy. Left: Kate is looking harassed , shepherded by her ever loyal (£10,000 a month) PA, Fiona Young. Right: the 50 or so paparazzi waiting outside were thrilled when, as the revellers began to stagger out in the early hours, Sadie Frost appeared like tabloid manna or a scene from a Russ Meyer flick: catatonic and with her ample left tit squeezed out of her red flapper-style dress. A lightning storm of flashbulbs created an icon. Another storm erupted next day, when Jude Law saw the mother of his children cruelly exposed in the papers. *(Chapman/Rex Features & Mirrorpix)*

Kate has made successive attempts to gentrify herself. Some of these have resulted in comical culture clashes. Here, she appears at ease with the Queen at an occasion to honour women of distinction in 2004. From left to right: Kate, JK Rowling, HRH, Heather Mills McCartney, and Charlotte Church. *(ROTA/Camera Press)*

Pete Doherty. The new love of Kate's life. "Colours and numbers crawling up in your skin, and stretching you and crushing you… these are the things that were haunting me since I was a kid. Hallucinations…Long before I took drugs." *(NXB/Rex Features)*

With photographer Mick Rock, who remarked: "She wanted to be the Keith Richards of the modelling industry, and she got there!" *(Matt Baron/Rex Features)*

Kate at the Glastonbury festival, June 2005 where she "married" Pete Doherty in The Chapel of Love and Loathing in Lost Vagueness. Kate's adoption of men's briefs as hotpants became one of her trademark styles, resurfacing in the Virgin Mobile ad of late 2005. *(Jason Bryant/Rex Features)*

Inset: One version of The Glastonbury Pants. Photographed in the London College of Fashion and analysed by the author. *(Vermorel/Paul Bevan)*

The constant warnings by family, friends and colleagues against Pete Doherty and his "sex and drugs and rock and roll" lifestyle failed to impress Kate. The Girl Can't Help It. Here, at one of Doherty's gigs at the Duke of Clarence pub in Islington in August 2005 she's indulging her fantasy of rock stardom. *(Danny Clifford/FilmMagic.com)*

The headline and pictures that said it all. These images of Kate Moss completed a perverse circle from Corinne Day's first pictures. They were as intrusive and raw. They stripped her privacy as once Day and Sorrenti had dispensed with her modesty… It was the beginning of a media blitzkrieg. *(Mirrorpix)*

Then began the cheesy saga of Comeback Kate: a lost soul in search of redemption, encouraged by a chorus of indignant celebs. But at this stage perhaps only a Hegelian-savvy impresario like Malcolm McLaren could unravel and transform the international scandal Kate Moss into fresh plots and products - negotiate the supermodel into a black hole where she might pop out the other side as anti-matter, or even a Sex Pistol. *(Mirrorpix)*

(Express Newspapers)

With mum in Arizona rehab, Lila has her third birthday party attended by a crowd of paparazzi. After having scared the child so much that she screamed, one of the snappers called out as her limo sped away, "Happy birthday, Lila!" September 29, 2005. *(HXL/Rex Features)*

Sarah Doukas: "I think she's metamorphosed. She's gone the next step... she looks more grownup, more sophisticated, more knowing, more together." From Poor Waif to Rich Bitch; Kate in 2005.
(Chapman/Rex Features)

Kate: "When I look at a billboard of myself 40-foot high in Times Square or on Sunset Boulevard, I don't see myself anymore. I just see an image of what someone's trying to advertise and that's sad. Sometimes I just want to be normal and think, 'Does my bum look big in that?'"
(Alisdair MacDonald/Rex Features)

Kate 'n' Pete at an impromptu Babyshambles performance at the Boogaloo in North London, 12 August 2006. "It was Spinal Tap for the noughties."
(The Sun/NI Syndication)

A style icon meets the fashion police. Kate with billionaire fashion retailer, Sir Philip Green, Topshop show, London Fashion Week, 2006. After Green signed Kate to "design" her own line the renowned Topshop designer, Jane Shepherdson, resigned. Later Shepherdson commented, "This whole thing of looking at what celebrities are wearing is so dull and unimaginative and desperately boring."
(Richard Young/Rex Features)

"These stark black and white snaps were vintage Corinne Day. They deglamorised Kate as not so much the girl next door as 'er upstairs." Kate poses in front of Corinne Day's images at the 'Face of Fashion' private view, National Portrait Gallery, 2007.
(Dafydd Jones/WireImage)

The journos also explored other angles. They remembered that Kate Moss was a mother. Calls went out: what was someone doing about all this? Spurious allegations appeared that Jefferson Hack, or Kate's mother or someone somewhere had called for Kate's child to be rescued or even put into care.

Predictably, *The Daily Mail* leaped on this angle: "Miss Moss ... faces a social services investigation into whether she is fit to be a parent to her two-year-old daughter Lila Grace ... Social services officers from Westminster Council plan to interview Miss Moss about her daughter when she returns from America ... later this week." The paper added disingenuously that, "A spokesman said: 'We would, of course, take seriously any allegations that any child in Westminster may have been put at risk or is suffering neglect or physical harm.'"

It then nastily upped the ante: "Sources said if social workers discover any evidence that Lila has been physically harmed or abused, she could be taken into care. A more likely scenario if reports that Doherty has taken cocaine and smoked marijuana in front of the child are true is that she could be placed on the 'at risk' register."

Here was a classic made-up story, a genuine crock of shite, with anonymous spokespeople tricked into making ambiguous statements re-contexted to seem faintly damning. No one close to Kate Moss was suggesting she was an uncaring mother. It is also unlikely that the child of a millionaire with a live in-nanny, four involved grandparents and Kate's personal assistant, Fiona Young – paid £10,000 a month to tie up any loose ends, would find themselves "at risk" from anyone except the very tabloids that were hounding her mother and, indeed, her three-year-old self (see below).

* * *

Around this point, people began behaving strangely. The matronly Anne Widdicombe, famous for her German helmet coiffure and fashion police dress sense, "Doris Karloff" herself, called for – even required, a prosecution.

The publicity hungry Sir Ian Blair, head of the metropolitan police, top cop in all Britain, diverted a press conference about international terrorism to berate Kate Moss on TV for being a poor "role model" and to announce that PC Plod would indeed be investigating: "We have to look at the impact of this kind of behaviour on impressionable young people and if there is evidence something should be done about it." Maybe a public spanking would do it. Or perhaps a penitential fashion shoot with Kate frozen leaping in a McQueen "heavy padded coat" and a D&G "suicide belt" over the ticket barrier at Stockwell station – as the British police had blithely misinformed us the Brazilian Jean-Charles de Menezes had done prior to being assassinated with seven dum-dum bullets to his head.

* * *

After her initial befuddled response, and as the implications sunk in and bravado vanished, Kate had locked herself away for several days in a New York hotel room with her commonsensical PA, Fiona Young. Pete Doherty meanwhile, flew off to Ibiza for a Babyshambles concert.

* * *

Eventually, Kate issued a belated public apology that sounded like a cross between PR bollocks, a stilted after dinner speech, and a sulk: "I take full responsibility for my actions. I also accept that there are various personal issues that I need to address and have started taking the difficult, yet necessary, steps to resolve them. I want to apologize to all of the people I have let down because of my behaviour, which has reflected badly on my family, friends, co-workers, business associates and others, I am trying to be positive, and the support and love I have received are invaluable."

* * *

And then she flew to Arizona for the ritual rehab, to be cleansed and born again in the cactus strewn desert. This was a 28-day rehab course at The Meadows clinic, known for its Spartan regime and hippie psychobabble.

* * *

Meanwhile as Lila's third birthday approached, the paparazzi, sensing a photo op, gathered in the street outside Kate's London home. Might Kate herself not sneak out of the clinic and fly secretly to this special occasion?

Early that morning, a *Sun* spotter was to be seen lurking, pretending to read a newspaper with as much aplomb as a spy from a Peter Sellers movie. He muttered to invisible colleagues on his hands free mobile. Things looked good. Intelligence suggested the party was to be at St John's Wood. The spotter produced a clipboard and methodically ticked off the party-going kids with their nannies and mums as they filed through the ornate gate.

Gradually, the street filled with paparazzi, greeting one another with the camaraderie of old soldiers. The freelancers arrived on scooters in black parkas and black shiny pants, swathed in belts, pouches and cameras. Salaried snappers came in flash saloons and designer separates.

Eventually, they were rewarded as Lila and her nanny appeared in a chauffeur driven limo. Lila was dressed like a sugary pink cake, in a pink fairy outfit with a pink tiara and gauze pink wings. They scurried in to a commotion of clicks. Then Jefferson Hack turned up in a black cab, looking anxious. He darted inside, shadowed by the cameramen, as if they were all joined in a peculiar dance.

As Lila, unseen, blew out three candles, and played her games, the paparazzi smoked or chatted to one another or paced up and down with mobiles clasped to ears. Some of them transmitted images to HQ on their wireless lap tops…

Around 5pm, paparazzi magic happened. They all knew exactly when Lila was coming out – before she could even have reached the vestibule. They clustered in a semi circle, bazooka-like lenses aimed at the gate.

Suddenly, Lila, who had run ahead, pushed open the gate. As she emerged, she was confronted by a nine unsmiling men, hungrily clicking. Lila screamed. She ran back into the garden. The nanny picked her up and they both emerged with Jefferson, who looked furious. They scrambled into the limo and sped away, the paparazzi lenses following them.

As they'd got into the car, a *Sun* cameraman had called, "Happy birthday, Lila!"

* * *

Talking of paparazzi magic, it was also remarkable how some tabloid journalists guessed the frequency and content of Kate and Pete's mobile phone calls. Almost as if they were listening.

Kate got increasingly frantic, Pete more and more forlorn. It seemed she wanted him to do the same rehab after she'd finished. He was thinking about it. Meanwhile, he confessed, "I just miss her. She says she just wants to be with me. She says she doesn't know why I love her, I don't know why she loves me, but that's just the way it is. Yeah, but no, but yeah…"

* * *

And then she came out and it was Pete's turn and he flew to Arizona to be cured. And it was Tibet all over again.

He lasted nine days and then quit. Later he commented, "With the amount of coke Kate was taking, it's amazing she got through rehab. I don't know how she stuck through five weeks, because I was bored senseless. I thought I'd be able to do five weeks. But if I'm honest, my head would have exploded. I only stuck at it because she paid."

He expanded, "I had to share a room with two people. There were lots of strange people in there. It was like a prison. They made me carry a teddy bear to show I had lost my inner child."

On a later occasion he admitted, "Maybe it was a bit of a rash decision, but I missed London, I wanted to play my guitar and I wanted my books."

Doherty also said of his lover: "Everyone believes she went in there to beat her cocaine addiction. That's wrong. She did it to save her career."

★　★　★

The real mystery might be why Kate cared about her career. She'd made her pile. What was left to prove? The anti-wrinkle cream was beckoning. The paparazzi were looking for cellulite. Maybe it was time to move on. Perhaps educate herself as Jodie Foster did, or settle like the wildest supermodel of all, Janice Dickinson, for: "Friendships. Health. Sobriety. Good works. Photography. And motherhood."

But whatever she might want, it seemed no one would let her go. She was too good a story. Too precious an asset.

★　★　★

Now began the cheesy saga of Comeback Kate: a lost soul in search of redemption, encouraged by a chorus of indignant celebs.

Naomi Campbell was predictably strident, "Kate Moss is my friend … I think it's like everybody is being bad to her … it's really like a vendetta." Twiggy denounced the press exposure of Cocaine Kate: "What they did is disgusting, completely out of order." Johnny Depp sent his commiserations via the media, (while carefully distancing himself by denying he'd contacted Kate in the recent past or ever met Doherty). Mumsy Sharon Osborn offered Kate a "big hug" and prattled, "Kate Moss, my heart goes out to her. She's got to be one of the most hard-working women I've ever met." Tracey Emin complained: "People should just fucking leave her alone. They are just jealous of her. I have never seen her touch the stuff once."

Elton John was cannier, "The great thing about England is that the media will give you a very hard time. They won't let you get away with it." He continued, "I wish Elvis Presley had lived in England because if he had, he would probably still be alive today. What this story has achieved is it has forced Kate Moss to get help. Plenty of people must have told her to do something about it. But plenty of people told me and it took me 16 years to go and do it."

Kate Moss now clawed her way back through an advertising campaign for the prodigious party-thrower, Roberto Cavalli … she was the cover on December *Vanity Fair*, wearing "a charcoal Chloe camisole" alongside the banner: "Kate Moss, Can She Come Back? (the answer was 11 pages long) but wearing rather less inside, sprawled in black undies with two kittens in a bed … she got hot and sticky for the 2006 Pirelli calendar … she became the new face of Longchamp – for whose MD she was that now tiresomely predictable thing, "an icon of our time" … and then – bingo! – was booked for the March 2006 issue of British *Vogue*, "For the millionth time," whinged the online www jossip.com, "Kate Moss shows us her boobs."

But for what purpose, for whose interests, was it important that Kate retain old modelling contracts or garner new ones?

★ ★ ★

You might equally wonder what went on in Sarah Doukas' head. From an interview she gave *The Times* after the story broke it seems not a lot: "We've spoken to one another every day for 18 years, but there are some things I know I can never discuss with her. We're close, but when you're an agent there's a line." Doukas blamed the media, she blamed Doherty, she blamed love, "When somebody's in love with someone like that, they're not going to listen to anything anyone else says." But she never blamed Kate. That wouldn't have been politic: "there's a line."

★ ★ ★

More tellingly, Doukas never showed any hint of relishing the affair. She was tired, shocked, distressed, apologetic. She wished it had never happened, that it would all go away, that things return to normal.

No way. Kate Moss was now cultural dynamite or she was dead – dead boring. But who had the imagination to manage all that? And did Kate have the balls?

★ ★ ★

A brand this big, concentrating such fascination, that contained and communicated nothing except itself, was a monster fetish. To unravel and exploit all the possibilities latent in that fetish you would need not Sarah Doukas or Simon Chambers, but Malcolm McLaren in his reckless and ruthless prime …

Only such a Hegelian-savvy impresario could unravel and transform the international scandal Kate Moss into fresh plots and products – negotiate the supermodel into a black hole where she might pop out the other side as anti-matter, or even a Sex Pistol.

But McLaren was unavailable. Who else? Step forward the man who "outswindled" the great rock and roll swindler himself (nicked his band and throttled his big idea while patting him on the back): Sir Richard Branson.

*   *   *

Branson had financed Storm from the start and thought of it as his fashion baby. And he had a (platonic) crush on Kate, counting her a dear friend. Branson's son too, the model and wannabe musician, Sam, was a close friend of Kate's. It was almost a family affair. Uncle Branson strolled to the rescue with sage advice, a soothing and welcome cynicism, and a £1.2 million deal for a video ad campaign for Virgin Mobile.

It's hard to doubt Branson's good intentions. Though Virgin founded its empire as the carrion crow of youth culture, he had a soft spot for this particular carcass.

It was also astute to feature Kate's coked-out cool to flog mobiles to children – Virgin mobile's core market. Kids are attracted by adventure and outsiderism, and are fiercely existential. A chat plan sanctioned by a disgraced supermodel flouncing in hotpants was just right for pay-as-you-go hoodies and microskirted chavs. But Kate's image also bridged that "demographic" with Virgin Mobile's aspirations upmarket, towards "contract" customers, the *Time Out* and *Sunday Observer* crowd.

The ad was duly rumoured, signed and screened. As a mark of Kate's new superstatus, it was downloaded millions of times before it aired that Xmas eve, trailed like a feature movie or big entertainment event.

As a video, it was drab. Kate in her Glastonbury 2005 hotpants and a story line suggesting lost and regained contracts. Branson was fulsome, praising his protégé as if she was an autistic daughter who'd just starred as Hedda Gabler in the school play. "She will impress a lot of people with her natural beauty, acting skills, great comic timing and ability to poke fun at herself." "Comic timing"? You needed a heart of Ham not to laugh.

*   *   *

We can suspect however, that was just to soften her up for the real scams. At the beginning of February 2006, it was leaked that Kate Moss might be taking a trip in one of the commercial space flights that the seasoned hot air balloonist, Branson, had lately been devising. This inauguration of space tourism would propel its customers into outer space at three times the speed of sound. Once there, said Branson, "They can experience weightlessness, they will check out that the Earth is round and enjoy space."

That was more like it: Cosmic Kate … And even if it turned out baloney, what matter? Attention had been focused on the project and its Virgin branding. Virgin was now the bedfellow of the most notorious libertine on the planet, and Branson was in his element, gulping the pure oxygen of hype.

Also mooted was an autobiography, courtesy of Virgin Books. Kate would get to tell "her side" of the story. Branson was said to have "convinced" her of the wisdom of this, and even said to be "helping" her write it. Whether as an authority or amanuensis wasn't clear. But how to stop her account being, well ... anodyne? Especially since frank admissions might scare off fashion labels and delay the coveted comeback? Maybe they'd go that extra bit and get a psychoanalysist to quiz her, a psychic to divine her ...

* * *

To get in first, I approached a "transpersonal psychotherapist." In a £50 "psychometric session," she was shown photos of Kate Moss from childhood and given personal items to handle.

Her first word was "fear."

Fear – [Kate] not knowing who she is ... huge unsureness – unsureness of who to reach and who she wants to be – no basement – she just grabs bits and hangs onto them – needs fame to keep her warm – but actually can't cope with it – she's very curious – but doesn't want anyone to know – a whole secret life of insecurity and very superstitious – little childlike superstitions – like picking up a pebble and if she didn't have it in her pocket she wouldn't win ...

The psychic speculated about issues with the mother, suggesting that the mother was "brittle too" and "quite hard", and that Kate's childhood may have been sometimes unhappy because she felt she was loved less than others – "a lot of jealousy ..."

And: ... horrible experiences with men – I think she has been used – because she is very wary – dark haired man who used to laugh at her – dismissive of her ... her femininity is a problem for her - she has no sense of her own femininity – as a female she feels desperately vulnerable ... an island person, but she would like to be a group person ...

Finally: tears in her eyes ... I'm drawn to the eyes – the eyes shine but it's almost like they shine with tears ...

* * *

Remember Pete? There was now almost a transatlantic bust up as the lovers communicated and rowed over the phone. Doherty was puzzled, hurt, and then bitter. He was also out of his depth. He complained, "People are obsessed with my missus. I don't know why ... she's just a bird from South London."

At one point Kate escaped the paps and the pair had a secret meeting in Paris. Things didn't go smoothly. Kate threw the £50 ring he'd bought for her back at him and it hit him in the eye. He suggested the real reason for her rage was that, "I can't buy her diamonds and my dick is too small." He complained, "I never know where I stand with her. It's either a black eye or a love-bite. It's like being in Afghanistan with her. I wish I could find some middle ground."

Meanwhile, he floundered along through increasingly desperate gigs, desperate drugs, in a tragi-comic cycle of drug busts and fiascos that once got him arrested three times in one day. The cops were on his tail, licking their pencils and frequently pulling over his "erratically driven" Jag...

* * *

People sniggered that finally she'd ditched the crackhead and good riddance. They misunderstood the woman. Like most addictive personalities she could only forsake one addiction by embracing another. George W Bush relinquished booze only to swallow God neat. Kate Moss gave up substances (as we suppose), but her major addiction has always been to the idea of being in love, the project haunts her biography.

As if to compensate for absent chemicals in her veins she now filled her life with *being in love* on an epic scale – to a pitch and point that left her friends and cronies bemused: she was gloriously and foolishly in that state of elated, ecstatic, wondering, breathless adoration for that one real person, the ONLY ONE, who ... happened to be Pete Doherty. And her anger at him, at the recent turn of events, and his seeming helplessness, was just another expression of that passion.

* * *

Meanwhile, Kate from Sanderstead had to kick her heels. So she reverted to her favourite waste of time: running. She was skiing, she was sunbathing, she was swimming. Occasionally she modelled in exotic places.

Then she was being chased by Paparazzi (according to UPI) in a Mercedes driven through night-time Paris by a companion at speeds of up to 150 miles an hour...

It also looked like she was on the run from the cops. After four months abroad a police spokesman was quoted, "We now think she is starting to behave like a fugitive." The Met Assistant Commissioner Tarique Ghaffur, admonished, "We would like to appeal for her to return, see us and tell us her side of the story. For everybody's sake, and for her to move on, the sooner she speaks to us the better."

Through third parties it was said that while she would be only too happy to help with enquiries she was just too busy "working".

This, as the press angrily muttered, while she was "enjoying a massage in Ibiza", sunning herself on "Richard Branson's paradise Caribbean island Necker", partying (yet again!) in New York and Paris... and even pole dancing at a topless bar with "Hollywood beauty Lindsay Lohan". What with all this activity it was estimated that in the four months after September 15 she travelled 34,000 miles.

Other stories enhanced this fugitive status. Kate was "endangered" or "threatened" by a Kate Moss fixated stalker, Peter Braunstein. The proof was a ten-year-old essay by this postmodern journalist (*Village Voice* and *Women's Wear Daily*): "I tried to kick Kate cold turkey. There will never be a next Kate for a simple reason: Kate is always the 'next Kate'. That makes her every woman I've ever fallen hopelessly in love with." Braunstein was on the run after attacking a woman in New York - so it stood to reason that Kate might be running scared ...

Even more tendentious was NAKED MODEL STABBED TO DEATH; BEAUTY DUBBED NEXT KATE MOSS BUTCHERED ON OWN DOORSTEP - a tabloid tale that started that September about the murder of 18-year-old Sally Anne Bowman, found "stripped and bleeding to death". Sally was not only an aspiring model with an agency contract but she lived in South Croydon, just like Kate Moss... a trope that was still surfacing four months later.

Then Kate Moss landed in a rented Malibu mansion overlooking the Pacific, "pool, spa, cinema, gym and three acres of land", an American dream once owned by Liz Taylor where she invited another Taylor, her special friend, the gorgeously proportioned and polymorphous Davinia, over for company...

★ ★ ★

This was some place in her head where maybe none of this had really happened... a place unreal enough to make it all seem like a dream - or where she no longer needed Linda's approval, Doukas' motherly concern, Doherty's madness... or the self immolation of yet another uncontrolled love affair - the self denial – or denial of self - of serial shagging and orgasmic binging.

Was that all?

What else was maybe in that deserted and forlorn almost-a-home back in the Cotswolds, where Pete Doherty's possessions stayed intact in "the potting shed" while autumn came and went and the gardener raked up the

191

leaves and that Christmas saw no presents or pudding and the drum kit in The Circus was silent for Kate's 32nd and where Dolly the housekeeper finally took down the bunting she'd put up in Lila's room to celebrate her return …

ACT SIX:

Sex and Drugs and Frocks and Roll

FOR once the Kate 'n' Pete roadshow proved too much, even for the rock'n' roll wild men of the New Musical Express.

Kate Moss and her boyfriend Pete Doherty were thrown out of the magazine's awards show after refusing to desist from what can only be described as overly amorous behaviour … They spent much of their time in passionate embraces instead of taking up their seats at the Hammersmith Palais … Eventually, the behaviour of the visibly worse-for-wear couple became so blatant and persistent that security was called to eject them. One source said: "They were caught trying to get into the toilets together and bouncers told them to get back to their table. Next they were caught in an alleyway out the back. So the bouncers got Kate and Pete's own security to put them in a car and take them home."

- *Evening Standard*, March, 2007

She says, 'Mum, do you think this is a good look?' Then she has a fashion crisis. I say, 'You'll wear what I tell you!' But she says she's the adult of the bedroom. We lay the clothes out before she goes to bed but she goes, 'Mum, I need options.'

- Kate Moss explaining in March 2007 that her five year old daughter, Lila, has inherited fashionista genes.

From the simple insight that humans can bond with manufactured commodities via stories has come the most important development of modern life: the endless tying of fictions to the fabricated stuff of everyday life.

– James Twitchell, *Branded Nation*, 2006

In Paris that autumn 2005, the designer Alexander McQueen, a Kate Moss stalwart who sported a T-shirt protesting, "We love you Kate", exposed a virtual Kate Moss on his ready-to-wear catwalk.

The show itself was sort of retro, summoning McQueen's "ancestral Gaelic roots", and fusing "a Highlands theme with a spin through Shakespeare's Macbeth." A collection brimming with "handsome riding coats, fan-tailed jackets and suits in misty plaids."

It also displayed McQueen's showbiz panache. Towards the finale, the runway suddenly blacked out. Then, a small speck of light appeared in a huge glass pyramid and slowly grew into a life-sized holographic image.

"Caressed by folds of white organza, with tendrils of blond hair, a ghostly mistress began to take shape. The apparition twisted and danced for a while before it became clear that it was a vision of Kate Moss."

Seeming to "emerge out of smoke", but also looking oddly trapped inside the pyramid, the ersatz supermodel floated above the catwalk, a synthetic and cosmetic and proxy and surrogate Kate, who "danced and turned, trailing large trains of floating fabric behind her."

As the fashionisti madly applauded the spectacle, this "symbolic resurrection for the supermodel" gradually became smaller and smaller until it disappeared, a vision which the *Financial Times* described as: "a ghostly, windblown, Kate Moss, swathed in rippling chiffon, [which] appeared and then faded, like the memory of a lost love."

McQueen's image said a mouthful. Kate Moss was everywhere and nowhere, ubiquitous but invisible, mute but cacophonous.

* * *

In this enforced hiatus, in exile, in the lurid spotlight of international fascination, the omnipresent absence of Kate Moss created new territory for fashion fantasies, media speculation and celebrity intensification.

A life already so unreal had now become phantasmagorical. As a spectre, she became a PR wet dream and the people's oracle. Her identity was chewed up and regurgitated in a media free-for-all, which everyone from Scotland Yard to Coty Inc. played for their own ends. But this was new territory. No fashion brand had ever gone this way or become so powerful or out of control. So some of these institutions got their fingers burnt – notably Scotland Yard. As for her, in the words of Little Richard, The Girl Can't Help It … But would this "bird from South London" grasp the power she had, let alone use it?

* * *

It's comical how celebs complain they've been "misquoted" or misunderstood by the media. As if it matters what celebrities *really* think or say or do. All that matters is that they create stories or have stories created around them. And all these stories have to be is diverting. It doesn't even matter if the public doubts the stories or takes them as a yarn. Just as long as they pay attention – however fleeting or ephemeral, attention is all: attention is revenue.

And now Kate Moss had indeed become the perfect foil for any amount of wishful thinking to float and commercialise her buzz. We could enjoy her sufferings from the safety of our smugness and in the comfort of our resentment at her lucky life – which just turned a bit unlucky – hah!

Media folks soon realised that the sordid fairytale of Kate Moss had become an unprecedented licence to print baloney. You could pretty well say any fucking thing you liked.

You could just make stuff up.

Here was a golden opportunity to follow the media rule that anything is believable so long as it's said *about a celebrity*. And that in any case all that counts is to TELL THE STORY. Never mind WHAT story, just tell it, fill the space, make a noise, stop the silence. The only scandal the media is in awe of, its nightmare, is silence.

* * *

In his biography of Marylyn Monroe, Norman Mailer coined the term, "factoids" for sub facts, or cod facts, "which have no existence before appearing in a magazine or newspaper." Neither true nor false, factoids just "are" by virtue of having once upon a time appeared. And as they get repeated they eventually become honorary facts which in turn generate new factoids …

Kate Moss had become a factoid factory: a cluster bomb of bollocks.

* * *

The Oscar for Kate Moss bollocks goes to "the director, Nick Egan", who invented an especially juicy viral factoid that can stand for all the others. Here it is:

Actor Johnny Depp has agreed to star opposite his ex-girlfriend supermodel Kate Moss.

Depp has signed up to star as Michael Hutchence in a film about the INXS frontman's life and death, Moss is currently in talks to play Hutchence's doomed girlfriend Paula Yates.

Moss and Depp were together for three years but split in 1997, however, Depp was keen to reassure producers that he and Moss were now friends.

An insider told the Daily Express: "Johnny was asked if it would be a deal breaker for him if Kate was cast.

"He said, 'Not as far as I'm concerned.' He figures there's been enough water under that bridge.

"Obviously he's [director Nick Egan]) hoping there's still enough chemistry between them that will translate to the screen. It has been claimed she never got over him and in the film they'll have to appear deeply in love."

Whether Ms Moss will actually appear in the film is yet to be decided.

★ ★ ★

Nick Egan's is one of those ersatz careers got off the back of a punk moment that never seems to die. A sort of odd job boy for Mclaren and Westwood (for whom he "designed invitations"), he rebirthed as an eighties stylist, then made humdrum commercials and music promos. Egan's website grandiloquently proclaims that "Egan's stylistic vision helped shape the punk aesthetic and shook visual music and fashion culture all the way from The Sex Pistols to the present." Which will be news to lots of people.

But there's an end to commercials for Cheerios breakfast cereal "Everything but the bowl" or jobs like Egan's unfortunate Oasis vid, branded by Noel Gallagher, no less, as "rubbish."

★ ★ ★

In itself, Egan's Kate Moss factoid was a more perfect product than any real movie could ever have been. See firstly how the keywords were drafted to chatter and linger in the agencies and Google news, newsgroups and blogs: *Johnny Depp … Kate Moss… Michael Hutchence … INXS … life and death … doomed girlfriend Paula Yates … Moss and Depp … split … he and Moss were now friends … if Kate was cast … chemistry … screen … deeply in love … Moss is currently in talks …*

The tone was masterfully judged: *Depp was keen to reassure producers … Johnny was asked … He said … He figures …*

Such reactions! Reactions being the manna of factoids. Here was Depp wondering and Moss pondering and Vanessa Paradis (presumably) fretting…

Then came Hutchence's father, who it was said had been approached for his blessing, but "slammed" the movie's conception. Was he perhaps angry at this desecration of his son's memory, or pissed off at his cut, or just an ornery old Crocodile Dundee seething in the outback? Then there was Hutchence's brother Rhett, who was allegedly "furious" about Kate Moss being "cast" and "blasted" the supposed casting. Hints here of sexual rivalry, fraternal ambivalence – and what kind of name is "Rhett" anyway?

The plot exploited the tetchy liaison of Depp and Moss – its maybe still smouldering embers: folk memories of champagne fizzing baths and dismantled hotel suites – linking this with the sordid ménage of Hutchence, sexually demented Aussie hyperjunkie, and Paula Yates, media superslag and grandslam groupie. It also sneakily summoned (by association) the long suffering St Bob Geldof who was bringing Fifi Trixabelle, Peaches Honeyblossom, Pixie and Tiger Lily up in Battersea while struggling to save Africa. And finally, here was a humiliated Vannessa Paradis weeping off-stage in the kitchen as Johnny risked their new found happiness for … cette sorcière!

★　★　★

Neither Depp or Moss had ever heard of this project. This was moreover, a movie without a script, or any scriptwriters. It also lacked a title. It had no budget, real or projected, and despite talk of "producers" in the plural the only "producer" around was Egan's long term partner, Ann Haugen, who had not exactly produced much celluloid, though she had produced their two children.

And then there was the ticklish issue that it was unlikely Kate Moss could act at all, let alone carry a feature film with an old hand like Depp.

But then, just as this factoid was whimpering down came the "news" that Bob Geldof's 17-year-old daughter, Peaches, the winsome partygoing and media friendly spawn of Geldof and Yates, had "been approached" to play a "cameo role" in the movie and that consequently Geldof was "livid" and had branded the aspiring movie makers "filthy opportunists."

"Obviously," crooned the PR, "they [Egan et al] know it will be difficult ground for her [Peaches] so they are offering to create a part where she doesn't have to interact with the two leads. They are thinking that she could play a photographer so she would be removed from the main plot."

In the end, Egan's bid for Hollywood proved as elusive as Hutchence's for an orgasm while hanging with a stiffie from a hotel door. But his factoid ran for six months, from April to September 2006, which is longer than many Cannes' Palme d'Or winners.

★　★　★

Kate's 32nd was more restrained than the bucolic scenes at her 31st – the venue for her tryst with Doherty. The day itself was feted in the US, but a week later she flew to Paris for the real party, which showed she'd lost none

of her zest for partying or deja vu. She stayed at the familiar Ritz where a
13-hour drinking binge was launched with an afternoon "champagne tea",
moving upstairs where the hubbub logged the usual complaints from fellow
guests.

Changing into a little black number and red stilettos, her blonde hair
loose, Kate then slithered out of a back entrance and was sped in a blacked
out Merc to a posh house on the Seine where she caroused with Naomi
Campbell and all the usual suspects – and then the gang raced back to the
Ritz in a convoy of limos buzzed by paps, and then partied till dawn crept
across the Place Vendome, as paps stirred their coffee in paper cups and
texted anxious editors ...

* * *

Meanwhile, Pete Doherty was gigging for Babyshambles in less salubrious
Stoke on Trent. He'd driven himself there in one of his dodgy Jags, which
sported an out of date tax disk.

Onlookers described him as looking "totally wasted". He had recently
written and released a poem about Kate which lamented, "I will never see
you naked again."

* * *

The British police also wanted her back, naked or not. While confirming
they'd not try to extradite her, in early January the Met Assistant
Commissioner, Tarique Ghaffur, issued the sternest declaration yet:

"It is very important that she comes back to assist us with this investigation. We hope that Kate [sic] will give us her version of events." He continued, "It is in her interests and everybody's interests that she does this as soon
as possible."

Ghaffur (or should we say, Tarique?) added: "There has been a lot of speculation about whether she has decided to stay in the United States. [Proving
that he too, like everyone else, read the tabs.] But we have an investigation
to carry out and we need to speak to her as soon as possible."

He then boasted, perhaps unfortunately, "The investigation is progressing
very well and the Met is closing in on those who are behind the supply of
drugs. But we have got to speak to Kate [sic]. I am making an appeal to Kate
[sic] to come back to this country."

This first name stuff was – excuse the pun, a Ghaff. It looked cheap and
opportunistic. As if Inspector Slipper, scourge of the escaped great train rob-
ber, Ronald Biggs, might have appealed to "Ron" or even "Ronnie" to
please come back from Brazil. As if to address the supermodel as "Ms Moss"

or "Kate Moss" or just "Moss" might make the Assistant Commissioner uncool.

Ghaffur continued in this mix of robust conciliation and gauche humility, "If she does [return] we will seek to see her by appointment. We will arrest her and interview her under caution. Whatever she says will be compared to the evidence we have collected and then presented to the CPS. I guarantee that, like anyone else, she will be dealt with fairly within the law. What we are seeking is positive information to help us with our inquiries."

Branching into the broader issue, Ghaffur explained: "Our position was made clear by Commissioner Sir Ian Blair. He said we would not just be taking up drugs at a street level but targeting the middle and upper classes who use cocaine.

"In particular," Ghaffur continued, sounding like Charles Dickens lamenting the effect of soot on child chimney sweeps, "I am very concerned about the harm created by drug usage in the entertainment, music and fashion industries. There are many impressionable young people who wish to pursue careers in those industries. They are susceptible to the drug dealers who infiltrate those worlds. There is also the danger that drugs are glamorised and vulnerable people take them and ruin their lives."

The detective heading the investigation, added: "Some celebrities have openly admitted cocaine use and think they're above the law. That is not the case."

Oh yes it was.

* * *

On January 31, 142 days after she had left the UK, Kate Moss flew from Paris in a private jet, landing at Farnborough Airport just after 11am. She was driven to London in a Mercedes with her legal eagle, Gerrard Tyrell, and accompanied by bodyguards.

It was agreed that she would avoid the humiliation of mere mortals of having to attend a police station. Instead, she was driven to the offices of the Met's Specialist Crime Operations Team at Wellington House, close to Buckingham Palace.

The British paparazzi exulted. *The Evening Standard* rushed out a photo of the errant supermodel in suitably large wrap around shades and a suitably demure cream shawl and black cropped trousers.

But inside the cop shop Kate Moss was tight lipped. She read a prepared statement and was frequently advised by her solicitor to reply to questions with, "No comment". Eighty minutes later she left through a back exit.

* * *

After the interview, a Scotland Yard source affirmed that the case "was a dead duck."

Photos were not admissible evidence in a British court. Moreover, though Kate had been filmed in flagrenti, the police could not prove whether the substance she'd been distributing and snorting had been the class A drugs cocaine or ecstasy, or class B amphetamines. Without knowing that, they feared the prosecution could not proceed.

* * *

Operation Finnean, as the Cocaine Kate investigation was coded, collapsed formally the following June.

Speaking for the Crown Prosecution Service on the 15th June, Rene Barclay spelled out capitulation with a touch of bitterness: "The film footage provides an absolutely clear indication that Ms Moss [whatever happened to "Kate"?] was using controlled drugs and providing them to others. However, in the absence of any forensic evidence, or direct eye witness evidence about the substance in question, its precise nature could not be established.

"Ms Moss declined to provide any explanation when interviewed, and the direct eye witnesses also declined to provide evidence. Expert analysis of the footage, however, narrowed the possibilities down to three particular drugs – cocaine, ecstasy or amphetamine."

Barclay elaborated: "But these three substances fall into two different legal categories of controlled drugs. To obtain a conviction, case law establishes that the prosecution must prove beyond reasonable doubt the legal category to which the substance being used belonged. Proving that it was a substance belonging either to one or other of two different legal categories is not sufficient.

"Accordingly, as the available evidence fell short of establishing the necessary crucial facts, we decided that there was no realistic prospect of conviction and that a prosecution could not therefore be started."

He added, "This was necessarily a protracted investigation in view of the need to obtain crucial evidence through a court order, the absence of Ms Moss from the UK for some months and the need to complete all reasonable lines of inquiry."

* * *

The way the drug was prepared in the *Mirror* vid and the fact it was snorted would suggest it was cocaine rather than amphetamines. Speed is rarely snorted. And, as every concerned parent knows, E usually comes in pills.

However, the CPS was right in assuming they couldn't prove beyond reasonable doubt that the stuff going down in the vid was coke.

But that is not the only reason the case collapsed. This "protracted investigation" through "all reasonable lines of inquiry" collapsed because the police failed to come up with corroborating or alternative evidence. This despite unprecedented publicity, despite the scene being awash with notoriously fickle hangers on (whom the press had no difficulty in manipulating at will), despite the endless scrapes of the fulsome and irrepressible and voluble and volatile Pete Doherty, despite ten months of trying, and £1/4 million of taxpayers' hard earned funds.

★   ★   ★

The police knew from the start they needed more evidence. So how did they set about procuring it?

To start with, it took 15 days for them to search the recording studio where the drug taking had been filmed. The *Mirror* story broke on the 15th September. It wasn't till Thursday 29th September that officers from the specialist crime directorate arrived at the studio with a warrant to search for class A drugs. These officers left after four hours, taking with them with "several bags." What was in those bags has never been divulged. Tampaxes, Kleenexes, Malboro Lite dog ends? It was unlikely to have been drugs.

15 days. Think about it.

In that time you or I could have organised a team of char ladies to fly in from Columbia to blitz the studio from skirting boards to striplights. Those same ladies could have hosed the car park and swept the streets all round, then visited Buckingham Palace and Abbey Road and shopped in Harvey Nicks before heading back to Bogotá. In fact, they could have done all this at least three times.

Fifteen days, during which over 30,000 British babies came into the world and 21,000 Britons departed it … As elections took place in Germany, New Zealand, Afghanistan and Poland … Hurricane Rita came and went, devastating the US gulf coast … the Danes enraged the Muslims by publishing cartoons of Muhammad … Monica Lewinsky caused a flutter as she enrolled as a student at the London School of Economics.

★   ★   ★

"All reasonable lines of inquiry."

So why were Kate Moss' two homes, in London and Gloucestershire, apparently never searched? After all, there she was closeted in a studio with at least three confirmed hard drug addicts. There she was handing out something that was not sherbet. There she was all over the media accused of and even confessing (in the famous apology) to something or other drug related. What's more, you can bet it was common sense in the canteens of Scotland Yard, just as it was in the hostelries of Fleet Street, that the circles this girl frequented were slags for substances.

Knowing about evidence, the police immediately grasped that the *Mirror* video would not be sufficient grounds to prosecute. It seems axiomatic therefore that the residences of the principal suspect (not to mention the homes of other suspects like Doherty and Jones) would be searched as soon as possible. Especially given that both of Kate Moss' residences were celebrated hives of Primrose Hill industry and entertainment. What was more, their occupant had effectively scarpered with no opportunity to cover up possible evidence.

Bear in mind too, that according to Sir Ian Blair no less, the police were definitely on *her* case. Kate was a principal, if not the principal suspect. Scotland Yard stated: "We consider it our responsibility and an imperative matter that … such a public figure [is] apparently flouting the law so brazenly. We are determined to come down hard on lawbreakers, no matter who they are." And referring specifically to Kate Moss, Blair said, "We have to look at the impact of this kind of behaviour on impressionable young people and if there is evidence something should be done about it."

"If there is evidence."

* * *

Intrigued by the Met's methodology, I applied under the Freedom of Information Act to ask whether any house searches had been envisaged or planned. I sent this application to the Met, as well as to the Gloucestershire constabulary. After some delay and deliberation over whether such information was "in the public interest", the Met declared it was not and refused to tell me. It appears, however, that her London home was left undisturbed. And replying on Gloucestershire's behalf, the Met declared that no discussions about Operation Finnean had taken place between them. This suggests they had never even anticipated searching her country home, venue of the fabled Circus.

* * *

House searches are pretty routine in drug cases. Even a casual glance at police activity for that month of September tells us that, for example, in Staines over a hundred officers stormed just two addresses, while in Beaconsfield, "20 police officers took part in three simultaneous dawn drug raids." Around the same time, in Yorkshire, "Operation Curriculum" involved over 21 drug searches in Rawmarsh's tiny Rose Hill Park and the nearby town of Wath, bagging a 19-year-old man for possession of suspected ecstasy tablets and a man cautioned for cannabis possession. A few days after that, police raided a Coventry home when, "About 18 police officers smashed their way in at 7am. Inside they found a man, his partner and a small child... Neighbours watched as police in boiler suits and trading standards officers wearing stab-proof vests searched the house."

Three days after that, South Gloucestershire police mounted "Operation Relentless", as part of which they raided the Swan pub in High Street, Thornbury. They sealed the pub while sniffer dogs sniffed out 35 wraps of suspected drugs. Two arrests.

Moving on to Sussex, 19th September saw Brighton police take a sniffer dog to raid a squat in Brighton for drugs. They'd been alerted, according to a police source because, "There was an illegal rave held at the property and officers noticed people leaving on Sunday who appeared to be under the influence of drugs. As a result we conducted a search of the building and found eight adults and one two-year old child." They found no drugs. But evicted the squatters.

Then, on September 23, Cornish coppers took to the skies in their force helicopter to pinpoint two "plantations of cannabis" growing on cliff top sites near the fishing village of Mousehole. Inspector Barry Tripp, from Penzance police station, announced, "This is a significant find. Undoubtedly there are other sites we have not seen, but we are on the look-out."

* * *

Then there was the case of the Cannabis Granny.

On 16th September, the day after the Cocaine Kate exposé, Northumberland police raided the village home of a grandmother, 66-year-old Patricia Tabram. This was Tabram's second raid in a year.

Tabram had previously been convicted of growing cannabis in her house and supplying it to friends. These friends, all old age pensioners, suffered like her from multiple sclerosis. They'd discovered regular doses of cannabis relieved the symptoms more effectively than prescribed medicines.

Tabram takes up the story: "Within three months there were five of us pensioners in a cannabis cookery club. We'd cook chicken and meat pie, lemon and lime cheese cake, casseroles, steak and kidney pies. We also played Scrabble and knitted. [Then] We decided to grow it ourselves and each put £200 into a kitty for equipment. I started 31 plants off in the garden hut and then moved them up into the loft.

"They were about 3ft and doing very well when there was a knock at the door. I knew it was the drug squad. Someone had tipped them off. I invited them in, admitted I was growing cannabis and offered them tea and coffee, and biscuits with it in, but they refused.

"I was… put in a cell for five hours. After being interrogated three times for 45 minutes I was given a caution and taken home.

"Four months later [16th September] I was raided again. I had 9oz of cannabis which I was putting in little bags for the ladies. I'd bought it the night before. I was fined £750 and given a six-month prison sentence suspended for two years."

★ ★ ★

So while Operations Curriculum and Relentless and the drugs war against the "Cannabis Granny" were busy raiding homes and cleansing the community of evil doers and wiping out pernicious substances, back in London "Operation Finnean" might have been coded Operation Finnegan's Wake: surreal.

Surreal in its lackadaisical pace, its apparent lack of zeal or initiative, its cutely phrased "appeals" to the missing supermodel sent forlornly via the media like radio signals sent into outer space hoping to connect with intelligent aliens …

★ ★ ★

It may be "no accident" as Marxists used to love to say, that the three people apparently most enthusiastic to prosecute in the Kate Moss case, and those most professionally embarrassed by the case's collapse, had all been involved in major enquiries into bent coppers.

In 1993 Sir Ian Blair headed a £1.5 million blitz on police corruption. "Operation Gallery" was the biggest such enquiry in London for a decade. While not a lot of indictable corruption was turned up, Gallery put the wind up a lot of rozzers. It also created lots of negative coverage. Morale plummeted. But Blair didn't let it go. He kept control of corruption enquiries long after Gallery.

Just as aggravating, Blair was an egghead in a force that didn't care for them. An Oxbridge contemporary of his namesake, the prime minister, a visiting Fellow of Nuffield College, an honorary member of the Senior Common Room of Christ Church … it was enough to make a redneck see red.

What's more, Ian Blair was known to be cosy with his namesake in number 10 and was dubbed "New Labour's favourite policeman." As such, he was seen as an agent of New Labour's bureaucratic fetish of box ticking and form filling "targets." Not to mention the encroaching machinery of political correctness.

As for Tarique Ghaffur, while Deputy Chief Constable in Lancashire, he too headed a major enquiry into police corruption. As the most senior Asian and Muslim member of the police force, after moving to the Met he'd also been behind anti race discrimination measures targeted at white officers. As a result he received death threats and hate mail at his office.

Then there was Rene Barclay, who was overseeing Operation Finnean for the CPS. Barclay was one of the principal lawyers reviewing cases involving prosecutions of police officers. (He was also the senior reviewing lawyer in the "Wormwood Scrubs" case involving assaults by screws on prisoners.)

* * *

So here was the eminent and ever so clever Sir Ian Blair making a fulsome declaration of war against Sloaney cokeheads. A public figure and trusted officer of the crown, perhaps recklessly aligning his braid-encrusted persona against wee waif Kate Moss. And there was Ghaffur, a man who took no prisoners on corruption or racism but who also maybe over-identified with this case – "Kate," innit? Were these distinguished officers cruising for a pratfall?

Some less exalted coppers assigned to the leg and spade work of this time consuming case might have thought Operation Finnean a PR stunt for Blair and Ghaffur, and rather a diversion from serious policing. So if this case fell apart would their superiors have red faces? Might they even look like silly, vain humbugs? In which case, might there be some chortling, even schadenfreude, in the lower ranks? Especially from officers discomfited by Blair and Ghaffur's anti-corruption crusades.

As for Rene Barclay's evident bitterness at the outcome, that might have seemed sweet to the coppers and screws he'd scourged through the CPS, an organisation not highly rated by some police officers, who suggested its acronym might interpret as "Clown Prosecution Service", "Criminal Protection Service" and "Can't Prosecute Sensibly."

* * *

But there was perhaps another, more "institutional" factor in this expensive cock-up.

Like everyone else, the police have caught the celebrity bug. Increasingly suckers for celebrity culture: hype, PR and spin, they relish the limelight: spouting opinions, briefing the press, leaking memos and reports. *Crime*

Watch no longer suffices. Cops now take camera crews on raids to show how much fun you can have bashing in doors and shouting "armed police!" while wearing fluorescent yellow jackets and space age body armour as helicopters chatter overhead and searchlights pinpoint fugitives. They increasingly market videos of such "raids" as well as car chases, car crashes, muggings, assaults and even murders. And they let us peek in on their work through fly-on-the-wall documentaries and reality TV shows.

As the line between such mediated policing and the media spectacle becomes murkier, as fantasy cop shows become grainy and jerky just like the real thing, and as the real thing becomes more entertaining and watchable, so showbiz values and priorities become touchstones of policing, investigation and prosecution.

That was evident in the Cocaine Kate debacle. For example, raiding the studio 15 days after the event seems more PR than evidence driven.

Equally, the Met's apparent shyness about raiding her homes might suggest another PR consideration – wariness about a paparazzi circus and tabloid backlash.

In which case, did the Met's impulse to manage the press compromise its collection of evidence?

We might also ask whether celebrities now occupy a distinctive legal category. The Met may have disbanded its elite Special Inquiry Squad, dubbed the "Celebrity Squad," after press derision, but still seems to tread softly when celebs are involved in a case. The human rights and privacy of the 32-year-old Kate Moss were tiptoed around respectfully, and her interrogation appears surprisingly cordial. Whereas the 66-year-old Patricia Tabram, in a case concerning a class C drug, heard the thud of police boots through her cottage not once but twice. She was also held in a police cell for questioning although she was prosecuted.

Finally, maybe there was a notion hovering around the CPS that any trial of a supermodel who just wants to have fun, with all the attendant rock and roll nonsense of Doherty, Mick Jones et al, would make the authorities, would make New Labour and New Scotland Yard, seem, well … uncool. Did the ghost of the infamous Redlands bust, with Mick Jagger debonair in cuffs and Marianne Faithful naked inside a fur bed cover haunt considerations?

We may never know.

* * *

After her taciturn encounter with the police, Kate was driven to Gloucestershire to spend the night in her country home. Wandering for the first time in months among its familiar comforts, the luxuriously fitted kitchen, the quaint rugs and chintzes, plump cushions scattered over floors, the photos and paintings and mementoes she'd accumulated over a lifetime, the picturesque garden with its familiar trees and arbours, she took stock.

She missed England, missed her friends and family. And she missed Pete.

And here was Pete's suite of rooms in the outbuilding he jokingly called "the potting shed", still containing his possessions moved in at the height of their romance: books and tapes, hats and shirts, and his prized Tony Hancock collection. This was her home, her country, her love affair.

Quietly, in the ensuing weeks, she moved her possessions and her daughter back to England.

And began seeing Doherty again.

And so the Pete and Kate Show began again in earnest. Except that now, the star was increasingly Doherty, and Kate almost a walk on.

* * *

"Where I come from, to be called middle class is fucking offensive. I never went to private schools, I don't own property. People think I'm loaded, but I'm skint. I bought this vintage Jag for 700 pounds through Loot. My other Jag, my London taxi and the MG I got Kate as a present, I bought them all second-hand. Kate looks so sexy in that MG, like a right Penelope Pitstop."
- Pete Doherty

* * *

By late February the secret was out: the pair were an item again.

Their romance had survived Doherty's dalliances with groupies and "mysterious blondes" and schoolgirls hopping on his tour buses and several "Kate Moss look-alikes." It also survived Kate's fling in Aspen, Colorado, with a public school toyboy, her close encounter with ex-addict and cadet officer of the celebritariat, Jack Osborne, and her brief encounter with Russell Brand, the "self-confessed sex-addict and former heroin addict."

Kate called her and Pete's love affair "star-crossed." People wondered whether she knew that meant "disaster-bound."

* * *

On 28th February it emerged Doherty had been arrested for the eighth time in 16 months, this time for suspected possession of a stolen car being driven the wrong way down a one way street in the city centre. A witness to the arrest reported, "He was being followed by a West Mercia car so they

207

must have followed him from the motorway. He looked totally out of it and was bundled into the back of a police van after being stopped by about two cars and motorbikes."

Doherty's addiction was becoming comically disaster prone. Indeed, it seemed he artfully – albeit perhaps subconsciously, engineered pratfalls. From driving erratically to signal to passing coppers that he was not entirely in control of his vehicle, to being caught in the toilets at a soccer match (QPR v Millwall) and thrown out of the grounds …

These were less cries for help than opportunities to chatter about his drugs, his addiction – and hence himself. Like all drug addicts he was more hooked on the idea of his addiction than any substance. Kate's concern, like his mother's anguish over his addiction, far from assuaging, actually fed it. The incessant pleading, the ups and downs, revivals and relapses were all fodder to his addict's mentality. The addict loves nothing better than to talk about his addiction, it feeds his victimised status and also the latent sadism: "I'd love to turn you on."

* * *

But what's most striking about the Doherty saga is the leniency shown him by the authorities.

It seems it wasn't only Kate Moss who could "get away with it" because of her fame. In Doherty's case, it looked like some of the judiciary were even bigger fans than the police or CPS, their judgement equally skewed by media coverage.[1]

Take for example, Doherty's protracted "courtroom romance" with "Miss Frances Jane McIvor", who had been appointed a district judge in January 2001. This began in March 2006. By then, Doherty had already stumbled through a roster of hard drug related offences, was a convicted burglar, had served time in prison, and was on parole. But he was also the most glamorous and known drug addict in the country.

At their first encounter, Judge McIvor chose to disregard Doherty's two "positive" results in drug tests the previous month – enough to have sent him to jail for breaching parole – and there were seven new pending charges of possessing drugs including heroin and cocaine which had been brought only hours before the hearing. (When officers had found plastic

---

[1] Doherty could perhaps expect sympathy from a New Labour administration that caved in to junkie convicts who successfully sued the Home Office for breaching their human rights after having undergone "cold turkey" withdrawal from heroin on admission to jail.

bags of crack in his right sock, Doherty told them: "I didn't think I had it in there.")

Indeed, McIvor asserted she had not even expected these drug tests to prove "negative." She then added mysteriously, "It's very good progress, a positive start. His determination seems to be increasing, not decreasing."

Telling the singer that she expected him to have tested "negative" by his next court review, she sent him away a free man.

Outside the courtroom, responding to a paparazzo's shouted question about his drug habit, Doherty quipped, "What sort of a question is that to ask on a Tuesday morning?" Told it was Wednesday, Doherty ran for the lift.

For his next meeting with McIvor on 23rd March Doherty turned up 50 minutes late in one of his Jags. McIvor was again accommodating, adjourning the case for four weeks while the singer straightened himself out.

She was maybe swayed by the eloquence of Doherty's lawyer, Sean Curran, "He has been cooperating fully with probation and has been regularly attending meetings with the drug treatment unit. He has been having more meetings than necessary [and] shown a desire and willingness to combat the entrenched problems he has." Curran continued, "He should be allowed to continue with the good work he has already done – this could be the start of him getting off drugs."

Doherty then engaged in a mock punch up outside the court, sparring with reporters who had gathered to witness his trials on our behalf. Kicking a pap he leapt onto a wall and snatched a mike from ITV reporter Monica Zilious – who snatched it back. Cameras whirred, onlookers cheered and guffawed.

The next meeting with McIvor on 20th April was even more favourable for Doherty. Doherty's lawyer admitted that his client's rehabilitation had failed to "run to clockwork" but huffed about his "slow but fruitful" progress.

The judge advised the singer that his rehabilitation would be a long and winding road, beset with temptation. "It's a long, slow process," she advised, "but you are showing sufficient signs of compliance and effort."

In this fantasy Doherty was the victim of his drug taking rather than its author. As though magic needles pursued him like the brooms of the sorcerer's apprentice, propelling him to acts beyond his volition. It seems that in McIvor's eyes, Doherty was that classic myth of our times, the liminal "out of control" rock star, a shaman gorged on excess and vanity – but we all love him to bits.

A twinned discourse was the singer's patently sincere and penitential stance, his very real (watch my lips, check the gaze, see the clean shirt and

Windsor knot of my tie) desire to get clean, to exorcise himself of this frightful demon of possession by an evil substance.

Sparing Doherty prison yet again, McIvor banned the rock star for driving for six months, and ordered participation in an 18-month drug rehab program, plus two years' probation. McIvor then warned the singer that if he broke the terms of his supervision he could be sent to jail. Finally, she noted with satisfaction that Doherty hadn't been arrested on drugs charges since 14 January.

* * *

A few hours later, Met cops stopped a car in East London after noting the "suspicious" behaviour of its occupants. Inside were Doherty and a male friend. They were arrested and held "on suspicion of possessing class A drugs with intent to supply."

There followed a flurry of drug related exposés and scandals. It seemed clear Doherty was still immersed in a hard drug culture.

Soon it was time to face McIvor again. But playing hard to get, Doherty now failed to show three times.

At the third non appearance his lawyer claimed the singer was being treated at a Portuguese clinic for smack addiction. It was also announced that Doherty was planning to have an opiate suppressing implant fitted. The lawyer confided, "I've spoken to the person who is managing him. I understand treatment is going well."

McIvor was Florence Nightingale, "It's a tough struggle for him."

When the boy genius finally showed in court she chided him that he had not yet achieved a negative drug test result. Then "You are going in the right direction."

At the singer's next appearance before McIvor on September 4, he was obliged to admit to a further five counts of possessing heroin and crack cocaine.

It was pointed out to the judge however, that the rock star was now staying in a branch of the Priory Clinic "specialising in the treatment of mental health problems" in leafy Grovelands Park, N14, paid for by his supermodel missus.

Perhaps empathising with the supermodel, McIvor cooed that Doherty had achieved "better progress than anyone could have believed." And while the new charges were a "deliberate flouting" of his drug treatment order she decided against jail: "I could sentence you today but it would be totally counterproductive and simply take you away from society for a matter of weeks and would undo the hard work that a lot of professionals have put in … [But] You must continue to cooperate fully with your rehabilitation."

McIvor then gushed about Doherty's recent single. "'The Blinding' is very good, but I'm not sure about the words."

So here was an appreciation, even a judicial endorsement, albeit veiled in a coy disclaimer: "But I'm not sure about the words." Was McIvor unsure about their quality or their meaning? Was she alluding to the somewhat monotonous repetition of:

Come and see the blinding
It's so blinding
It's the last thing that you'll ever see…

Or was she alive to the promise of:

But you might be happy oh, happier
Than you've ever been

Realizing that musical talent was now admissible evidence in British courts, and seizing the moment, Doherty's lawyer chirped about "significant progress" and about his client's performance at the Get Loaded concert on Clapham Common.

"Since he was last at court he has made a public appearance at a concert which by all accounts received very good reviews … When he is getting treatment he is capable of giving very good performances. His last concert was one of the best he has ever done."

So that was alright then.

Doherty again left court a free man, telling the crowd of cheering fans, "I'm really happy I've not been jailed. Now I just want my life back." He then got into a stretch limo which sped him back to The Priory.

McIvor and Doherty next met in October. This time the judge had to admit that the singer's rehab was not "as successful as expected." She added however, that the outlook was "optimistic-ish", a nice mumsy phrase.

The singer warbled, "I've been going to NA meetings and seeing a counsellor separate from the Priory." More leniency ensued and another review was ordered for the following January.

* * *

I had the great good fortune to be born in a mad village. It was the kind of village that you could not actually invent.
- Dario Fo

* * *

In the early hours of Sunday, 3rd December, Doherty was at a party thrown in the Whitechapel flat of 51-year-old Paul Roundhill. Roundhill was a known and convicted druggie reputed to have once been a useful aide to Boy George.

He had also been present at the Cocaine Kate incident. In fact, Roundhill was the only person charged as a result of the police enquiry and had been given a 12-month conditional discharge after pleading guilty to possessing Class A drugs.

Roundhill had subsequently fallen out of favour with Kate herself, but not with Pete, who used Roundhill's flat as a regular haunt. Roundhill chuckled, "Apparently, [Kate] calls me 'that crackhead in Whitechapel'." He added, "She's got a furious temper." Roundhill's flat displayed several of Doherty's paintings, notoriously done in blood.

* * *

The party was swinging when a 30-year-old actor and part-time bookseller turned up.

Mark Blanco was a bright spark who'd gained a first in philosophy from Trinity College, Cambridge and recently began acting in alternative theatre. That very day he'd been rehearsing as The Maniac, the lead part in Dario Fo's play, *Accidental Death Of An Anarchist*. The production was being staged at the George Tavern in Stepney, among whose regulars were Blanco as well as Doherty and Kate Moss. Blanco was an ebullient and well liked regular at the pub, "He was in here every day and was the heart and soul of the place."

Paul Roundhill recalled, "There were about six of us there including Pete [Doherty]. When Mark [Blanco] arrived he was extremely excited about the play. He couldn't stop talking about it. He had had quite a lot to drink and was aggressively excited.

"At one point he had Pete pinned to the wall and was waving a rolled up promotional poster for the play at him. Pete looked a bit white and Mark was getting out of order."

Roundhill has admitted that at one point he snatched Blanco's trademark trilby from his head and set fire to it. Another witness, textile designer Anna Smith recalled, "There was this ashtray on a stand. Paul poured lighter fuel over the hat and set fire to it, stuck it on the stand. It was all put out quickly, but Mark didn't even notice."

Roundhill then ejected Blanco from the party. "I dragged him out because he wouldn't leave and was being aggressive." According to Roundhill, Blanco was escorted to the second floor balcony outside the front door and the door was closed.

212

Then, about 15 minutes later, Anna Smith left the party. Exiting the stairwell she saw Blanco lying on the ground. "He was quite still, twisted and breathing but in a very laboured way. His eyes were glazed, blood had poured out of the back of his head. It was obvious he was very badly injured." She ran upstairs and raised the alarm.

Doherty reacted swiftly. Before the emergency services arrived he left rapidly with a group of friends. They gingerly stepped over the actor's smashed and bleeding body. Doherty later explained, "I legged it. Yes, I saw he was badly injured on the ground. I ran, but I run everywhere."

In fact, he and his party ran to the Malmaison Hotel in Clerkenwell. Far from subdued by the Blanco incident, they began drinking and throwing glasses around, and then fighting with other guests. Then Doherty retired to room 204 with a blonde "Kate Moss lookalike" and other companions.

Around 2.30am the occupant of the room next door, a Welsh newspaper reporter, Nathan Bevan, was awakened by "the unmistakable sound of someone or something having the seven bells kicked out of them on the other side of the wall." He continued, "I felt like I'd fallen asleep under the table at a Greek wedding reception, what with the amount of crockery that was being broken." Then, "Pressing my eye to the spy glass in the door, I heard a broad Cockney yell of, 'But I love you, you slag!' – something I thought people only ever said in bad TV shows – followed by loud, urgent pleas of 'Pete, Pete, leave it mate. Leave it!' Then came a dull, heavy thud and silence."

Bevan called reception and two security guards arrived. They were reassured by Doherty: "Nah mate, it's fine honestly. Everything's cool, no need to call the Old Bill. Come in."

It seems however, that security was not impressed by the scene inside. The singer's "wrecking spree," according to Bevan, had seen him "smash mirrors, rip out light fittings, boot in the TV and swish stereo, upend furniture and smear his blood on the walls and the bed sheets."

The police were called. But before they arrived, "Doherty and about three hangers-on fled, his tall skinny frame, replete with guitar, hoofing it across the cobble-stone court yard until the billowing tails of his coat eventually disappeared beyond the glare of the orange street lights."

★　★　★

Next day, Monday, 4th December, Doherty appeared in court to answer yet more drugs charges, this time involving possession of crack cocaine, heroin and cannabis, and yet again before the understanding Judge McIvor.

Bleary-eyed but be-suited, he appeared for all the world a contrite lad on his way to redemption. McIvor certainly thought so. As Mother Theresa, she pronounced that the drug offences were still not serious enough to warrant jail. She fined Doherty £770 and told him this punishment was about "hitting your pockets."

That same afternoon, at the Royal London Hospital, Mark Bianco's life support machine was switched off and he was pronounced dead.

*   *   *

Ironically, the character of The Maniac that Blanco had been rehearsing dies in a mysterious fall from a police station window.

Dari Fo, the playwright also had his character say, "If people come to understand what's really going on, then we are in deep trouble."[2]

*   *   *

By the end of March a third biography of Pete Doherty had appeared. This was penned by Alex Hannaford, who told us her subject was in a line of wasted boy geniuses stretching from Byron, Keats, Shelley, Rimbaud – and even the anaemic and homebound Emily Dickinson. Hannaford also confided that Doherty was "one of the most charismatic individuals, not just in rock, but of his generation."

Less enthusiastic was David Cohen who reported for *The Evening Standard* a spine-tingling drive he'd had with the disqualified Doherty, alleging that the singer was "tearing along" the M1 in the early hours at 100mph while smoking a crack pipe.

*   *   *

Linda Moss was predictably unhappy about the re-emergence of Doherty. She knew her daughter, and feared a self-destructive streak was the source of the relationship.

But now she had her own worries. Her long term relationship with Geoff Collman – the relationship that had shattered the Moss family home and led to the divorce that unhinged the teenage Kate, had ended. She had also had a health scare.

Meanwhile, the melancholic Morrissey saw it from the other side: "Kate Moss has just dragged him [Doherty] down to her level. I think it is

---

[2] Subject to any new information coming to light at any subsequent inquest, it now seems that Blanco had died after attempting to jump from the balcony to a nearby lamppost.

unfortunate that he is more associated with the silliness than he is with music."

* * *

Music, Shmoosik. By April Doherty was hearing wedding bells. He chattered at an Austrian porn club, "We are going to marry. It's going to happen at a Scottish castle somewhere between September and November. A posh Scottish castle. That's gonna be so cool." Then he confided: "Drugs or sex – they are both great. The best is a combination of both of them. I really love sex on substances – nothing beats that."

Not even vampirism.

In a classic piece of tabloid hypocrisy, the *Daily Mail* splashed pictures of Doherty apparently extracting blood from a female fan to use in one of his blood paintings, shrilling: "We apologise to readers who find these pictures, and the account that goes with them, offensive. But we believe they and their children need to know the truth about Pete Doherty, pop star lover of Kate Moss, junkie, criminal … and hero of the oh-so liberal media."

"Other pictures," the *Mail* claimed, "show [Kate] Moss, her beauty shrivelling like fruit going bad, lying limply in a bed."

* * *

But this limp fruit look was going down a storm in the fashion industry.

And stories associating Kate Moss with Pete Doherty's villainy enhanced her naughty cachet and kept her name alive and bankable.

The pair were now a "power couple", known by the US media as PeteMoss, "ranking alongside the likes of Brangelina (Brad Pitt and Angelina Jolie) and TomKat (Tom Cruise and Katie Holmes)."

They were Liz Taylor and Richard Burton minus big budgets, Frank Sinatra and Ava Gardner without the talent, Gainsbourg and Birkin without the sophistication … but perfect for an era of cheapskate celebrity, trash aesthetics and reality TV.

"And we keep watching because the romantic part of us wants to see a happy ending" opined an excited American journalist. Missing the point that what we really wanted was a car crash.

The column inches meanwhile added noughts to Kate's bank account. In April 2006 it was calculated she'd rung up £9 million in the last year – almost double her previous annual earnings.

* * *

The art industry also prospered from the Moss brand. The British Artist,

Marc Quinn, created a life sized brass statue of Kate in a contorted and carefully suggestive yoga pose that fairly cried, "CUNT."

Enthused Quinn, "She is the contemporary version of the Sphinx"

* * *

This sphinx had a temper however, as Doherty was rediscovering. Their relationship was as unpredictable and tempestuous as ever. Paparazzi lurking outside her London home consoled Pete after the model had allegedly ejected him into the street by his collar. Doherty complained to a reporter, "She was furious. She hit me until I was black and blue. She whacked me with her fists and feet. I'm OK now but she injured my finger."

The paparazzi also found themselves at the sharp end of a Moss tantrum when she turned on them after leaving a friend's house. She unexpectedly ran at one paparazzo and kicked him several times, before attempting to punch him, and then stamped on his lens cap. Reporters gleefully reported she had "lost it" and "was really laying into this guy." Images of Kate looking like a Thai kick boxer flashed around the globe.

Doherty's fascination with blood resulted in an equally newsworthy attack on reporters. During an interview with a TV crew, back stage after a gig in Berlin, he squirted a syringe full of his own blood at the MTV camera crew, yelling, "That was a wicked shot. That's going to make a cracking link that is." He then fled, leaving his band mates to apologise: "I think the interview is over. I'm really sorry mate, that's fucked up".

The incident was showcased on the MTV website.

* * *

Explaining the durability of Kate Moss, Darryn Lyons, the owner of the Big Pictures paparazzi agency mused, "Kate is always a story. She's the only celebrity model left for us really. Cindy's gone, Elle's old and Naomi's such a pain that no one wants her. [But] Kate's the one who'll make the money because she has that dangerous quality about her, you just never know what you're going to get – and the cocaine story reflected that."

Adding, "We all love the pantomime baddies and Kate is like Sid Vicious' Nancy of the Seventies." Then, in a touch which suggested Kate's canny collusion with the paparazzi she claimed to detest, he pointed out, that she "changes her outfit three times a day, which gives us three times as many pictures."

* * *

"You love them [drugs] more than you love me/So that's why I could cry all day

long/that's why I can't breath(e)." – Poem in Kate Moss' hand, scrawled in one of Doherty's journals.

"I love you so much...To say it on paper is a bit off but marry me and I'll do the crack off (sic) if you want." – Pete Doherty, Journal entry

* * *

Mumbling his love for the supermodel to the chat show host, Jonathan Ross, Doherty confided that his drugs were the reason they kept splitting up. "It's right and wrong, up and down. She's had enough, I think. I love her bones, I always will.

"[Am I] Trying to stop? Yes, absolutely. Being skint, drunk, paranoid, no, I don't wish that for myself. Being clean means I can sit down and rediscover writing. My song writing suffered, being on drugs."

* * *

She too, loved his bones and stood by her man. Onlookers marvelled they couldn't keep their eyes or hands off each other.

By August she was flashing a vintage diamond engagement ring. Pete too, was sporting a pewter-coloured ring to mark their engagement. (Pete's ring however, seems to have been a poor fit. A couple of months later, while "larking around" with Kate, the ring became stuck on his finger, causing acute pain. He had to be rushed to the private Princess Grace Hospital where the ring was cut off and his finger bandaged. The public was reassured that "the incident had left no lasting damage.")

* * *

The exposure of their couplehood had become essential to Babyshambles' appeal. Kate was increasingly an item of Doherty's stage routine. She would conspicuously ferry supplies of fags and Guinness to her man, posing and jigging around the stage area in suitably sexy attire. "Kate was sat on the bar wearing a tuxedo, frilly knickers and a hat. She'd get on stage, dance then sit down again. It was like a burlesque routine where she would wiggle her bum at the audience." At one point in the set Pete would sing 'What Katie Did Next' into his lover's eyes. Then they would duet sweetly on 'La Belle Et La Bete'. Finally, they might snog and hug before leaving the stage hand in hand.

It was Spinal Tap for the noughties.

* * *

That appeal counteracted Doherty's wacky unprofessionalism. Aborted Babyshambles gigs were almost *de rigueur*. Pete was off his face, or recovering from a fight with Kate, or sleeping off the day before … Booked for Ibiza the singer failed to show as he'd lost his passport. So the record company arranged for emergency documents which needed an ID photo. Taking the piss, Doherty posed grimacing with his head lolling forward. The picture was rejected: Ibiza was cancelled.

* * *

Pete's mother, Jacqueline Doherty now steamed into the Doherty publishing industry with a weepy, if not creepy, memoir. It had a title as sentimental – and as long – as a Victorian Temperance pamphlet, *Pete Doherty My Prodigal Son: A Child in Trouble, a Family Ripped Apart – The Extraordinary Story of a Mother's Love.* It contained charming pictures of the rock legend reading the Beano at seven, joining up to the Beaver cubs, 13 years old in white cricket togs …

Catherine Shoard of *The Evening Standard* complained about, "pages and pages of self-pity optimistically dressed up as self-help … a sad, sanctimonious read."

But the coda, provided by Doherty's father – who now refused to see his son until he was drug free – was shrewd: "In the Doherty home there has been much sadness, marked at times with a deafeningly silent anger that screams at you from every wall in every room. Mixed with the sadness and the anger is the constant pain, the sorrow, the feeling of foreboding, the embarrassment, the guilt, the shame, the unhappiness, the helplessness and the utter hopelessness of our situation.

"Peter's greatest misfortune was to become famous. I watched as he was voted one of the most influential rock heroes of all time in *NME*. People seem hell-bent on perpetuating his wretchedness — a pathetic, limp figure."

* * *

In late August this "pathetic, limp figure" appeared before Judge Alison Rose, who proved less forgiving than her colleague, Judge McIvor. Pleading guilty to five counts of possessing heroin, crack cocaine and cannabis, Doherty was only released on condition that he "live and sleep" at a Priory rehab clinic in London.

A curfew was now imposed: from the hours of 10pm to 8pm he had to be present at the Priory. This proved a wrench. He was soon desperate, and at one point smashed up his room and allegedly punched a male nurse in the chest.

An onlooker commented, "His behaviour was appalling. He was out of control. He's lucky that the nurse was not hurt." Kicking his door and slamming the walls with his hands, Doherty had to be restrained and was threatened with forcible sedation.

He also screamed abuse at staff when told to attend drug therapy sessions, "I don't fucking want to be here! I've fucking had enough! Fuck off!"

He was also screaming that he wanted Kate.

* * *

She was abroad but they were constantly on the phone to one another. He was maudlin, she consoling. "If I hadn't fucked things up," he mourned, "we'd be married by now. I thought you were going to leave me." They exchanged excited declarations of love.

Then he got into trouble again, this time for allegedly supplying cocaine to a teenage inmate. The Priory management warned him that any further trouble would get him banned from the clinic. The alternative was jail, a prospect that terrified the singer.

* * *

The fact that he had just been evicted from his Hackney flat may also have sobered him. Like all things Doherty, this eviction became tabloid fodder. "Shocking pictures" were splashed: "Walls of the £350,000 pad are covered in blood and red and blue spray-paint graffiti. Drug syringes, broken glass and rubbish are strewn across the floor. Dirty scraps of cloth are pinned over the windows to block out daylight. Scrawled across one wall is "Martell Grande National", [referring to] his drug use."

One neighbour complained: "It's been like living next to a building site with comings and goings at all hours and a non-stop din."

What was more, the star owed over £10,000 in unpaid rent. The disgruntled landlord, Andreas Panayiotou, described Doherty as the "worst tenant" he had ever encountered. "As well as not paying rent, there's graffiti and blood on the walls, and goodness knows what else. We have never known anyone like him."

* * *

"I want to be with him [Doherty]. It's just a case of when. There are certain circumstances which we have to get over and then we'll be together. I love him so much. He's the sexiest man on the planet." – Kate Moss, to a friend

* * *

Instead of sending a cheque to Mr Panayiotou, Kate now began to think seriously about having Pete move into her London residence. To clear the way, and mindful of their stormy relationship, she asked Lila's live-in nanny, Jade Davidson, to move to her own nearby flat in Primrose Hill. She also arranged for her personal assistant, Fiona Young, who had been living in the six bedroom house, to stay elsewhere.

*   *   *

Meanwhile, Pete was marooned at the Priory, where Kate became a frequent visitor. Whenever they could, they got physical. Several times they were surprised entangled in the extensive Priory gardens.

*   *   *

In late September Doherty was released from his stint at the clinic. He immediately celebrated by travelling to Ireland with Kate for a Babyshambles gig.

Despite rehab, Doherty seemed unfit. He sported a black eye, his face was "bizarrely swollen and he generally looked exhausted and overweight." The exhaustion was not diminished by a night on the town with the legendary piss artist, Shane MacGowan – which also left Kate "dishevelled."

Performing later at the Ambassadors Theatre in Dublin the famous couple flaunted contempt for stringent Irish anti-smoking laws. In a black mini skirt, singing along with Pete, Kate conspicuously chain smoked while her man puffed away like a steam engine. These "offences" were on show at the next gig at Carlow's Music Factory where Kate, now in denim micro pants, shook her hips and duetted with Pete, albeit rather tunelessly.

Doherty apologised, "Sorry we haven't had a chance to practise much lately what with my probation and then The Priory. I did meet lots of Irish people in The Priory though."

The crowd loved it. They'd come to see a freak show not a musical performance.

*   *   *

Later that week, the first sign of a crack in Doherty's rehabilitation came when he was caught sneaking into a pharmacy, the Health Express store on Millennium Way, where he bought not one, but two, syringes.

"Wearing a scruffy white T-shirt and black suit he slipped the needles into his pocket before rushing back to supermodel girlfriend Kate Moss."

About an hour later, Kate left the hotel for Dublin airport and flew back

220

to the UK alone. A reporter who spotted her at Heathrow noted that "The model was sporting some nasty bruises on her legs – no doubt the results of a couple of big nights out."

★ ★ ★

Shortly after returning to the UK Pete found himself in Kate's doghouse. She had not been pleased with his Dublin drug drama. Following a Babyshambles gig at the Brixton Academy, the couple had "an almighty bust-up" which resulted in Doherty's hasty departure from Kate's London house, half dressed and with only one shoe, at 3.20am.

One of the paparazzi outside smirked, "Pete burst out of the door looking pretty angry and was going on about how he had smashed his guitar. He was looking everywhere for a taxi to get home but he couldn't find one, this made him even more angry."

He took his frustration out on the paps, wrecking one camera, before legging it into the darkness.

★ ★ ★

The Brixton gig had been poorly received by the press. In *The Guardian*, Lynsey Hanley wrote: "The chief appeal of the Libertines was the obsessive tactility of Doherty and his co-singer-songwriter, Carl Barat. They shared a single microphone and showered each other's half-naked bodies with sweat and spittle. Watching them play live was like watching romantic poets engaging in Roman wrestling. Here [at the Brixton gig], Doherty stayed buttoned up in a shirt and grey pullover, like a giant schoolboy who'd bunked off to live his secret parallel life as a pop star. He ducked out of the microphone's range when not singing and looked out at us shyly rather than defiantly.

"Without the protective shield of his old band or the self-assured professionalism that would have come from spending the last three years gigging and songwriting, rather than skanking around his beloved East End trying to score drugs, Doherty's live presence appeared vastly diminished. When not yelling back every word of Babyshambles' aptly shambolic hits 'Killamangiro' and 'Fuck Forever', the crowd chuntered to each other loudly, and thinned out significantly during the set, except for a rabid core of fans who squished one another in order to be closer to him."

Hanley wondered about Doherty's appeal to fans. "What is it about him? Babyshambles' limited repertoire – based on one underwhelming album and a forthcoming EP, 'The Blinding' – is muddy-sounding, half-baked and relies almost embarrassingly heavy on the jangly indie sound patented on the Smiths' first album.

Hanley then commented scathingly, "Kate Moss, the gorgeous 'missus', skittered on and off stage for a brief few seconds during 'La Belle et la Bete' to sing some backing vocals that matched her other half's for mud-like clarity."

* * *

In early October, Jefferson Hack was reported engaged to another, younger, supermodel, the Belgian, Anouck Lepere, 24. The demure and domesticated Lepere cultivated a cordial relationship with Kate, playing step mother to the now five-year-old Lila when the child stayed with Hack.

Hack's father Douglas, meanwhile, had spoken out – not for the first time, about his concerns for his granddaughter.

"We're worried about Doherty and his drug situation. We don't want Lila around him or drugs. But Kate is headstrong. She's going to do whatever she wants and who can tell her otherwise? It's not like she listens to us anyway," he complained. "She just loves the whole rock thing. She'd love to be a rock star herself. That's why she hangs out with that crowd the whole time. She doesn't really like modelling that much."

Douglas Hack also commented that, "Jefferson doesn't like Pete at all. They've been in the same room a couple of times, but really just by accident. He left as soon as he saw him, Jefferson can't stand him."

As for Anouck Lepere, she wryly observed of Kate, "It's quite difficult to be in love with someone who's so destructive, and everybody has to have a bad boyfriend once in their life. They're the hardest to break up with when they should be the easiest."

* * *

But Pete was no "boyfriend." He was Kate's mission.

Since their last bust-up they had become "surgically attached." Doherty was now established at Kate's London home and even assigned the odd domestic chore.

However, around now, potential cracks began to appear. Increasingly, Doherty chafed at Kate's temper. He began to think her unreasonable, even paranoid. For her part, Kate began wondering about her hold on him. It was possible that once he found his feet, mastered drugs and achieved that coveted hit, he might do a Johnny Depp – decamp and find someone compatible with his ability – his own Vanessa Paradis.

While Kate was forgiving about Pete's escapades with groupies, she was less understanding about his apparent lingering fondness for the singer, Lisa Moorish, who'd given birth to Doherty's son, Astile (and Liam

Gallagher's daughter, Molly). Kate was also edgy when Pete began warming to the gifted and outspoken singer, Lily Allen. Allen, who was 11 years younger than Kate, had once declared that Pete was a "wanker" who should be "exterminated" because his addictions were "a bit dull." Recently, however, they'd been swapping presents and enjoying prolonged phone conversations.

★　★　★

In late October, the Pete'n'Kate show – AKA Babyshambles, toured Italy. But in Florence, despite taking up the drum sticks, Kate was booed off stage during a rendition of 'La Belle Et La Bete'. The circumstances were singular. A witness reported: "Kate looked out of it. She was buzzing, she could not sit still. She was perched behind the band's drum kit with a glass in her hand all night and kept leaping up and down and running around. [She] was chain-smoking – I never saw her once without a cig in her hand. To be honest she looked all over the place. In contrast, Pete was looking sober and getting on with the gig. The crowd went absolutely crazy for him – they loved every minute.

"But it all changed when Kate got up on stage. They did a duet but it didn't go down well. The crowd were booing and hissing. Kate seemed very emotional and upset and when she finished she dashed off."

It was also reported that at some point Kate had injured her arm and "blood poured on to her hand and splattered all over her metallic top, jeans and bag."

"There was a huge amount of blood – she looked very distressed."

She was rushed from the concert by minders.

★　★　★

Maybe this experience accounted for her foul mood a few days later at a masked ball at Strawberry Hill House in Twickenham, London. The place was heaving with celebs and media sorts when Doherty tried a version of the Small Faces' 'Itchycoo Park'.

The ex *Daily Mirror* editor, Piers Morgan, thought Doherty's performance was "a tuneless whining noise akin to a lobster being boiled alive." When the singer finally stumbled against a wall, Morgan laughed so hard his mask fell off.

He recounted, "Kate saw my face and gasped in horror. 'Oh fuckin' 'ell, what the fuck is he doin' in 'ere? Just fuckin' get 'im out of 'ere!'"

Bodyguards escorted the giggling newspaper man from the venue. He recalled, "And so I left my masked ball, frogmarched out by security, to the cheers and jeers of the entourage. I glanced back at Kate, who scrunched her face into a tight merciless ball of blind triumphant fury."

Exacting revenge, he later wrote: "Well, just as I thought, she's a drunken, foulmouthed, ill-mannered, paranoid Croydon girl with a cocaine-desecrated hooter and spots. And Pete's a filthy talentless junkie who can't sing."

* * *

Kate was not the only person bloodied in Italy. Pete was becoming increasingly aggressive. In Florence he became involved in a vicious fight with a photographer which ended with both covered in blood.

The other members of Babyshambles were getting worried. According to them, to compensate for his lack of hard drugs, Doherty had taken to excessive boozing. While the drugs, paradoxically had kept him stable, the alcohol allegedly made him violent.

A confidante claimed, "Adam, Drew and Mick are terrified that Pete is drinking more than ever now he's trying to kick the drugs. The booze is making him bad tempered and he's lashing out a lot."

* * *

In early November, Kate Moss won one of the highest prizes of her profession, Model of the Year at the London Fashion Awards. "Kate Moss is a fashion icon and without doubt one of the most prolific models in the industry," enthused the awards panel. "She has now been modelling for over 15 years and remains at the top of her game."

It was an award tailor made to stir the kind of "controversy" in a teacup relished by the fashion industry. And duly pounced on by the press with ritual tut tutting and rhetorical outrage, "Is this the wages of sin?", "Is this the way to set an example to ..." [name your pet demographic], "What kind of message does this send out?" [as if we didn't know].

The Guardian fretted, "In terms of career turnarounds, it is like [the Jew baiting] Mel Gibson winning best actor at the Oscars this year, or [the alleged paedophile] Michael Jackson being given a lifetime achievement at the Grammys." The *Mail* sniffed that "Just over a year ago Kate Moss's career was in tatters [but] Luckily for Miss [sic] Moss, the industry has a very short memory."

George Ruston, director of the drug education charity Hope U.K., complained that the companies exploiting Kate Moss and the awards panel were effectively glorifying drug use. "They're making decisions to reward the behaviour," he stated. "I really don't think people should be making personal gain out of stuff that is causing lots of problems in the world."

Someone else who knew about cocaine was the Colombian Vice President Francisco Santos. He was in the UK on a tour of Europe designed to heighten awareness of the harm (practically a civil war) the cocaine trade was causing in his country. "To me it's baffling," he told *Newsweek,* referring to Kate Moss. "When she snorted a line of cocaine, she put land mines in Colombia, she killed people in Colombia, she displaced people in Colombia, she helped finance kidnapping." She even, he alleged, "destroyed the environment. We have lost two million hectares of pristine rain forest to drug trafficking."

Perhaps mindful of all this devastation Kate didn't turn up at the awards to collect her trophy. Instead, she sent the grand old lady of punk, Vivienne Westwood, to the event to collect it on her behalf from a grinning Brian Ferry.

"I love Kate," announced Westwood, "She is true to whatever she believes in." Then, "She is absolutely brilliant."

* * *

Like everything in the fashion/media universe all this was as bursting with significance as it was devoid of meaning. If Kate Moss really was "absolutely brilliant", what exactly was she brilliant at? Why, at being Kate Moss. And why was that brilliant?

It's the economy, stupid!

Because everything she touched turned to gold.

Allegedly.

Because this commerciality was largely a self-fulfilling prophecy. And the evidence was often from interested parties.

Thus a £2.99 charity bag from Superdrug supposedly saw a "tenfold" increase in sales. And Burberry reported an "extraordinary" demand for the £750 handbag she sported in their current ad campaign. But how were such claims documented or verifiable? Moreover, Burberry would hardly claim that the fee they lavished on Kate Moss was wasted.

In a replay of the happy "coincidences" underlying the initial launch of Kate Moss in New York, the "comeback" ensured that money spent was well spent and happy outcomes ensued. Cosy compacts, nods and winks, friendships and favours, gifts and freebies, all ensured that scepticism never reared its unattractive head and that the discourse stayed within safe realms of simulated controversy and mock outrage.

* * *

Another friend of Kate's was Joe Corre, the son of Vivienne Westwood and Malcolm McLaren, and founder of the lingerie empire, Agent Provocateur. It was in Corre's Marylebone home that Kate had staged Episode Two (pink flowers and moodily flickering candles) of her 30th birthday revelry.

Corre set about featuring Kate in a number of "provocative" videos. Naughty they were not. Rather, cod surrealism with Kate wandering around looking and sounding stoned in undies. Kate was directed by the talented Mike Figgis like a cross between Betty Page and Betty Boop – or as if he really couldn't be arsed.

But launched with aplomb. Corre's yarn went: "Whenever we do collaborations with Kate we get such a huge response, with millions of hits." Such millions he claimed that his web site "crashed" under the onslaught of curiosity.

Picking up this factoid, Vogue.com also trilled that the Moss video "crashed [Corre's] site when it first went live." The online Life Style Extra headlined, "Kate Moss' knicker flick crashes net," adding, "staff are now desperately trying to get the site up and running again and preparing for the next rush of fans." You could smell the panic. *The Sunday Herald* told us, "The suite, called Dreams Of Miss X, proved so popular when it premiered that the Agent Provocateur website crashed." The online First Post went one better. Not only did the website "crash" but, "So many people wanted to see Kate Moss in her underwear, the server exploded." Crashing websites, exploding servers.

Images for the rampant desire Corre might like his undies to inspire. But do sites really "crash" because they are clicked on? Not really. Your PC might crash if you download dodgy software from a site. Or your connection to a site might falter if traffic to that site is intense. But that is your connection failing rather than the site crashing. The site itself will not crash just because people are attempting to access it, as the server will not pass on these attempts. And what might an exploding server look like? Pretty unusual I should think.

But hey, party pooper! – "crashing" sounds so good, a metaphor for hedonism, bohemianism …

Partygoers "crash" out, gatecrashers "crash" in, stock markets "crash" and obliterate empires, and James Dean crashed in a Porsche 550 Spyder driving west on Highway 466 – "crashing" is cool.

*   *   *

Kate's Model of the Year was a well earned award, mused Sir Philip Green, the high street fashion tycoon and owner of Topshop. But he too had a vested interest. While not claiming to be a friend (not yet, anyway), in May that year he'd paid £60,000 at a charity auction for the prize of kissing the supermodel (only to pass the honour to Jemima Khan). He was equally keen for Kate to embrace his Topshop brand and paid a reported £3 million for Kate to "design" her own-label range of clothes, bags and shoes.

But Topshop already had a designer, Jane Shepherdson.

Shepherdson, a driven and rebellious entrepreneur, had overseen a Topshop revival which saw profits soar from £9m to £110m in eight years. The influential style guide, *Drapers*, dubbed her "the most important woman in fashion."

Shepherdson and Green were already at loggerheads over strategy and management style. The trim and trendy designer and the portly billionaire made an odd couple.

Shepherdson was noted for her sense of style. Not so Green. His idea of a wicked stunt was to arrange for the passé and risible Michael Jackson to visit the Topshop flagship branch in Oxford Street at midnight. Green flitted through the shop with the bleached superstar who emerged with "a couple of shirts and a jacket from Topman."

It seems that the Kate Moss appointment may have been the last straw for Shepherdson, who had not apparently been fully consulted about the arrangement.

This imminent falling out was not evident at the party thrown by Green to celebrate the Moss signing. Here the tycoon gushed, "It's not every day you sign up Kate Moss." Adding "Every retailer's dream is to build the best global brand, and I believe that with Jane Shepherdson and Kate Moss we have the best team for the job."

A week after that announcement, Shepherdson left. "I hadn't been planning it, it was quite sudden. I, um, yeah, it, it just came to a point where I thought, OK now is the time I have to go. I am quite impulsive, if not normally that impulsive."

Since then, she has – rather nervously – denied that Kate Moss had anything to do with her sudden exit. In any case, her departure was said to have precipitated a serious talent drain from the company. It seemed that many on the design staff were loyal to her rather than the brand. And sceptical of Green.

There was an added factor to Shepherdson's pique. As everyone knew, Kate Moss would hardly be knitting her brow in front of design software or roughing out slinky outfits on the backs of envelopes. She was there for her name rather than her brain. But the "ghost designer" brought in at Kate's insistence was not a practiced designer either. In fact, she was one of Kate's famously tight clique: Katy England, wife of Bobbie Gillespie, the Primal Scream frontman.

England and Gillespie went way back. Kate had done a routine for the psychedelic Primal Scream vid, 'Some Velvet Morning', jigging in a see-through frock, and she read a poem to bless the couple's wedding in July 2006, dressed in a sort of safari outfit with short trousers, like Sanders of the River. Kate had also splashed out around £20,000 to fly the happy couple to a Rolling Stones gig in Amsterdam for some honeymoon déjà vu. As one of the gang, Gillespie had recently confessed on Channel 4 that: 'I used to do loads of it [cocaine]. Me and my mates used to get sniffed up and play table tennis at my house. That's the way to do it … Cocaine and table tennis it's a great recreational activity. That's when I'm at my best. You know what I mean?"

But England, while known for her commitment and flair, was more of a stylist than a designer. She had worked as such for Hack's *Dazed & Confused* and *Another Magazine*, as well as for Kate's other close friend, Alexander McQueen. Maybe this was all too incestuous for Shepherdson, who was certainly in a different league and not one to be seduced by rock star connections.

This cooption of Kate Moss and her chums into the Top Shop design department smacked of celebrity marketing for its own sake. It was slightly hysterical, if not daft – the kind of scam an undergraduate at the London College of Fashion might come up with. Who was taking design decisions in Topshop post-Shepherdson? A supermodel? A starstruck tycoon?

* * *

By now the supermodel of all supermodels was the focus of 14 ad campaigns. She had also tripled her annual income to an estimated £30m. Claire Beale, the editor of the advertiser's house magazine, *Campaign*, marvelled, "In advertising, I can't think of anybody who has had the kind of longevity or been associated with the variety of brands that Moss has. Most celebrities ally themselves with at most two brands."

Crucially however, all these campaigns stemmed from the same merry go round of media and fashion gurus, an inward looking clique indeed. This same clique manufactured a consensus around Kate's fashion "influence."

Thus, *The Guardian's* deputy fashion editor, Hadley Freeman, claimed that "[Kate Moss] is credited with kickstarting nearly every major fashion trend on the high street for the past few years, from skinny jeans to ballet pumps."

But credited by whom?

Undoubtedly, as a celebrity and model, Kate Moss was a touchstone of taste, an exemplar for some punters. But these punters saw her in outfits created by designers and made available by retailers, and in images selected by picture editors. To ascribe such influence to a model – even to this model – was disingenuous. Fashion is a vast and intricate industry that sprawls globally from fashion forecasting to promo to distribution to retail. And the people who really count behind the scenes are the Tom Fords and Anna Wintours. The trickle-up, street fashion view of the business, where a Kate Moss can force the pace or raise the stakes, was a Romantic post punk and essentially academic daydream.

Note that Hadley Freeman was also a contributing editor to *Vogue*, the "fashion bible" which is a byword for the slippery interstices of advertising-as-editorial, and vice versa, where celebs rule and journos drool, and where everyone is a friend of a friend.

Explaining *Vogue*'s seemingly obsessive recycling of Comeback Kate themes, the editor Alexandra Shulman pouted, "I don't do this because she's a friend of mine but because, as a model and a personality, Kate Moss sells."

But would the public swallow the Kate Moss legend as easily?

The Kate Moss brand could open hearts and wallets in boardrooms, it could proliferate clicks to gossip sites, but could it shift frocks off racks?

Lorna Hall, executive editor of *Drapers*, thought the answer was yes … but no.

"The PR machine behind these launches is very sophisticated. Retailers boost the pent-up demand before the launch, and the fashion cognoscenti get excited. But these things are really self-perpetuating. The media frenzy creates customer demand, and if we're honest, a lot of that demand is people buying racks of the stuff and putting it up on eBay – people seeing a commercial reason for buying it rather than anything to do with the designs."

The last word here is from Jane Shepherdson, speaking after her timely exit from the Moss Topshop circus:

"This whole thing of looking at what celebrities are wearing is so dull and unimaginative and desperately boring."

* * *

Not to be outdone, in November, Pete Doherty made it known that he too was a fashion "designer." He'd been recruited by the trendy Gio-Goi to create a range of garments reflecting his "personal style." These would be launched through Selfridges.

The co-founder of Gio Gio, Anthony Donnelly, enthused, "Pete looks fantastic as a model. We are very excited and we look forward to having Pete's influence as a rock icon in the design process."

* * *

"Icon." Uh, oh – that word again.

Announcing a forthcoming exhibition, Face of Fashion, the National Portrait Gallery boasted it would feature no less than nine "iconic" photographs of Kate Moss.

Corinne Day was duly commissioned by the gallery to revisit her first triumph and create a brand new Kate Moss icon.

Day explained, "I asked Kate if we could have a serious conversation. I wanted to find her character, in a serious way. We never see Kate in that way. So I went to her house, we sat down. I put a little light on her. She didn't wear anything, it was just head and shoulders. And we just sat and talked. And I snapped away … Some of the expressions I had never seen before. Because Kate is a very happy girl. You always see her, the party girl, she loves to have good fun. You never see her really sad and down. Not often. Not in the public eye anyway."

These stark black and white snaps were vintage Corinne Day. They deglamorized Kate as not so much the girl next door as 'er upstairs: frumpy and grumpy.

* * *

Also marvelling over Kate's iconic status was the *American Idol* rock promoter Simon Cowell. He announced, "I would like to offer Kate Moss a recording contract, whether she can sing or not."

"The thing about Kate," he explained, "is that she's a star – it's the 'Kate factor'. People attach themselves to her and instantly become interesting."

Adding, "There's no way I would take [Pete Doherty] on. I doubt he'd turn up for anything."

* * *

Both Pete and Kate turned up for a party in mid-November at the Serpentine Gallery to mark 90 years of *Vogue* magazine. But only just. By now, Kate was getting bored with the glitz, tired of the fashion scene. She and Pete slipped out of the *Vogue* party after 15 minutes and the couple resurfaced in the Golden Heart in Shoreditch, quaffing ale like real people in Eastenders.

Kate's new taste for gritty realism Doherty-style was also evident in her appearance in a charity performance of *Little Britain*, the bad taste TV show.

The performance was at the Hammersmith Apollo and Kate played the younger sister of *Little Britain* star, Vicky Pollard. Wearing "a polyester sports top with skin-tight leggings and lashings of gold Creole jewellery" Kate delivered the lines: "I'm the easy one … I'm a total slag. I'll do anything for a packet of Quavers." And, "I'm off on the rob." The "star studded audience" "rocked with laughter" as Pollard shouted at Kate, "Lose some weight, you fat bitch!"

* * *

The great question that has never been answered, and which I have not yet been able to answer, despite my thirty years of research into the feminine soul, is "What does a woman want?"
– Sigmund Freud

* * *

The question most women ask about Kate and Pete is, "What does she see in him?"

Firstly his mind. He may be a twat, but he is a bright twat.

Kate has only been serious about men she thinks she can learn from. Her Eliza Doolittle complex draws her to people with class and education. Doherty has brains, as his scholastic record showed. He could also feed her the lines and anecdotes that made her feel a cultural "insider."

And his culture was excitingly outsiderish and rarefied. With what people call a "dark side." While he borrowed from Tony Hancock a surreal whimsy that made Kate laugh, he also flirted with Hancock's eventually suicidal melancholy.

Plus, Doherty was a sort of rock star, and a proxy role in that game suggested a way out of the tedious grind of supermodelling. And a way into what she imagined were the highest realms of cultural achievement, The Rolling Stones and all that.

Doherty also fascinated her in his contradictions. Overpowering in his vulgarity and loudness, he's a sweetie in poetic moods: equally explosive and brittle, a combination of Iggy Pop and Harry Potter.

Then there was his body. Detractors point to his clammy look and pasty face, but there's no denying he's pretty, and in a feminine way. That girliness combined with a robust physique attracted her. At six foot two he towered above her, and she loved to nestle in his broad chest and look up at him.

And he had animal charm. Lots of it. For contrasting with his nattily besuited style, Doherty had a fascination with flesh and blood and gore – and all sorts of excretions.

231

Here was a man who loved to expose his body to surprised onlookers, who would share intimate physical functions as well as hypodermic needles with strangers, who would drop his trousers PJ Proby style for fans, or lift his shirt to exhibit his heroin implant with pus oozing from it, who spurted blood at onlookers from a syringe, regularly painted blood paintings and graffiti in his own and others blood, wrote Kate messages and poems in blood – she returning the favour – and who revelled in the grime and disorder of his refuse-piled squats, as well as the messes he loved to make of other people's places – or hotel rooms. (It also seems from the detritus of the couple's love making that a variety of bodily fluids were commingled and celebrated.)

All that was about spreading himself, commanding and swamping his surroundings, and manipulating others. Indeed, his charisma was founded on that appeal: a vulnerable spillage, a potlatch of talent, opportunity and looks.

Then there are Pete Doherty's "hygiene issues."

Notorious for rarely brushing his teeth, his foul breath and rotten teeth – mostly the result of drug abuse, were mythical. Quipped a friend, "They're so rotten you could probably flick them and they'd break."

Unfamiliar with washing machines and such like gadgets (he discards shirts rather than washing them), Doherty's sweaty torso, his chipped and dirty fingernails, his redolent underwear, were legendary.

But aphrodisiac to Kate – who is quite a crusty herself.

We might call this the appeal of Doherty's dirty realism.

Kate is an uninhibited, tactile and sensual woman, an instinctive toucher, who thinks nothing of climbing onto a stranger's lap to ask a favour, teasing and giggling in your ear. It's also often been noted that she lacks – or refuses – a normal sense of boundaries, both in her behaviour and expressions, and choice of surroundings. She is a good-time, instinctive and unabashed "dirty girl" in the sense celebrated by Pink Floyd ("Oooh, I need a dirty girl …").

So habits, odours and manners that might have made other women recoil, reassured her that her man was a real man, that Doherty was FLESH AND BLOOD, and that their love was properly existential: uncompromising thus authentic – something to salvage and cling to in the self-indulgent frivolity of fashion with its perfumed hypocrisies.

* * *

Fragrance Partnership With Global Icon Kate Moss
Fragrance Venture Marks First for Supermodel
Coty Inc., the world's largest fragrance company, announced today the signing of supermodel and fashion icon, Kate Moss, as Coty's latest beauty partner to develop and market her own line of signature fragrances.

... said Bernd Beetz, CEO, Coty Inc. "There is no one better to embody a new fragrance than Kate, who epitomizes the look and feel of today's fashionistas. We are very excited about this fragrance collaboration and look forward to a long and fruitful partnership."
- http://sev.prnewswire.com

*   *   *

How many times can a rock star get done and banged up and then let off? How many hotel rooms can he trash, how many dying actors step over? The Doherty-disaster movie was now so well worn that in early December yet another Pete publication appeared. This was an illustrated children's story book, "a cautionary tale of pop star who comes to sticky end."

A Boy Called Pete related the rise to fame of a notorious rock singer who "sings songs and wears hats." "Pete plays guitar, eats special sweets and falls over a lot." Pete also meets a famous girl called Kate and they eat special sweets together that make them go "ballistic." But because of their fondness for "mind-bending drugs" Pete and Kate are "always getting into trouble."

The book was couched as a moral tale, warning its young readers that "Class A drugs are not very good for you. They make you smelly and a bit untidy-looking." In the end, Pete, even though "once upon a time he was a very clever and handsome man," discovers that he's no longer famous as a rock star. He is incarcerated in "a very big house with high walls" because "London has lots of rules and lots of authority."

The book became a Christmas best seller. But was not found in Lila's stocking.

*   *   *

"Budgie is the bravest, nippiest, cheekiest, friendliest little helicopter Harefield Airfield's ever know. If he isn't getting into trouble, he's getting out of it. If he isn't dozing off, he's flying off and if he isn't in need of a wash, he soon will be."
- Sarah (The Duchess of York) Ferguson, *Budgie the Little Helicopter*, 1989

"At twilight, when lotus flowers are floated on the surface of the swimming pool, the picture of tranquillity is finally complete."
- Suzanne Trocmé – in an article for *Interior Design* describing the Phucket resort of Amanpuri

*   *   *

As predictable as the perils of Pete were the caprices of Kate. That Christmas she jetted off to one of her favourite venues, Phuket in Thailand. Here she stayed at the Amanpuri resort, a former coconut plantation overlooking the Andaman sea on Phuket's west coast.

Named for the Sanskrit word meaning "place of peace", the resort was described by *Interior Design* as, "a hotel and 30 private residences, created under the watchful eye of Paris-based architect Ed Tuttle. The first impression is one of bougainvillea, orchids, and gloriously perfumed trees." The report quotes a visitor, "It doesn't even seem to belong on earth."

Kate's villa was within hailing distance of her new good friend, Fergie, Duchess of York, also vacationing on paradise.

Fergie, formerly dubbed, the Duchess of Pork for her ungainly looks and fashion howlers, had recently endured a weight loss regime and now espoused the company of the chic. Already a pin-up in Tamarah Mellon's book, *Four Inches*, sporting only a string of diamonds and a pair of stilettos, the royal was due to appear in a glossy hagiography of Vivienne Westwood, alongside Jerry Hall and, naturally, Kate Moss.

Doherty obtained permission from his probation officer to join his missus and the couple saw in 2007 with a fireworks display on the steps of the Amanpuri Hotel. Also present were Fergie and her two daughters, Princesses Beatrice and Eugenie, who later shared a New Year's bevy with Kate and Pete in the hotel bar.

* * *

Then suddenly, the British tabloids were energised by a rumour that Kate and Pete had secretly married in a Buddhist ceremony on a beach! *The Sun* revealed that:

"Kate Moss and junkie Pete Doherty were 'married' yesterday -in a bizarre Buddhist ceremony on holiday.

"The lovers had water sprinkled over their heads as a Thai priest pronounced them man and wife.

"Friends and family clapped and cheered – even though the New Year's Day union at a villa overlooking a Phuket beach is NOT legally binding in the UK."

Not to be outdone, the *Mirror* ran the same story, telling us that Kate had worn "flowers in her hair for the simple exchange of vows witnessed by close friends."

The *Mail* headlined: COCAINE KATE'S ISLAND WEDDING.

The *Chicago Sun-Times* expanded that Kate, "wore a silver Galliano gown and was barefoot, [while Pete] wore his usual black suit and that stupid hat. There were some Buddhist prayers and something about entwined wreathes of flowers …"

Unusually, the Kate Moss machine issued a denial. Kate's PR man, the ex *Sun* editor Stuart Higgins maintained, "There has not been any kind of marriage ceremony in Thailand. She is on holiday."

But the *Irish Independent* insisted, "There was no denying those blurred paparazzi photos that showed the pair of them standing together, she in a silver dress, he in a trademark trilby, wearing flowers in their hair and pouring water on each other's heads." It continued, "Reading between the lines, the most likely scenario is that the lovebirds enjoyed a non-legally binding Buddhist marriage ceremony, as a show of their love for one another."

Phuket locals had the answer. Explained one, "There's a custom to hold a seaside blessing for soulmates, a spiritual bonding with scattered flowers and incense."

So it was just Pete and Kate and their chums and Kate's mum all being hippies together.

And nobody laughed.

★ ★ ★

Later, another, seamier side to their "wedding" emerged. Pete it seemed, had been fretful in paradise and escaped to the nearest concrete jungle.

Here, he'd been recognized by an Australian backpacker fan, Jess Lea, as he was buying syringes in a chemist. (What else would he be buying?) Lea invited the star back to her hostel to party with two female friends. Pete obliged. One of these girls then filmed Doherty with her mobile phone, naked from the waist up, and sitting on a bed strewn with a "drugs paraphernalia of a spoon and syringes, plus scattered banknotes in British, US and Thai currency."

Doherty allegedly injected cocaine three times in two and a half hours. "It was a bit mind-blowing. He asked us if we minded. Initially we were like, 'OK, go for it.' But as time went on we began to get nervous."

It was also claimed that during this time he had several agitated conversations with Kate on Lea's mobile. "She [Kate] did seem quite pissed off, with him constantly pleading, 'What's wrong? I love you.' After one conversation his mood changed. He was quite upset.'"

He also disclosed his anxieties about Kate, "Pete kept telling us Kate was paranoid and wanted to know where he was and who the girls he was with were. He kept telling her there were no girls." When asked about their impending marriage, the rock star commented, "No, I love her but I wouldn't marry her if she was the last woman on Earth. She's too paranoid."

The girls then decided to get rid of their guest but it appeared he couldn't recall where his villa was, even while joking he'd had breakfast there with "Princess Fergie."

Lea reported that as they were leaving, Doherty asked the receptionist where he could buy heroin. "Then he went up to every taxi driver asking if they could score him some drugs."

The singer was now in such a state that they dumped him in a well known cafe and Lea, "sent Kate a text reading, 'Dropped Peter off at the Bob Marley café. He's a bit out of sorts'. That's the last we saw of him."

* * *

At the beginning of our media age, Daniel Boorstin noted the transmutation of celebrities into pseudo-people, beings in his phrase "known for being well known", who floated through fogs of mediated pseudo events.

Nowadays, we know such celebrities don't exist. Not like you and me. They are made-up freaks, media spooks. You may protest that Kate Moss is a real person. As I write this and you read she is no doubt busy about her life, nattering to Davinia on her mobile, wondering what that noise was just then in the back garden … Yet to all intents and purposes, as a celebrity, as Kate Moss, she's an object made of newsprint and silicon chips, cardboard and cathode rays. She's equally a magnetic fetish to which all kinds of mysterious and magical attributes attach. But none of that comes from her. It all comes from me and you.

In fact, all celebrities are blank screens onto which we project our fantasies and failings. The blanker – more ambiguous, indeterminate – a celebrity persona is, the more useful for this purpose.

And who – or what – is blanker, in every sense of the word, than Kate Moss? Famously blank faced. Famously silent. A clothes horse. A mannequin. A Mme Tussaud's waxwork.

* * *

Now pose with Kate Moss at Madame Tussauds!

A wax figure of Kate, reclining on a couch in a Manhattan loft style apartment for a photo shoot, has been placed in a section of the world-famous attraction which is reserved for only A-list celebrities.

Now visitors will be able to pose with "Kate" and be photographed to produce a fictional glossy magazine cover called Iconic.

– http://www.zeenews.com

* * *

Sharon Dowsett is Kate's favourite make up artist as well as a confidante.

She knows the "real Kate" well. Attempting to convey her appeal she gushed what a "fantastic personality" her client was. When I suggested "fantastic personalities" just like that might be found in any fashion college canteen, or in any high street, Dowsett smiled conspiratorially. She acknowledged I had a point.

Yes, Kate Moss is bubbly, she is a laugh, she is a looker.

But to quote The Anti-Nowhere League, "So Fucking What?"

* * *

Dowsett herself is known not just for being well known, but for being superb at her work (google it). You might – and some do – argue that Kate Moss is also superb at her work. Several photographers for example, enthused to me about Kate's "professionalism." But on enquiry this turned out to be turning up on time, sitting around for hours, posing to order, and being chatty between shots.

* * *

Voicing his incredulity at Kate's uncanny status, and breaking ranks with the faithful – as befits an artist – is Juergen Teller. Teller has been an intimate of Kate since she was 15, and created some of her most memorable post Day and Sorrenti images. But now he confesses in the *New Statesman*, "I'm astonished about the Kate Moss story, full stop. I don't quite understand it. ... to get to be such an icon, to have exploded like a rocket – I don't really get it."

He continues, "She is beautiful, but so are many others." He also suggests, "I don't think she looks any good in any photos of the past five years. In fact, she looks crap in all of her recent huge advertising campaigns. Chanel, Burberry, Rimmel. She looks awful. It's as if it's enough just for her to look something like Kate Moss."

Teller concludes, "It's a dreadful life for her, to live in this position."

* * *

Back in March 2006 *The Sun*'s front page had featured yet another cruel picture of Kate Moss. Headlined "COKE FIEND", here was Britain's most famous supermodel every bit ecstatic. And on the table in front of her, lined up neatly, was an alleged quantity of cocaine.

The substance was helpfully ringed with a white-edged red ellipse, like a halo painted by a Renaissance artist. A halo might equally have hovered over Kate's glazed gaze – she looked more beatific than beautiful with palms spread like Christ revealing the stigmata in a kitsch etching – even while her eyes were fiendishly red in reflected flashlight.

Accompanying this image were allegations made by a South African model booker, Gavin Maselle. Maselle alleged that Kate had taken cocaine at a reception for Nelson Mandela, snorting from the lavatory seat in the liberation fighter's home, and once even snorted it off the floor in a changing room – painting a pretty picture of the supermodel on all fours with her "bum in the air."

* * *

Yesterday the world of fashion was rocked to its foundations over the grisly double suicide of Kate Moss and Pete Doherty. The star-crossed couple were discovered by a housekeeper in a final embrace under an apple tree in the grounds of Kate's Gloucestershire mansion. It seems they had taken a simultaneous drug overdose in a last act of defiant passion. Daubed on the tree trunk in Doherty's blood was a message to his fans, telling them that he loved them, but that it had all gotten too much.

* * *

We are as celebrity mad as Freud was sex mad and like him we impute every motive and outcome to our madness. Kate Moss is only explicable through a culture super-saturated with celebrity. Today, even Scotland Yard and the Crown Prosecution Service, are impressed by the media clout of a supermodel – or her media afterglow. Billionaire execs babble like hippies on acid as she appears to disappear and disappears only to appear again. Kate Moss the brand and the catwalk holograph, the leggy hooligan and cheeky escapee, omniscient cover girl and convulsive headliner, paparazzi fodder and factoid staple …

But there's another dynamic at work.

Because underneath fashion's velvet knickers is an iron dildo.

Fashion is a totalitarian regime. It may seem to float on whimsy but it breathes fire. The obverse of its seductive whispering is its blurting of Orwellian newspeak and enforcement of censorship. It airbrushes inconvenient facts and shuts up awkward customers. It excommunicates heretics and blackballs scoffers.

After Corinne Day pissed off *Vogue* with her "heroin chic" Kate Moss images she found no fashion work for years.

When the mask fell, Kate Moss summoned her minders to frog march the hapless Piers Morgan from the party, and "scrunched her face into a tight merciless ball of blind triumphant fury."

And when Kate Moss sashayed into the *New Musical Express* awards in March 2007, an *NME* insider (who tellingly refuses to be named) affirmed that The Supermodel ordered NO PICTURES apart from ritual arrival shots. She then engaged in over an hour of very photogenic sexual exhibitionism with Doherty. My source recalls his amazement at how "incredibly weird" that seemed: Kate and Pete in deep tongue clinches, writhing and gasping, "with a massive crowd of people gathered around watching."

Much weirder was that the *NME*, spiritual guardians of rock and roll, rigidly enforced this whimsical ban on photos, a ban which, combined with the exhibitionistic fantasies of this supermodel, added up to as petulant and dotty a display of power as you would find in any half baked diva – and all because they were "terrified" of pissing said supermodel off – because she'd agreed to feature on an *NME* cover.

So snap the woman anyway and put *that* on the cover!

Why not?

Who cares?

NME does.

In the same vein of fear and trembling, when I once approached the iconoclastic www.showstudio.com, brain child of the once-upon-a-time Factory Records rule breaker, Peter Saville, the site's editor-in-chief, Penny Martin, coyly emailed that, "As you know, Kate Moss is a valued contributor, who has submitted numerous unique projects to our site. Of course, her agency are being super careful about her coverage at the moment and out of loyalty, therefore, I am afraid we really are not able to support any unauthorised projects on her."

Fashion models who take a line of coke and a tumbler of champagne for breakfast will embroil newspapers in law suits they can't win (because they are in the wrong) but which they also know will ruin the publications through legal costs. That is all normal behaviour – serves the bastards right, press scum!

The fashion industry has no conception of truth or independence, nor any need for such quaint nonsense. Its discourse is fantasy, its reality is hype.

Meanwhile, it terrorises through patronage and embargo. And particularly controls images, its main currency, deciding not just what you should and shall see, but also in which context.

It sees no problem in that.

*   *   *

Once upon a time there was this picture of Kate Moss. But then it disappeared. Only that wasn't magic. It was censorship.

You may recall my description (in Act 1) of a remarkable image of a naked Kate Moss aged about 15, clutching her crotch, and looking, well… victimised.

I used this image to sum up the chemistry of her early potency – an adolescent stripped of dignity and clothes. These snaps showed a pubescent Kate Moss naked, rather than nude. There were many of them, but that particular picture, by Mario Sorrenti, crystallised their mood most brutally.

A core element was that they were often taken (by Kate's own accounts) in the aftermath of agitated or tearful rows about whether she needed (or wanted) to strip off. The photographers, principally Day and Mario Sorrenti, who insisted she get her kit off prevailed. The results duly exposed the teenage Kate churlish or resigned, sometimes reconciled, but never at ease. That was their hook: a cutely rebellious and suitably (and recently) chastened Kate Moss. You could almost smell the tears and taste the humiliation.

And these portraits became the "look" that launched the Kate Moss industry. They appealed firstly to the style bloods at *i-D* and *The Face*. Then they seduced Calvin Klein, who'd been alert to the potency of "underage" allure even before Brooke Shields.

When I first wrote about that image, it was the most popular – clicked on and linked to, image of Kate Moss on the Internet: No 1 of tens of thousands. You could tell this because the Google (and other search engine) rankings consistently showed it as the first picture during any image search for "Kate Moss" or "katemoss".

And then it vanished.

And today you will hardly find it anywhere in cyberspace. To paraphrase the Monty Python sketch, this picture has passed on … it is no more! It has ceased to be! IT IS AN EX-PICTURE!

That suggests someone got mighty pissed off with this image being ubiquitous. Maybe too, someone was peeved I'd highlighted and dissected it. In any case, the fact that it was "disappeared" in such a draconian manner suggests considerable resources of time and cash, and lots of warnings to fans and bloggers to, in the legal jargon, "cease and desist."

Meanwhile, approaching Sorrenti's people to get the picture reproduced in this book, elicited: "To enter into approval process and fee negotiations for Mario's image, have you received PR approval from Ms. Moss?"

Er, no.

★ ★ ★

A celebrity, in short, does not make her public image, her meaning for others, in anything like the way a carpenter makes a chair from a block of wood. She is not the sole and sovereign "author" of what she means for others.

*When a quintessentially "postmodern" (that is, openly and unabashedly deriva-
tive) performer like Madonna [or Kate Moss?] complains of unauthorized appropriation of her image, she is seeking to have it both ways. Having drawn freely and
shamelessly on our culture's image bank, she is trying to halt the free circulation of
signs and meanings at just the point that suits her. She is seeking to enforce against
others a moral norm that her own self-consciously appropriationist practice openly
repudiates. The law need not be party to such contradiction.*
– Michael Madow, "Private Ownership of Public Image: Popular Culture
and Publicity Rights," *California Law Review*, 1993

* * *

There is a network of control in fashion that extends from *Vogue* to
avowedly "independent" websites. This creates and polices a consensus that
inhibits and finally crushes opposition. Everyone imagines and acts as if they
are in thrall to a supermodel's temper and to the priorities and goodwill of
agencies, the dictates of PR and all the associated "interests" – from Coty to
Burberry to Testino to Virgin.

This ensures that artists who use the likeness or name of Kate Moss are
cronies, and that none of them considers – or even envisages – speaking out
of turn or imagining anything that might offend, disturb or provoke the status quo.

While "subversive" is an accolade artists like the photographer Rankin or
Mark Quinn award themselves, Rankin's visions of Kate Moss in scanties
are subversion lite, while Quinn's fetish of the Moss quim dares not risk a
laugh, covering itself under the snigger of bronze tights. As for Mike Figgis'
Agent Provocateur vids, they suggest Johnny Rotten's sneer, "Ever had the
feeling you were being conned"?

Elsewhere, Kate Moss is a trophy walk-on to music vids, wriggling
through visual clichés: verse, chorus, verse, chorus, middle, verse, choruses
out …

It seems an unholy truce has descended between fashion and art.

* * *

The only subversives around, hence the only true artists, are the paparazzi.
Their agenda provides a refreshingly caustic and outlaw aesthetic. These guys
who relentlessly camp in Kate Moss' cul de sac, or park bumper to bumper
in her Gloucestershire village, swapping stories and munching burgers while
waiting for Kate or Pete to show their faces, who race after her Range Rover
though winding English country lanes or drink at the pub table next to her
select party at Sunday lunch, they feed the frenzy but also up the ante.

Derided as mercenaries, paparazzi are artists who go wherever their project takes them – do whatever it takes. Nor do they hide under the skirts of fine art practice. As Wayne Koestenbaum comments, paparazzi are "a kind of perverse artist … the artist who doesn't merely represent a desire, pilgrimage, or inquiry but performs it, and thereby crosses the risky borderline between mimesis and praxis."

Their "money shots" are the only artworks today (apart perhaps, from Alison Jackson's work) that effectively probe the boundaries, expose the politics, and suggest the breaking points – and thus threaten, the increasingly omniscient power of the celebritariat.

What price a Mario Testino royal portrait for a snap of Diana's smashed up body in that Mercedes? What price a dainty Jefferson Hack movie on youtube (Kate With Kane) for the wonderfully infectious and sublimely disaster provoking Cocaine Kate vid?

In the bonanza of Kate Moss "icons" shown in the 2007 National Portrait Gallery show, Faces of Fashion, that vid was the only "icon" missing.

But it haunted the place.

ACKNOWLEDGEMENTS

It's been quipped that the anonymity of these acknowledgments is better suited to a book on the mafia. I rest my case. Fashion is an incestuous business that deals in Sicilian style patronage and revenge. Luckily however, people - especially fashion people, love to talk. In fact, this book was built up from contacts initiated from 1994 while researching *Fashion and Perversity* (about Vivienne Westwood), Kate Moss being one of the models I interviewed then back stage at a Westwood show in Paris. Then, a decade on, when, a few months into my research for *Addicted to Love*, the "Cocaine Kate" scandal blew the lid off Kate's Id – maybe because Kate herself then became AWOL and the whole thing seemed so unreal, informants became bolder. Albeit still wary about getting mired in what had become a reputational minefield. So in the end, I thought it politic not to acknowledge anyone publicly.

However, my warm thanks to all those from Sanderstead to Lechlade to London and Paris and Dublin and New York, who gave me so much time and information and insight. Thanks also to my researchers and collaborators, notably Olivia Dowle, Gary Holder and Gilly Booth. Not to mention my indispensable agent, Leslie Gardner, and understanding editor, Chris Charlesworth.

And now I'm off to Waitrose to buy a large, juicy venison steak …

5/07(62371)